From Sri Lanka with love

with love

a tapestry of travel tales

by

Margaret L Moore

I hope you enjoy reading about our holiday exploits!

TSL Publications

Margaret L Moore

Published in Great Britain in 2020
By TSL Publications, Rickmansworth

Copyright © 2020 Margaret L Moore

ISBN: 978-1-913294-56-4

Contents

Thanks

I know I rarely look at the acknowledgements page in a book and perhaps many readers will skip over it too. But now I realise how important it is to put in writing my immense and heartfelt thanks to those without whom this book wouldn't have come into existence.

Firstly, thanks to husband Douglas, and sons David and Andrew who have been key in my life and therefore in my holiday experiences. Hopefully I haven't misrepresented you too much!

Thank you, Iain, for introducing us to the delights of Sri Lanka in 2015; somewhere we would probably not have considered as a holiday destination, but we're so pleased we'd our first holiday there with you.

George and Sylvia, you quickly made us feel welcome as we chatted on the veranda in 2015. Thanks for inviting us to join you on tours then and to return with you to Sri Lanka for a second holiday in 2017. Your friendship and kindness was, and is, amazing.

A thank you must go to all my friends and family for the encouragement and advice given during the long process of preparing this book for publication. An extra special thanks to my sister, Jean, whose help and insightful guidance was provided when I needed it most. (Thank goodness you'd finished your PhD and had time to spare, Jean!)

Special thanks go to cousins Lorna and Dallas, and Glenn and Helen who went way beyond anything we expected when hosting us in Australia, and to George and Bunty who did likewise in Canada.

In fact, all those named in the book deserve thanks as the holiday wouldn't have been the same without you.

Finally, to those who helped, advised and guided me along the learning curve required to convert holiday emails to the published work now in your hands, thank you.

In giving thanks, there's also the worry of unintentionally missing someone. If this is you, please accept an even bigger thank you and let me know so I can rectify matters.

Dedication

To everyone who has been a part of my life –
even if you feel you've only played a small part,
you're important to me.

And in the words of a hymn sung at Douglas and my wedding:

To God be the glory, great things he has done.
So loved he the world, that he gave us his Son.

(by Frances Jane Crosby; 1820-1915)

Who's who

Having mild dyslexia, one of my difficulties is remembering names of people when reading a book. I often resort to writing a list of who's who. In case you are like me, I've prepared such a list. Many of the characters only appear once, so this will mean you don't have to worry about trying to remember them all.

Douglas	My husband
David	Elder son (born 1990)
Andrew	Younger son (born 1992)
Julia	Andrew's fiancée and now wife
Leah	David's girlfriend and now fiancée
George & Sylvia	Our friends from Newcastle with whom we shared our holidays in Sri Lanka
Iain	Friend who introduced us to Sri Lanka in 2015
Jacqui & Paul	Another couple in Sri Lanka in 2015 and 2017
Milinda	Sri Lankan guest house owner
Janaka	A tour driver in Sri Lanka
Granny & Grandad	My Mum and Dad
Jean, Sheila, Jennifer & Clare	My sisters
Uncle David	Jean's husband
Jill	Friend since we've been at senior school, with whom I toured Scottish Highlands and Islands
Lindsay	My cousin. Jill and I met him when touring in Scottish Highland and Islands
Cecil	Lindsay's work colleague we met when touring in Scottish Highland and Islands
Karen	Friend who bought our caravan with her sister Julie
Kristina & Elisabeth	Friends since early school days
Mabel & Olivia	Kristina and Elisabeth's daughters
Dave & Chris	Friends we holidayed with in Austria and Dubai

George & Bunty	My cousin George and his wife in Canada
Dallas & Lorna	My cousin Lorna and her husband in Australia
Sarah, Suzy & Charlie	Dallas and Lorna's daughters and grandson
Hugh	Lorna's brother
Emily	Lorna's friend
Glenn, Helen & Alex	Douglas' cousin Glenn, his wife Helen and son in Australia
Philip & Diane	A couple we met at a dinner under the stars in Australia
William	The waiter who served us breakfast when in New York
Antonio	Guide on Levada walks in Madeira
Alessandro	Tour guide in Italy
Gabriel, Richard & Lin	Work colleagues when in Hong Kong
Euan & Kathleen	Directors of Ayrshire Fiddle Orchestra
Jan, Chris & Roberta	Postscript friends who were invaluable in lead up to Andrew and Julia's wedding

Introduction

I've got a terrible memory which, in terms of my wonderful travel experiences, can be infuriating. Reminiscing, for me, can be challenging as photographs don't always spark my hesitant memory brain cells. So, I write when I'm on holiday, hoping the words and accompanying photos will light up those memories with laughter and "Remember when's". I record the happy and not-so-happy times, emailing daily updates to family and friends.

Encouraging email recipients have repeatedly said, "You should write a book." I have now taken up their challenge, editing and drawing together some of those emails.

This book centres around a wonderful holiday my husband Douglas and I had in Sri Lanka in 2017 scattered with memories of holidays as a couple, with sons David and Andrew or friends and relatives.

In Sri Lanka, we had the joy of spending time with friends George and Sylvia exploring our immediate surroundings and travelling further afield in this wonderful island. Each day brought new experiences ranging from relaxing to exhausting, amusing to thought provoking, straightforward to the very opposite!

When writing, I try to capture humour integral to my travelling experiences, many recollections to this day still lead to me laugh aloud. I've often heard it said, "laughter is the best medicine" and even if I'm not laughing, I'm happy when writing. It's even therapeutic writing about the downsides of our holidays – the mishaps, accidents and when things go pear-shaped. For such is the nature of life, and the not so good experiences make me value the good ones even more.

My approach to writing reflects my age and the progress of technology. I began with pen and paper, moved to a Dictaphone with write-up later, and ultimately to a tablet or laptop. The Dictaphone "phase" caused much family amusement. From my perspective, it was quick and easy to use when things happened. To clarify, I was not Margaret Moore, Private Investigator, suspiciously hiding behind pillars and quietly speaking into the gadget so as not to be overheard. I used the Dictaphone in the car when travelling with Douglas, David and Andrew. At such times they relished teasing me, bombarding me with comments solely aimed at putting me off my train of thought; the challenges of being part of the Moore family where a wonderful sense of humour clearly flows from generation to generation.

I got my own back asking them to contribute to the recording. It's enlightening to reflect on what was note-worthy to David and Andrew when they were young. When touring in California in 2001, we stopped at Oakhurst in the wonderful mountains surrounding Yosemite. Did David and Andrew comment on the fantastic scenery we'd just driven through? No. David (aged 11) recorded,

"Dad and I saw this sign in the bathroom which said, *If you sprinkle when you tinkle, please be neat and wipe the seat.* There was another sign which said, *A bad day when playing sports, is better than a good day at work.*" The recording continued with him guffawing with laughter.

Andrew (aged 9) contributed, "I saw a puppet which looked like a bin. When you put your hand in the puppet, a cute wee[1] racoon appeared out of the bin. Bye." Short and sweet.

Progressing to a video recorder also had pros and cons. Recording was easy but editing, time consuming especially wading through the mistakes I'd made with the on-off switch. I was annoyed with myself when I reviewed the footage from a wonderful boat trip lasting several hours on a lagoon in Sri Lanka's Colombo in 2015. While thinking the recorder was off, I'd filmed the bottom of the boat, my skirt, the inside of a pocket and the incessant sound of the boat's outboard motor for most of the tour. Then thinking I was switching it on, I recorded fantastic footage of monkeys and enormous fruit bats whose wingspans were 120 to 150 cm (4 to 5 feet). But this footage didn't exist as I'd unwittingly switched the recorder off instead of on.

Fortunately, life is easier now as I've discovered how simple it is to do everything on a tablet or phone including making mini daily movies of photos and videos.

The re-reading required for this book has reminded me of the many happy family mealtime conversations which started with, "Do you remember when ..." and we launched into recounting memories from family holidays. Like: "Do you remember the huge table of bread in the hotel restaurant in Oslo (2002). We'd never seen so many varieties of bread before. And we'd to slice the loaves ourselves holding the bread

[1] Wee = Scottish for "little".

with a napkin in one hand and the knife in the other." At the time it was amazing but now more commonplace. This sparked off another memory about the same dining room, as David recalled:

"And Andrew and I went round the unoccupied tables looking at the pictures on the lids of the individual milk cartons. We wanted to collect one of each of the different animals pictured. We swapped any we didn't have for duplicates from our table then drank the milk so we could keep the lids."

Recipients of my holiday emails told me they felt they were on holiday with me as they read, and I hope it will be the same for you. Hopefully too my writing will trigger your own "I remember when ..." holiday reflections and conversations, and maybe even encourage travel to some of the amazing places we have visited.

So now please journey with me as we holiday in Sri Lanka and reminisce about holidays in our Scottish homeland, Iceland, America, India, Hong Kong, Norway, Spain, Italy, London, Madeira, South Africa, Dubai, Canada, Austria and Australia.

PS: I've included dates in the text to allow David and Andrew's ages to be established in the various holidays described. David was born in May 1990 and Andrew in May 1992, two days apart. (I was making David's birthday cake on the evening I went into labour indicating Andrew was on the way. The train made of mini chocolate covered swiss rolls with train candle holders was hidden away until Douglas brought it to the hospital on David's birthday.)

Sylvia, George, me and Douglas on top of rocky outcrop behind Aluthapola Buddhist Temple

Sri Lanka – here we come

"Well," I said to Douglas, "one day when we're going on holiday, I'll be organised well in advance rather than rushing at the last minute." His reply was, "We'll see."

I'd been determined to get things right *this* time. I visualised myself having a leisurely breakfast, going to church as normal (after all, it was Sunday and Douglas was the minister so had work to do before his holiday could begin!), coming home for lunch followed by time to sit down, relax perhaps reading a book and having a final cuppa before leaving the house to start our long journey to Sri Lanka.

I started packing many days in advance, trying to emulate my friend Jill. Some would say I'm a bit over the top about cleaning and tidying the house before I go on holiday. But this time before starting any new task I cross examined myself: "Is it vital this is done before I go away?" Surprisingly, I became good at saying "No". You would think therefore I had it sussed. But I didn't.

The taxi arrived. There were things still to be done: dishes to be dried and put away, and when did I last brush my hair? Neither was vital and I decided I could do without brushing my hair. But did I really want to come back and see dishes still in the draining rack; a reminder once again my ambition to be totally organised hadn't been realised? This was a step too far, so I thrust the dishes (still wet) into the cupboards, then changing my mind, grabbed a brush and ran it through my hair before running to the waiting taxi. Douglas sighed, he'd seen me rushing like this many times before, but my arrival only delayed the driver by a few seconds, I reasoned.

We hadn't planned to go by taxi to the airport. However, Leah, our son David's girlfriend, let us know of delays in her journey earlier in the day which could similarly affect ours. She was meeting our son Andrew's fiancée, Julia, and Julia's other bridesmaids in Glasgow to search for dresses for the imminent wedding. At the local train station Leah discovered the trains were all stopping at Kilwinning and a replacement bus service would follow resulting in a much longer journey time. Wisely, Leah opted to use the alternative direct bus to Glasgow, but further problems arose. The first bus didn't turn up and the next had only a couple of free seats – not nearly enough for the long queue of people wanting to get on board. In consultation with David, a plan evolved. Leah walked back about a mile towards Ayr to an earlier stop. Success! Another bus arrived with a whole four empty seats, and fortunately Leah got one, arriving safely, but a little later than planned, in Glasgow. Heeding Leah's warnings and keen to get to the airport in a stress-free state, we ordered a taxi. I felt really spoiled!

The taxi driver was delightful and chatted all the way to the airport taking us a scenic route rather than the motorway telling us this was shorter and quicker than the motorway route other taxi drivers prefer.

The conversation turned to the terrible food waste in supermarkets. Our driver mentioned how the local Lidl supermarket in days gone by put unsold food on a shelf at the end of the day and people could take it for free. This brought back memories for me as I remembered us being happy recipients of such free food on several occasions. Loaves of bread and other perishables were gratefully received at a time in our lives when we'd to count our pennies carefully.

"The feeling of getting a bargain is hard to beat," I said as my mind drifted to a special family holiday. In 2000 we heard about an Icelandair special offer: half price flights and accommodation in New York including a stopover in Iceland. Only a little supplement had to be paid for the accommodation in Iceland. All we'd to do was collect tokens from four newspapers then phone to book. Despite thinking the offer was too good to be true and expecting to be unsuccessful, we planned for one night in Iceland followed by four nights in New York.

The phone lines opened at 9 a.m. on the following Monday and I remember it well. Douglas had come off a night shift but rather than going to bed, he was tasked with walking David and Andrew to school, something I usually did. In the meantime, I stood in the hall beside the phone, the handset attached to the base by its spiralled and slightly tangled cord ready to phone at 9.00 a.m. on the dot.

As I waited, my stomach churned and my head was in overdrive. Questions bombarded my mind, strengthening my doubt about us getting this special deal. How long would it take to get through? Would I get through at all? Would the phone line automatically cut off after twenty rings? Would I have to keep redialling? How quickly would I be able to tap the numbers in again? What if I dialled the wrong number?

Would the dates we wanted be available? Probably not, I thought, because we wanted to go during the Easter school holiday, and I was sure *everyone* waiting would want the same dates. If I could book though, this would be David and Andrew's first overseas holiday.

I dialled a few minutes before 9 a.m., hoping to get into the queue for when the phones started being answered. The engaged line suggested others had had the same thought. My third attempt was about 15 seconds before the clock chimed 9. This time the phone rang! I waited for the recorded message telling me they "were experiencing a high level of calls." But the message didn't come and instead almost immediately the phone was answered. I've dialled the wrong number, I thought. But no, on checking with the man on the other end of the line, I was through to the booking department. I couldn't believe it! But I knew this was just the first hurdle.

As I gave him the dates, I was shaking like a leaf. He checked, "Yes, these dates are available," he said. I couldn't believe this either! I don't know how many times I thanked him as all the details were finalised.

When I pressed the "end call" button on the phone I immediately phoned Douglas' mobile. After I came off the phone, I had a thought. I phoned him back.

"I was just thinking," I started, knowing Douglas dreaded hearing these words from me. "Are we daft going all that way for so short a time especially as jet lag will affect us? Would it be better to add an extra night to our stays in both Iceland and New York?"

I'd no idea if it would be possible to change the dates.

"It's worth trying, but don't build your hopes up," Douglas said.

Thus, phone back I did, and again the phone was answered immediately. I explained my request and after checking the hotel availability the booking was changed without any cost to us. Lots more "thank-you-s" from me!

On the day we left I was very excited when the train arrived to take us to the airport. We were on our way! I was surprised David and Andrew were so calm. I think I expected them to be wired to the moon with excitement. Once we were settled in our seats Andrew said, "I can't believe it."

"What can't you believe?" I asked.

"That we're actually going. I kept expecting something to happen and we wouldn't go to Iceland and New York," was his reply.

Yes, he was excited but in his quiet kind of a way.

"Not only are we going abroad for the first time, but this is the longest train journey Andrew and I have been on," David added. "It's 45 minutes and our longest train journeys so far have been with Granny and Grandad when they've taken us to Irvine. It only takes 11 minutes to get there."

And thus began an amazing holiday.

Looking forward to our flight to Sri Lanka we said farewell to the taxi driver, and in the airport found several changes. The need for the new "Repacking" area became apparent as we checked in. Next to our Emirates check-in was a check-in for Whizz flights. We became aware of constant to-ing and fro-ing statements between a customer with two bags and the check-in lady.

"Your ticket only allows for one piece of hand luggage – not one plus a handbag," she patiently told the Whizz passenger.

"But I've paid extra for luggage."

"You've paid *separately* for luggage, but this is for one item – your small suitcase. There's no free luggage allowance in the ticket price to cover your handbag." (The handbag was a substantial rucksack). "Can you put your handbag into your case?" she offered as a solution to the lady's problem.

This question remained unanswered, "But I paid extra for luggage," she said again, and the same explanation followed. Eventually the check-in lady had heard the argument enough and bluntly told her to go and "repack" at the repacking area or pay for an extra piece of hand luggage. Off the traveller went to the repacking area. We didn't find out if she squeezed all her belongings into the case. Or perhaps she put on extra layers of clothes to make space in her case for her rucksack.

"Some flights are particularly bad for customers trying to take additional luggage onboard," our check-in lady told us. "I've had families of three people arriving with 20 pieces of luggage." I wondered if she was a teeny-weeny bit like me and prone to ever so slight exaggeration?

Another lovely surprise followed in an unexpected place – the lady's toilet. Refurbished a few years before (my surveyor's hat has not left me), the pleasant surroundings were further enhanced by something simple but so effective: two vases of daffodils and tulips. (Did I hear or read somewhere mixing daffodils and tulips in a vase isn't good as the flowers don't last so long? Reminds me of the long-gone *Call my bluff* TV programme: is this "true" or a "bluff"? I don't know the answer to this question!) On commenting to the lady cleaning the floor outside the toilets about the flowers, she said she'd been amazed at the number of people who'd said the same thing to her – and today was the first day the flowers were in place. Hopefully this becomes standard practice.

As we approached the security conveyor belts where we would be removing our electronic gadgets, liquids etc., I pulled myself up short. I was in "work" mode, zoning out and rushing along trying to get through the security process as quickly as possible. I reminded myself it was over a year since I stopped making regular work-related flights up and down to London Heathrow airport. I didn't need to try to get through this hassle as quickly as possible anymore. I was going on holiday!

We got through security without a hitch which was amazing. Douglas is invariably stopped. This despite him being fastidious in his attempts to ensure anything and everything with the slightest possibility of setting off the alarms as he walks through the screening is put into the trays on the conveyor belts. EVERYTHING is removed from his pockets, his watch is removed, his belt is taken off, his clothes are removed (no they aren't – only joking! Mind you, if he did, it would save him emptying his pockets, and double and triple checking he *had* emptied them). Fortunately, his trousers stayed up even without the belt. This is more than could be said about another traveller who had to quickly grab his trousers as gravity caused them to fall rapidly towards the floor.

The airside vending area was bright and attractive with several new shops and eateries open, but few people were purchasing. Personally, we find even the "duty free" prices are extortionate. Having said that we don't tend to buy designer clothes or accessories so don't know the "real" price of such items.

But airport shops are part of the holiday, so we had our customary look round, putting on a skoosh[2] or two of perfume/aftershave hoping we'd like them. I've discovered there's nothing worse than being on a long flight wearing perfume I thought would be worth a try but subsequently found it to be horrible.

But what has happened to all the free chocolates once offered in the shops? Regretfully for me this seems to be a rarity. Mind you, it avoids the mistake Douglas and I once made in Dubai airport when we tried some chocolate from a dish only to discover it was incense! Absolutely disgusting and despite our best efforts it took ages to get rid of the awful taste from our mouths.

If only all airports could be like Hanoi Airport in Vietnam. When there

[2] Skoosh = Scottish word for "a spray" or "a squirt".

in 2015, we found the shops fantastic. Many of the things we'd seen in a craft factory were available here too – and not at massively inflated prices. We ended up buying more than we'd done during the previous few days in Vietnam as there was a much better selection than when we'd searched elsewhere for souvenirs and gifts.

Our journey to Sri Lanka today involved two flights. At Dubai, we disembarked, waited a few hours in the airport before boarding another plane. On the second flight, I found myself writing: "Our first flight was on a A380 plane." I was feeling very pleased with myself and thought Douglas would be ultra-impressed when I pointed to this all-important reference to the "A380". (Douglas had worked in Air Traffic Control and knew all about planes).

Now picture the scene. All is quiet as passengers snoozed or watched a film.

"It wasn't an A380. It was a 777- 300 series plane," he corrected me.

But it wasn't just *me* he told but *every* other passenger on this flight too. With his headphones on he didn't realise he was yelling at the top of his voice. All I was aware of was everyone's head turning in search of the source of this verbal disturbance to their peace and quiet. This was even more embarrassing when I noticed they all had headphones on just like Douglas and yet they had still heard him. (OK – I admit it … slight exaggeration – only 99.9% of heads turned around. The 0.1% represents the passenger who had died on the flight.) [Note from "Editor Douglas": "She's havering."][3] (Authors revision: No deaths, but everything else written is totally and utterly true! Oh dear – now I'm having a slight twinge of guilt about telling fibs.)

We noticed some differences in the Emirates flight from our flights to Sri Lanka two years earlier. There was no pack waiting for us when we arrived at our seats with eye mask, toothbrush, toothpaste and socks; no hot facecloth after embarking or just before landing, and fewer offers of drinks during the journey. Oh, for the good old days.

At one point I was listening to an Emirates' "propaganda" discussion on the entertainment channel. Some high heid yin[4] from the company was telling us about all the planned "improvements", all of which would be "great for passengers". Those travelling in First and Business classes would be offered more and a greatly enhanced travelling experience. Economy passengers were not forgotten either. The gist of it was tickets

[3] Havering = Scottish for "talking nonsense".

[4] High heid yin = "someone in a senior position in a company".

would change so *less* was included in the price and passengers could choose "extras" like food on the planes or families being able to get seats beside each other – all for appropriate additional costs. "How fantastic!" I thought sarcastically. I was overwhelmed with these thoughtful changes. Imagine families being able to sit together! The way he talked you'd have thought this hadn't happened before and there had been an eureka moment in the Board Meetings where this possibility was decided upon. I got the impression Emirates was taking a leaf out of some of the low-cost airlines.

We landed in Colombo, Sri Lanka four and a half hours after leaving Dubai, at about 17.50 local time (5.5 hours ahead of UK). The outside temperature was 30 degrees just as it had been when we arrived here in 2015.

We joined the inevitable queue at immigration. Even though the queue was short, it was a slow process.

"Do you remember when we were in Hong Kong in 2013 when I was on one of my lecturing trips and you were helping to carry my suitcase?" I asked Douglas. What he was really doing was having a holiday while I was working but I let him believe he was a great help to me.

"What in particular am I to remember?" I suppose this was a relevant responsive question.

"Well, I had to go one way at immigration to the short queue and you had to join the separate long queue for normal passengers."

"They clearly wanted to separate out the abnormal passengers like you," was his witty response. He knows how to make me laugh. I'd a work visa so got special treatment.

While standing all alone in my special queue, I found myself getting nervous. I've no idea why as I'd made a similar trip twice before. I was wondering what would happen if there was something wrong with my visa and I was refused entry. I had five full days of teaching ahead of me, and the other lecturers also had full timetables, so they wouldn't be able to take my classes. Fortunately, the short queue moved quickly so I didn't hang on to these thoughts for long. I was waved through as normal and waited patiently for Douglas to join me. If only the journey home had been as straightforward but that's a tale for later.

"Oh, and there was the time we were in Madeira with David and Andrew, when they had to go one way and we another. Remember, they had new electronic passports and we the old ordinary ones." I could see Douglas tuning into my thoughts.

"Yes, it was the first time we, and I'm sure everyone else on our flight, had come across the passport scanning machines. It wasn't a good welcome to Madeira," he replied.

The automated electronic route caused many problems. People didn't know how to use the machines they were faced with. There was no clear signposting, so some people joined the queue not realising it was only for people with the new passport. When they tried their old passport in the machines they didn't work. The poor folk had to go and join the separate queue for a manual inspection of their passports.

Douglas and I using the old-fashioned manual route were processed quickly and stood watching the slow progress David and Andrew were making. We watched as people wearing glasses, realised they had to take them off. Each had to stand on two yellow footprints on the floor and look into a camera, making sure they didn't smile, as smiling was forbidden. (Not, I'm sure, that any were in the mood for smiling anyway.) Once recognised, the barrier opened and with a sigh of relief, they could proceed.

One problem, we witnessed, related to the height of the camera for facial recognition. We saw parents surrounded by their young offspring, none of whom wanted to stand in a queue close to their parents so were making constant bids for freedom. The poor parents were multi-tasking as they tried to keep control of their roaming offspring, fathom out how the machine worked while lifting up a wriggling and uncooperative child towards the camera only to find the child did not understand the concept of needing to stay still while looking at the camera way above their heads. Parents became flustered, people in the queue behind impatient.

Finally, one of the immigration officers came out of his booth and sauntered over to tell the already exasperated parents to go and join the manual passport processing queue. The electronic route, they were told, wasn't for children. Wouldn't it have been so much more helpful if he had stood at the entry points to the queue to direct the families away from the electronic system in the first place?

Eventually, David reached the front of the queue and got through with his electronic passport. Then it was Andrew's turn. After inserting his passport, an error message appeared on the screen in front of him. "Children" apparently included 17-year olds! He wasn't impressed at being called a child and subsequently the immigration officer wasn't pleased as Andrew should have gone through "with his parents".

Anyway, he was allowed into Madeira and through this experience we learned a lot about electronic passports and associated processing technology.

"Mind you, I don't think I have been as worried as I was when you and I went to Australia," I recalled. We'd prepared ourselves for the horrors of Australian immigration having watched TV programmes about people being stopped at customs there. At Glasgow airport I'd wanted to buy suntan cream.

"Where are you going?" the man at the till asked.

"Australia."

"You wouldn't be able to take this into the country because it was over 100ml and you're stopping at Dubai."

"But it will be in a special Duty-Free bag," I countered.

"It doesn't matter."

The sun cream wasn't bought, and I wondered about all the other bottles I had in my suitcase which was heading for the hold in the plane. I warned Douglas these might be confiscated.

Getting through immigration when we arrived in Australia took a ridiculously long time, with only one girl checking the immigration forms and passports of all arriving passengers.

"It was funny when you remembered about the packet of lemon biscuits in your pocket from the flight," I reminded Douglas. "You were worried about them being found when our luggage was checked, but I'd a great solution. I'm sure we were the height of inconspicuousness when we stopped and ate them behind a large column supporting the roof!"

Actually, I was pleased Douglas had found the biscuits as I needed a wee bit of sustenance in my mixed-up time-wise stomach. We made sure we carefully examined each other (a bit like monkeys grooming each other searching for insects) and wiped away any crumb residue around our lips which would provide evidence of our latest misdemeanour. Then we confidently stepped out from our hiding place.

We eventually arrived at the desk where the aforementioned paperwork-checking lady checked our paperwork. We were prepared to be directed to the waiting custom officers who were checking suitcases – just like on the TV. However, she waved us through another exit point which I'd assumed was only for those with Australian passports. This route took us straight into the arrivals lounge without the baggage check we'd anticipated. We'd made it into Australia!

You would have thought we would have learned a valuable lesson after the biscuit-in-pocket scenario. But no. Later in the holiday we were in Perth waiting to board our flight to Adelaide.

"Where is the banana you bought the other day but didn't eat?" Douglas asked, having heard an announcement detailing a long list of items we couldn't take onto the plane in hand or hold luggage including, you've guessed it, bananas.

"In the cool bag which I put in your suitcase." I assured him. I wasn't going to be caught with food in hand luggage again.

"But it's not allowed in hold luggage either."

"Oh well," I shrugged, "we'll just need to wait and see what happens." (OK, the word "banana" wasn't actually used, but I reckoned was included in the generic "fruit".)

While we were waiting to get off the plane at Adelaide, I was aware of Douglas rummaging in his hand luggage once again. This time, I too heard the announcement about forbidden fruit. And low and behold, what did he find in his rucksack? The banana. Clearly it wasn't where I'd assured him it was.

Trying to conceal the banana without attracting the attention of the authorities (there could easily have been fruit spies on board) he worriedly asked me what we should do.

"I'll eat it," was my reply. (I was getting good at destroying evidence.)

Aware this was a serious business, I sat down and quickly consumed said banana. Well most of anyway, the skin as far as I'm concerned is unpalatable, so I wrapped it in a paper hankie.

I was sure I'd heard mention of bins at the front of the plane where forbidden items were to be deposited, so wasn't overly worried. I would pop the package in, and we would proceed guilt free. But there wasn't a bin. We walked on. Taking the you-know-what from me, Douglas took on the task of trying to look guilt free. He put it into his pocket and stuffed his hand in trying to conceal its shape while all the time rather than looking guilt free, looked very dodgy. Finally, we spotted an ordinary bin in the café area, so we parted company with the banana skin. One relieved Douglas was now walking beside me! I'm sure he was six inches taller than moments earlier as the weight of guilt had been lifted from his shoulders.

The end of the tale; or is it? I suppose there could be DNA evidence for anyone who wanted to find it ...

Later in the same holiday, Douglas said, "Elephants, bears, kangaroos, chihuahuas, chimney pots, extension cables, hedgehogs, porcupines, half eaten Christmas pudding." I had to interrupt.

"What are you talking about?"

"Have you got any of these either in your hand luggage or in the suitcase, or have you put any of them in my luggage?" It was more of Douglas' sense of humour at my expense as we approached the doors into Adelaide Airport, Australia.

I admit I'd fallen a bit short on our previous flights, but this list was even more extreme than the one we'd seen when we were about to board a ferry to Kangaroo Island a couple of days previously. There were signs stating what passengers were forbidden to take: honey, potatoes, foxes and rabbits. I couldn't understand why honey and potatoes were included on the list. During our two-day tour we learned the island was the one place in the world to have only Ligurian bees and beekeepers wanted to ensure they're kept pure. The bees are exported around the world because of their placid nature. The restriction on potatoes is because the farmers produce seed potatoes and didn't want to run the risk of disease arriving with other potatoes. The sign made sense.

Yes, queuing at immigration in Sri Lanka provided opportunity for reminiscing.

The next stage of travelling can also be tedious – waiting for suitcases to arrive from the plane.

One of our cases came off the conveyor belt relatively quickly. What joy – we were going to get on the final leg of our journey soon. Our hopes were premature. We found ourselves watching with increasing trepidation as case after case came through the flapping doors and round the conveyor belt in front of us. When would our case number two join case number one on the trolley beside us? After a long wait and with a sense of relief we finally saw it appear through the doors.

Two years previously, when we were last in this airport, I was surprised to find a duty-free area of shops after immigration. It was no different this time. There was what I would regard as a normal duty-free selling alcohol, perfumes, cigarettes etc. But following this was a long row of shop units selling, it seemed, anything and everything. When I say shop units, they were not High-Tec as in a departure lounge at London Heathrow airport for example. Instead they had flimsy looking walls, were open fronted and their goods spilled out into the passageway. It was more like walking through a market where we could have bought all manner of things including a cooker or a fridge without any difficulty.

Finally, we were in the Arrivals area and a wonderful sight met us – a row of drivers wearing dazzling white shirts holding aloft cards with names on them. Amongst them we saw our name and gratefully followed our smiling, happy driver, immediately feeling the wall of heat as we stepped outside the terminal building.

We were looking forward to seeing friends George and Sylvia who we were spending the holiday with. They had already arrived from Newcastle and would be waiting for us at the guest house. We first met and got to know them as we sat chatting under the shade of the veranda when last on holiday in Sri Lanka. During that holiday we went on great trips with them.

The drive to the guest house gave us an opportunity to feel like knowledgeable experts as we saw and heard the familiar sights and sounds; the busy roads full of tuk-tuks, cars, very bashed buses plus motor cyclists all vying with each other for position on the road, achieved through beeping of horns and a good dose of daring.

This year we weren't surprised when we saw fancy material fixed to the roofs of the higgledy-piggledy low-rise roadside buildings and draped down over the edge of the veranda to the kerbside.

"Do you remember when we were first here, we walked past the material, even walking on the road to avoid it? It's strange now to think we didn't realise it hid the small shops behind and was helping to keep them cool. This year we'll know to draw back the curtains to reveal the delights in the hidden shops."

We passed the many small religious shrines often built at the end of buildings at a road junction. These were brightly coloured, and often had plastic flowers and fruit, multi-coloured garlands and old looking net or cotton material at the back.

"Do you think you will be visiting there this time for Lion beer?" I asked Douglas pointing to the floor to ceiling prison-bar-like frontage of the government-run off-licence store. I knew the answer before I heard it as it was the only place to buy alcohol for evenings at the guest house. Seeing the store meant we'd nearly arrived. And it was only a few more minutes before we were at the guest house where we were greeted by a very excited Sylvia and a more reserved George.

Our holiday had well and truly begun.

Type of catamaran used by
fishermen though this one
used for tourist voyages

Sand, sea and fishermen

It's two years since we were last in Sri Lanka. This time we were in a new guest house which Milinda, the owner, had recently built.

I'd forgotten what lovely smiles the female members of staff have and how quietly keen they are to please, though not always understanding what we're saying. At breakfast for example, we learned a gentle shaking of her head accompanied by, "Ah", meant the waitress had understood our request. Until this happened, we knew we hadn't explained ourselves clearly.

A table was slowly and meticulously set for us when we went down to the canal bank where breakfast was served. Beside the cup and saucer was placed another smaller and differently designed saucer which served as a plate. We ordered our food selecting from what we affectionately called the "full works" which comprised fruit juice followed by a large plate with two boiled or fried eggs, sausage, bacon and two varieties of curried vegetables – one potato, the other tomato and onion. Oh, and there was a rack of toast and dish of delicious strawberry jam. All this would have been more than enough, but we knew there would follow equally enormous oval plates of fresh fruit: papaya, banana, orange, mango and pineapple. A very pleasant way to finish the meal and we were well on the way to having our "5 fruit and veg a day" – based on the recommendations of the World Health Organisation at the time.

Douglas and I enjoying our first enormous breakfast

I didn't have eggs having heard from Sylvia and George they had a strange taste. Douglas risked it and while saying they were OK; said he wouldn't have them again. There were plenty of other things on his plate; an odd egg or two wouldn't be missed.

Although there was no peppermint tea, based on experience I knew it would be brought in specially for me for breakfasts to come.

Small, young cats wandered around the garden together with a few large dogs. The dogs were guard dogs but once they knew we were guests were docile and happy to let us come and go as we pleased. One of the cute cats crept under the table without me noticing. I got such a fright when it brushed against my leg and let out a yell giving the other guests a fright too. They wondered what awful thing had befallen me.

We walked to the beach with Sylvia and George and plonked ourselves down on sun loungers under the palm trees at "The Beach Lodge". The massive deserted expanse of fine sand beach and the sea lay in front of us. Sun loungers could be used for free providing a drink or something to eat was ordered. I expected someone to come as soon as we settled ourselves, but no one appeared. An example of the relaxed attitude here.

"There's a bell attached to the tree trunk over there," I said to Douglas, pointing, "and a sign telling us to ring it." Yes, I wanted Douglas to unsettle himself from his comfy sun lounger while I continued my laziness.

"I'd like mango juice please," I said to the waitress when she finally arrived. The others placed their orders, which arrived, but my juice took a *long* time to come. I was convinced the girl had gone to the shops to buy the fruit.

I tasted the juice and passed it to Douglas.

"What do you think of this?" I asked.

He had a sip.

"Seems fine to me. It's just like the watermelon juice we had in Hong Kong."

"Yes, but I ordered mango juice."

"Well that explains why it's orange in colour. Strange it doesn't taste of mango though."

I'd no idea what ingredients were in my glass. But it was wet and cold, so fine.

Two lady beach traders selling their wares approached with all sorts of dresses and shirts piled over their arms and in supplementary bags. The questions began, in their quiet, gentle manner:

"Where you from?"

"How long you stay?"

"Been here before?"

Niceties dispensed with; the persuading to buy began. Unsurprisingly, they thought I would suit every dress they held up to show me! Initially I said "no," even though there was a blue one I really liked. Eventually I relented, "OK, I'll try it on."

Returning as if in a fashion parade, I gave my verdict, "It's too long."

"No, no it's fine," I was assured.

"I think it's too long."

"You just lift up when you walking," was the pidgin English solution provided.

Finally, I agreed to buy the dress, but remained resolute I didn't want to buy another.

"I'm not going to look as posh tonight as I envisaged, with this dress hitched up to stop me falling flat on my face!" I mused with the others.

We'd a refreshing swim in the sea, enjoying the waves before Douglas and I spotted local fishermen further along the beach pulling in a fishing net. We went to investigate.

Pulling in the net involved twenty men. Firstly, the long length of rope to which the net was attached was pulled in and carefully coiled on the sand. The enormously long colourful net followed made of numerous smaller sections of red, blue, orange, green and yellow net. White polystyrene floats were attached to each section. The men laid the net along the beach in a long line making for fantastic photos as the bright colours contrasted with the light-coloured sand. The men sang as they pulled and slowly walked backwards using the rhythm of the song to ensure the stamping of their feet into the sand was in unison. After every few steps, the man at the back let go of the net and walked slowly down past the line of men, taking up his position at the front near the water's edge. It was fascinating to watch.

Finally, the last and important section of the net was brought ashore, revealing the catch.

"I can't believe how few fish are in such a long net," I commented. "And the fish are so small. I wonder how many of the twenty men pulling in the net will share this catch. Few hungry mouths will be fed with this haul."

A crowd of both locals and tourists had gathered to witness this daily activity, the final part of which was loading the net back into a boat to be taken back out to sea.

A few of the fishermen assessing their catch after pulling in the long fishing net

Meandering back to the Beach Lodge we were disappointed to notice a sign saying food wasn't being served until 3 p.m. Our tummies needed sustenance. The four of us left to find somewhere else. There were oodles of eateries along the Main Street but which one to choose? We chose one and walked through the restaurant and back outside so we could sit under the canopy overlooking the beach once more.

"Not sure I would like this carpet at home. It's functional but high maintenance," I observed.

The others agreed. It looked beautiful as we walked in, but we quickly ruined it.

"We can't be taken anywhere! How could we have done such a thing on our first visit to this wonderful establishment?"

I suppose it was inevitable, unless we could have flown to our seats. The intricate pattern on the "carpet" had been created by carefully raking the sand on which we trod.

Lunchtime chat began.

"What do you think of your room?" Sylvia asked.

"It's certainly huge and bright," I said, "and in many ways better than the guest house we stayed in previously. Everything is so fresh and new. I'm not sure, though, why there's what looks like a window opening without a window in the wall between the bedroom and the bathroom."

"No, me neither. And do you have a fridge?" Sylvia asked.

"No."

"Neither did we and there isn't a communal fridge like in the guest house we stayed in last holiday. We got a fridge given to us yesterday though."

"Oh, good. We'll no doubt get one too. I get the feeling they're still completing the rooms."

"Mind you, Jacqui and Paul had a fridge in their room when they arrived. Smacks of favouritism!" Sylvia joked. Jacqui and Paul were another couple we met two years previously.

Contrasting the rooms made me think of a similar comparison we made on our first overseas holiday with David and Andrew; the one I'd booked with vouchers from a newspaper.

We arrived at our New York hotel tired from the flight, feeling jet lagged and the stationary traffic for much of the journey from the airport had made the taxi ride wearisome. We were relieved a price for the journey had been agreed at the outset and so did not worry as we watched the meter clicking round indicating ever increasing costs, way beyond the quoted fare.

We opened the door to our bedroom. It was dark and dingy. Despite this we looked in expectantly. Through the gloom we saw there was only one small double bed in it.

I phoned reception.

"This is the only room available," I was told.

"But I booked a family room."

"This is the only room available."

"How are four of us expected to sleep in this small double bed? It's not a king or even a queen size."

"I will send up a spare single bed, but it will cost $25 a night."

This was a ridiculously high amount when compared to the amount we'd paid for the "family room". After arguing, he finally agreed there would be no charge and we would be moved to another room in the morning.

We put the boys to bed and Andrew was soon fast asleep. After a long wait and no sign of the bed, I phoned reception again, "We haven't got the single bed yet."

"It's coming."

Thankfully, shortly afterwards, there was a knock at the door. Now to let you understand more fully our predicament, it wasn't only the double bed that was small, but also the room. It therefore proved difficult to get the un-foldable single bed into the room and once in, there was scarcely any space to move around. A traffic light system was set up in our minds to avoid collisions with each other and movement was kept to a minimum.

In the end, I slept on the single bed, and Douglas joined David and Andrew in the double bed. Not an ideal way to start our holiday in New York, especially after the amazing couple of nights we'd just spent in Iceland.

The hotel accommodation in the Hotel Loftleidir in Reykjavik had been very different.

"Would you like two adjoining rooms instead of the family room?" the receptionist asked.

"How wonderful," we replied, totally taken aback by the offer of an upgrade. We'd paid very little for the family room with breakfast and what we were allocated was out of this world for us.

Douglas and I had a Deluxe room, one of only a few in the hotel, and David and Andrew had an adjoining twin room. What an experience for David and Andrew; a room of their own and the ability to watch programmes on their own TV.

The twin room was large and the Deluxe room three times its size. The Deluxe room had not only a king size bed, but also a three-piece suite, plus a bathroom instead of a shower room. I mustn't forget the trouser press. This was the first time we'd been in a hotel room with a trouser press and we immediately started pressing our trousers – well the spare ones in our suitcases – not those we were wearing. None *needed* to be pressed; we just wanted to use this gadget. There was one drawback to having two rooms: I'd only brought one tube of toothpaste! This was a miniscule difficulty we were happy to deal with.

"You will therefore realise our room in New York was an enormous contrast," Douglas finished off this tale.

"Douglas, do you remember the awful owner we came across at a motel in Huntingdon when touring California with David and Andrew a year later?"

"Yes, we hadn't booked accommodation in advance and after trying a few and finding they were fully booked, we accepted the first one with availability. Big mistake."

"Unlike our room in Iceland, this one was expensive, and we expected better. Plus, we'd a very grumpy owner to deal with."

He gave us strict instructions, "Do not enter the hotel after being on the beach opposite until you've washed your feet with a hose outside to get rid of the sand."

"I couldn't believe it when we returned from the beach later and saw him waiting at the bottom of the stairs to make sure we hosed our feet!" Douglas said.

"And there was only one towel in the room for the four of us. I didn't mind going and asking for more, nor returning later to ask for shampoo when we discovered there was none in the room. I was aware he was getting grumpier with each request I made," I continued.

"Do you remember, we ended up tossing a coin though to see who would have to go and break the news to him when we couldn't find a remote controller for the TV?" We decided to go as a delegation.

"There's a controller in the room," was his response.

"We can't find one."

"It was sitting beside the TV when you first went into the room," he told us.

"No, it wasn't," we assured him.

Eventually, he gave us one, but more strict instructions rang in our ears. "Hand it in to reception when you leave."

On failing to find a hair dryer in the room, we had a committee meeting and decided even with all four of us going, it wasn't worth the anticipated aggravation. Basically, we were scared. Letting my hair dry naturally was an easier option. These things all made us laugh though – when we were well and truly out of his earshot.

Prior to checking out of the hotel, we checked the room thoroughly to ensure we hadn't left anything.

"Look what I've found," I heard Andrew say. Turning, I saw held aloft not one but two remote controllers. He had found the second one down the side of one of the beds. Clearly the room hadn't been very well cleaned before we arrived, but we didn't confront the owner with this fact.

This tale reminded me of a short break Douglas and I had in a hotel where we'd booked a no-smoking room. As we walked along the corridor leading to our room, we were just about knocked out by an awful smell, like a burst sewer. We went back to reception.

"I'm ever so sorry," a very nice receptionist responded. "The carpet has just been cleaned and we can't get rid of the smell."

"I have never smelled a newly cleaned carpet smelling like a sewer!" I replied.

"I can change your room but unfortunately there are no rooms available in the other no-smoking corridors. Here, take the keys for rooms 1, 2, 3, 4 and 5 and see which is the least affected by the smell of smoke. Let me know which room you choose."

In and out of rooms we went, sniffing the air. Room 5 was the least bad.

However, having moved all our belongings into this room, we found the self-locking door, wouldn't self-lock, so could be pushed open by anyone in the corridor. The receptionist came, checked and agreed we couldn't use this room. We moved everything into room 4.

In this room we found several problems but couldn't face trying to find an alternative room. In addition, the level of smokiness increased with each change of room.

"Oh yes," Douglas remembered, "The hot water tap wouldn't turn off. It wasn't just a drip, but a stream of water. I tried to turn it off more tightly but the whole tap turned round. Fortunately, it didn't come off in my hand! Decided it was safer to put up with a running tap. One of the drawer handles came off in my hand as the paper wrapped round the screw trying to secure it failed. The lid to the kettle was broken and it was a two-person job to shut the curtain – one person holding one end to anchor it as the other carefully pulled the other end to the required position. We discovered this because initially the whole curtain went flying along the curtain rail and came off at the other end."

There was one further issue.

"What's that noise?" I'd asked Douglas.

"I can't hear anything," he replied. Douglas has a hearing problem, so I wasn't surprised.

"It's a loud, buzzing sound. There's no way I can stay in a room with such a noise." An audible, deep sigh came from Douglas.

"I don't want to change to another room, but I'll see about getting the noise stopped," was my solution.

I wondered if the buzzing was coming from the rooms on either side of us, so pressed my ears against the walls. No, the buzzing didn't get louder, so I surmised this wasn't the root cause of the problem. It wasn't coming from the corridor either, so perhaps it was something outside. I sneaked past reception and went round the back of the building but couldn't pinpoint a source of the buzz.

I had to admit defeat and spoke to the receptionist on my return, who came to the room and like us couldn't work out what the noise was or where it was coming from. He too went outside to investigate but came to the same conclusion – it was a mystery.

By now we were tired and weary of all the problems so said we would just stay in the room, despite the buzzing sound, the running tap, the broken handle, kettle and curtain. Hopefully, we thought, the buzzing would stop.

The receptionist bade us farewell and the door shut behind him. There was nothing for it now – we just had to settle ourselves in this room. Unpacking was therefore next on the agenda. Douglas opened his bag of belongings, and I followed suit.

Well, talk about dying of embarrassment – the situation I found myself in. The source of the buzzing noise was identified. It was my electric toothbrush. It must have switched itself on. I'm embarrassed now even thinking about it!

I went to the receptionist to confess. Fortunately, he thought it was very funny!

"I must tell you one last story before we pay the lunch bill," I said to the other three, "about our stay in Adelaide when Douglas and I were touring in Australia. We had been booked into apartments much more often than hotels, even if it was just for one night. We stayed for one night in Adelaide, went to Kangaroo Island for a couple of nights before returning to Adelaide, to a different apartment in the same apartment block for another single night."

It seemed ridiculous having such wonderful accommodation for just one night. Because of our pickup times we didn't even use the kitchen or dining facilities to make breakfast.

In our first apartment, I was doing something when I heard Douglas say, "Oh, that's really good!" He'd just found how to pull out the extractor fan above the cooker to make it work. He was clearly impressed by the technology.

"Oh gosh, trust me," was the next rather deflated sounding phrase to emanate from his lips. He couldn't push back in whatever he'd pulled out. I visualised having the extractor going all night. I knew he'd rather not ask someone for help fearing it was something very simple he'd overlooked. He'd also be worrying he'd broken it. I was no help as I couldn't stop laughing.

I realised for Douglas though, this was a serious matter, so trying to contain myself I got up to see if I could lend a hand. Just then, he managed to push the extractor back in.

"It's obviously defective," were his closing words on the subject. This made me smile to myself, but I wasn't going to argue.

The next apartment had a different layout with a much bigger kitchen/dining/living room space. We put our cases into the bedroom and unpacked what we needed for the night.

Back in the kitchen, I noticed a large cupboard, not something we'd had in our last room. Being investigative by nature, I opened the door and found to my delight it contained a washing machine and tumble dryer. Brilliant! Even though it was after 11 p.m. and not a normal time for putting on a washing machine, Douglas was immediately told to give me his clothes for washing. I got my clothes too, by the way.

When I came out of a shower, Douglas for some reason walked to the window at the far end of the living room area. As he turned, he saw a door we somehow hadn't noticed before. We were intrigued but rather more cautious than when I discovered the washing machine and tumble dryer. Holding onto each other for protection, we edged our way to the door, carefully turning the handle and slowly opening the creaking door, broken cobwebs falling onto our hands.

We gingerly peaked our heads through the opening, Douglas' head above mine, he's taller than me after all. Deciding it was safe to proceed we opened the door a bit further before taking a few steps in. Lo and behold, we found another much bigger bedroom with an en suite bathroom! How we missed the door earlier I have no idea. We couldn't blame the cobweb camouflage as this part of the tale's a bit of poetic license.

Unbeknown to us we'd been given a very upgraded room. It was too late for us to be bothered moving bedrooms, so we settled ourselves in the ordinary, non-en suite bedroom. It was such a pity we had to check out early the next day. Enough time to dry our laundry though!

"OK, time to pay the lunch bill now," I concluded this story telling.

It was time to walk over the sand carpet once more before a trip down memory lane as we walked along the Main Street looking in the various touristy shops. Memories flooded back:

• The small shops with a young boy in charge of each, in darkness but illuminated when the light switch was flicked as we entered. An energy saving measure.

• The shelves in the shops usually understandably unclean looking because of the dusty roads outside and the mountains of "stuff" on the shelves. It would be a never-ending task to keep the shelves clean, and it seemed there's no inclination to do so.

• Very few shops had air conditioning though some had fans which were switched on like the lights.

"Right, I'm on the lookout for gifts," Douglas said resolutely. My heart sank. Douglas had started a family tradition a few years before when he bought cheap tacky gifts for David and Andrew. This turned it into a challenge. They set out to find even cheaper and tackier gifts from holidays for us and succeeded on several occasions.

After all the stress involved in looking for such gifts (as I find it harder to buy such awful things) I needed a boost only an ice cream could bring. The ice cream shop we knew from our previous holiday had shut down. Fortunately, we found a new one. It had no curtains concealing its entrance. Instead, it was modern with a fully glazed frontage but cool inside due to wonderful, permanent air-conditioning. We opted to sit on the sofa inside rather than at the roadside tables to ensure our ice cream didn't melt too quickly.

As we opened the door to leave, we braced ourselves for the heat we knew would hit us. Walking along the back streets to the guest house we passed mounds of rubbish. Bonfires were the means of disposing of rubbish for those who don't pay to have it uplifted. It's not ideal passing either the piles of smelly, rotting rubbish waiting to be set alight or the lit bonfires fuelled with plastics or rubber but it's the way of life here and has the advantage of keeping mosquitos away when the fires are lit.

Douglas went for a cooling swim in the pool while I spectated and chatted with George and Sylvia before we all went for our first evening meal together. I wore my new dress, no doubt looking ridiculous as I walked with it well hitched up. But I didn't care.

"What's the difference between 'rice and prawn curry' and 'prawn curry'?" I asked the others as we perused the menu.

George explained, "Prawn curry is just rice and a bowl of prawn curry. When you order rice and prawn curry you get a plate of rice and bowl of curry plus five little bowls of accompaniments."

The rice and prawn curry sounded completely different and I ordered this, ensuring I said "not hot" being wary in case "normal" recipes are too spicy for me. The accompaniments on this occasion were carrots, onions, potatoes, dhal and grated coconut. I don't know why we didn't try Sri Lankan rice and curry last time we were here. What a special meal it turned out to be.

We met and chatted to some lovely people when we went to a bar for a drink after our meal. We perched ourselves on high, long wooden bench seats at even higher bench tables. Just like with the ladies on the beach, we started asking one young couple questions:

"Where are you from?"

"Austria," was the reply.

"What are your holiday plans?"

"We're going to do a tour of Sri Lanka by train."

"Oh, we went on a train when we were here two years ago. It was brilliant!"

They were keen to hear all about it.

"Our train journey was just part of a three-day trip. Most of the time we had a car and driver so we could sit back, enjoy the scenery, towns and villages we passed through and most importantly didn't have to drive on the roads ourselves. Driving etiquette is different to what we're familiar with and at times is very frightening. Our way of dealing with it was either to grab hold of each other or anything static in the car, shut our eyes and/or squeal out in alarm – whatever was the most appropriate in the given situation."

Our aim was to see elephants in the natural surroundings of Udawalawe National Park, rather than going to elephant orphanages where we were told the elephants are trained for the benefit of tourists.

On the way, our driver stopped to show us a gem mine in a field. The flat, grass field was below the road level. Steps had been formed with bags filled with soil and these provided a challenging, uneven descent from the road to the field.

The mine was a very small affair – a couple of shafts dug into the ground in the field, overlooked by a tree covered hillside. A tunnel linked the two shafts which were about 10 metres (about 33 feet) apart. Over one of the shafts was a shelter built with four posts supporting a pitched roof covered with thatch. We were told anyone can mine for gems in Sri Lanka if they own the land and pay an official for a permit.

The shaft had earthwork support and a long ladder to the bottom. A noisy generator worked a pump to remove the water from the bottom of the shaft. One of the eight workers climbed down the ladder to fill a bucket with soil. The bucket was hoisted to the surface where the contents would later be washed in what looked like a large paddling pool made of a canvas covered frame. Sieving by hand would hopefully reveal some gems.

"Do you want to go down the shaft and crawl through the tunnel?" one of the workers asked.

"Eh, no thank you," we all replied, not wanting to offend, but not wanting to put our lives in danger either! I wasn't convinced the earthwork support (if there was any in the tunnel) would have passed UK Health and Safety Regulations.

"So now if you see little thatch roofed structures in the middle of fields, you will know they're probably gem mines," we told the young Austrians.

"And we can also highly recommend Udawalawe National Park. Go early – we left our accommodation at 5.30 a.m. in the pitch dark to make the half hour journey to the gates of the National Park. We were in a large jeep with two rows of tiered seating behind the driver, each row overlooking the one in front, so we all had fantastic views."

We saw our first elephant through the gloom but discovered this elephant is always at the same spot close to the road because men sell bags of food to folk who want to feed it. We therefore decided not to count this as being a real sighting of a wild elephant.

By the time we arrived the sun had risen.

The driver got out at the entry gate to the National Park and joined the queue of about ten other drivers waiting to buy their entry tickets. When he returned, he was accompanied by a guide who climbed into the jeep and stayed with us throughout our safari. Both driver and guide were fantastic at their jobs.

We soon discovered the driver liked a challenge and whenever there were two optional routes along the rutted tracks, he took the most difficult one adding to our excitement. At one point we stopped to rescue another jeep stuck in the muddy water we all had to cross. A rope was attached to the two jeeps before revving of engines and pulling began. We felt we were on a thrill ride at a fairground as we were tossed about even more violently than before. We held on tightly to the bars in front, so we weren't injured or worse – thrown out of the jeep!

Later, we came to a river with very steep sides. Driving down this was scary not just because of the depth of the water or steepness of the sides but because of all the ruts and trees we had to drive over or around.

When we got up the far side, our driver stopped and jumped out. We wondered what he had seen and quickly started scanning the area around us.

"Can you see anything?" we excitedly asked each other. "Is there an elephant or other wild animal about?" We got our cameras ready to snap a photo, checked to see which direction the driver was looking in, and turned to do likewise.

But the driver hadn't seen an animal. No, he was focused on the driver who had previously got stuck in the mud and was following us. Our driver wanted to make sure he got across the river safely, though I wondered if he was enjoying the prospect of seeing the less experienced driver tackle this difficult part of the route. I suspected he was secretly hoping he would witness the jeep getting stuck again thus proving his own skill. He shouted instructions across the water.

Our driver laughed merrily as he filmed the second driver slowly driving the obstacle course towards us with a terrified expression on his face. Watching, we realised why we'd felt scared. I was amazed anyone could drive this route. Yes, our driver was good.

"What animals did you see?" we were asked by the interested Austrian newcomers.

"Well we were very fortunate. Initially we saw a variety of birds, then bigger creatures including water buffalo, iguana and crocodiles."

"Don't forget about the domestic cows," someone chipped in. "They were a real surprise to us."

The guide told us they had "broken into" the park! Why? Because of the good pasture.

The highlight though was seeing a family of 14 elephants. The jeep stopped close to the elephants, so we had a brilliant view. They were right beside the track. At one point, two of the larger elephants walked across and stopped at the front of the jeep, linked their trunks and proceeded to make a lot of blowing and snorting sounds. I admit, I felt threatened and scared, but everything must have been OK as the driver made no attempt to move. We stayed for ages watching them feeding and walking back and forth across the track. My favourites were the baby elephants. They were so cute. I loved watching their little trunks swinging around as though they had absolutely no control of these appendages. It was amazing to watch.

I was also pleased and surprised only six jeeps stopped. There wasn't a mass influx coming from all directions to view the spectacle.

We didn't see the single leopard living in the park. We didn't join the group of jeeps waiting in the hope of seeing it come to a tree it visits every day though at no set time. Considering we only saw about a tenth of the elephant population in the park during the three hours we were there I don't think there was much chance of seeing a single very shy leopard.

We'd a few other sightings of single and pairs of elephants as we continued driving but no more large groups. Other tour groups on safari at the same time only saw a couple of elephants far in the distance. We counted ourselves very fortunate to have seen so many and at such close range.

"We'd better tell our new friends about our train journey. After all it's a train tour they're doing."

"Oh yes – the train. But to let you understand, after the safari, we drove to Ella. It was from here the next morning we'd a relaxed departure time as we were catching a train at 10.56 a.m. (our driver told us this train is never late). The four of us were to be on the train until 1.45 p.m. when we would arrive at Nanu Oya. We would meet the driver there for the drive back to the guest house. So, the race was on – would car or train arrive first?

"We were booked in the Expo carriage and lunch was included. Another advantage of this compartment was there was a large open-air viewing section at one end of the carriage. As the purpose of this train ride was to see the magnificent scenery this was ideal."

"I saw a very annoyed lady who had paid extra to travel in the first-class carriage," Douglas added. "Our carriage was joined to the first-class one and she had opened the door at the end of her carriage, expecting to be able to walk into ours. But locked gates prevented this. The poor attendant in our carriage had to listen to her complaints."

"I want to come across to the viewing section," she demanded.

"This section is not for first-class passengers," he replied.

"But there's no open viewing section in the first-class compartment."

"Yes, I know."

"Well, let me come across. I have paid more for my ticket, you know, than the passengers in your compartment," she said aloofly.

"I know you have paid more, but this is just for people who have booked the Expo carriage. This compartment is fully booked. So, you can't come across."

"But there are only a few people in the viewing section. There's *plenty* of room for me." She was getting increasingly annoyed.

"The space has to kept for other passengers who are sitting inside. They could come out at any time. You cannot change compartments."

She turned round briskly and stormed back into the first-class compartment, slamming the door behind her.

The scenery on our journey was breath-taking. Up in the mountains, looking down onto the arable land below gave a much better feel for the way of life than during the car journey. And there was the contrasting scenery along the way as we passed through forests and tea plantations. It was wonderful.

Our driver won the race and was standing waiting for us on the platform as the train drew into the station.

"Train travel is a great way to see Sri Lanka," we concluded.

Wedding material, coffee and fridges

There's always something to watch in the quiet canal while we eat breakfast. Yesterday a boat went slowly by, the two men on board looking carefully over the side, every so often stopping to lift something out of the water. On one occasion it was a coconut. The man held it towards his ear and gave it a good shake to find out if it had milk in it so still intact. Other times, plastic bottles were extracted from the murky water – and there were plenty of them floating by.

Today there were splashing sounds. I thought someone was throwing bricks into the water. The canal is used as a disposal point for many things. However, looking towards the sound, I saw a man shaking a tree. Coconuts were falling into the water below. After getting into a small boat he retrieved his harvest.

Breakfast finished, Sylvia, George, Douglas and I had our first tuk-tuk ride of the holiday and we went in luxury, hiring not one but two tuk-tuks. They're only designed for two passengers but during our holiday here in 2015 on one occasion four got in one, Sylvia lying across the knees of the other three who were squeezed into the seat behind the driver.

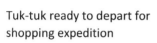

Tuk-tuk ready to depart for shopping expedition

"Hello again," came a friendly and familiar voice as Douglas and I approached our tuk-tuk. What a lovely surprise to see and be remembered by the driver who had often taken us around two years previously.

Our destination? CIB, a large department store selling clothes, material, soft furnishings – everything material related really. The material department on the top floor is amazing and was where I bought material in 2015 and had it made into tablecloths and placemats by a lady near to the guest house.

This time I was on the lookout for something else – material to be made into an outfit for Julia and son Andrew's wedding. Unfortunately, I only thought about this just before we left home so had done no research into outfit designs, how much material to buy, type of material required or anything else a well-prepared person would have done. And as I'm not a dressmaker I hadn't much of a clue about any of these things.

I was back to the drawing board as far as an outfit was concerned as my initial suggested outfit spotted by Douglas and me when in a tourist shop in Edinburgh met with a pretty negative response from Andrew. Will I ever understand why the tartan off-the-shoulder dress with matching tartan shoes, clashing tartan tights and different clashing tartan Rodeo hat wasn't to his taste? Probably not, but the youth of today clearly have different ideas of good taste and I suppose I must, on this occasion accept it.

Sylvia and I saw a range of material we thought appropriate – each bale was a different pastel colour with white flecks. Not knowing which colour would suit me, I did the logical thing and asked if there was a mirror somewhere so I could decide which went with my rosy complexion. The poor guy I spoke to hadn't a clue what I was asking for, so I started miming in the hope he would understand. After about 10 minutes of me playing this game of charades, with over-exaggerated gesticulations, he eventually said, "Ah – glass."

"Yes!" Sylvia and I yelled in unison, unable to conceal our delight. Or at least we hoped *glass* meant *mirror*.

We prepared to head in the direction of his pointing, into the adjacent gent's department.

Still in a state of excitement and joy at our ability to communicate so effectively, 1 grabbed armfuls of bales of cloth, swung round, and in so doing sent another of the assistants flying skywards over the parallel aisle of material. I honestly didn't know he was there and think he had sneaked up behind us, inquisitive to establish the reason for the rumpus. Fortunately, he recovered from this ordeal with little sign of concussion, but this clearly served as a warning to the other assistants who dived for cover as I approached.

In the gent's department, the assistants were unaware of what had just happened in the fabric department, but I was aware of every eye turning our way. I felt I could read their minds; they were wondering what on earth this woman was doing with large bales of material under her arms marching purposefully through their department, followed in hot pursuit by another lady – Sylvia. I got the distinct impression such happenings rarely occurred in CIB. A mirror came into sight.

The large bales were unrolled sufficiently to allow me to hold up a length against me while not allowing any to touch the ground. As if this wasn't enough of a feat, it was also necessary to call Douglas for a third opinion, decide, roll up the bales again, then march equally purposefully back to the department from whence we'd come. Here I asked for advice about the quantity required. Nothing like shifting responsibility as far as decision making is concerned.

"2.5 metres will be enough, madam," he assured me.

I wasn't so sure. Maybe I would want to have a coat or jacket made to match?

"Let's make it six metres," I countered before adding, "I will need lining too."

"No, madam, lining not necessary."

"But this material is for a dress I'm going to wear in the UK. Lining will be good in case it's cold, and if by chance the sun is shining, it will stop my legs being seen through the material."

I'm not convinced he understood my reasoning and wouldn't blame him for thinking the easiest way to deal with this strange customer was just to agree with her.

"OK, madam, get three metres."

As well as not being sure if I have bought enough material, I have found myself admitting I wasn't sure if what I bought would be suitable. But at least I was trying to get organised for the wedding. And, worst case scenario, the fabric would ensure I won't be short of tablecloths for the rest of my life!

After our traumatic shopping experience coffee was required to reinvigorate us. Here communication too caused a problem.

"Can we please have two white and one black coffees and a bottle of water," George asked the server.

"Only Nescafé, sir," was the reply.

"Yes, that's fine, two white and one black coffees, please."

Do you remember the song "There's a hole in my bucket" which basically talks about how to mend the hole? After various verses identifying ingredients required, the final verse identifies a problem as the final ingredient is water. But how can it be collected as there's a hole in the bucket? We felt we had a never-ending problem too.

'Just Nescafé, sir."

A new strategy was required – notice the switch: "Can we have one black and two white coffees."

This seemed to do the trick as we heard a different answer.

"Only white coffees, sir."

George was by now a crumpled heap on the floor in desperate need of caffeine and agreed to forgo black coffee.

"Three white coffees, please," he said weakly.

We sat down triumphant and having paid, we commented on how inexpensive it was especially as Douglas had more easily added cake to our order.

We'd a wee while to wait but it was going to be worth it, we told ourselves. Our anticipation was met with deflation as three very tiny espresso sized paper cups of frothy white coffee were brought to the table. I reassured the coffee drinkers; this could be overcome by ordering second cups.

We discovered "Nescafé" coffee not only comes white, but also ultra-sweet. It was pre-mixed coffee, dried milk and sugar to which hot water is added. It was so sweet Sylvia's face was a picture of horror as she took her first sip and her mini cup was quickly passed to George, who needed it anyway to fully revive him, and she rushed to the counter where she was relieved to be able to buy a safe carton of juice.

The waitress forgot about my water but when I reminded her, I reckon I got the best deal. Unlike the coffee where the choice was Nescafé or Nescafé, white or white, I was given a real choice, "Chilled or non-chilled?"

Reinvigorated, we left the café and wandered around the nearby market-type shops and were glad we did. We discovered a new kitchen gadget, something we hadn't seen before – a coconut scraper.

We headed for the bus station and the 905 bus to take us back to our board and lodgings. The local buses are functional but very rickety and bashed. Some buses had large slashes along their sides making us wonder what they had hit or been hit by. Our bus was sitting at the stance and we were pleased we'd arrived early while there were few people on board. It wasn't long before all seats were taken, and people were standing. The bus departed and along the route more and more people squeezed on. It made it very difficult for the bus conductor to collect fares and for those wanting to get off to physically do so.

Buses are highly decorated inside and maybe accidents are the reason for the little religious sanctuary at the front, created by the drivers according to the religion followed. I think drivers are very wise to say a prayer or two before starting a shift having seen the dangers they face.

"The driving is bad here," I said to Douglas as we looked out the window, "but nowhere near as bad as we experienced in Vietnam."

We'd added a few days holiday to Vietnam after my last ever trip to Hong Kong as a Quantity Surveying lecturer. During our own on-foot sightseeing in Hanoi, we immediately discovered pavements weren't necessarily for pedestrians. Often, we'd to step off the pavement and walk in the road gutters as there wasn't enough room for both the motorcycles parked on the pavements and us.

This danger though was miniscule compared to crossing the roads. I'm not a person who is easily scared but standing looking at the zebra crossing in front of me, I realised my feet seemed to be glued to the pavement, unwilling to step forward onto the black and white stripes ahead. Why? Because zebra crossings are not safe places for pedestrians as we know them. Here traffic did not stop to let us cross.

"You just have to start walking," the travel rep told us on the way from the airport to our hotel. "Keep walking at the same speed and don't look at the traffic or try to guess which way it will go. It will drive around you."

All very well but we were not in the habit of stepping into an absolute mass of motorcycles with no real gaps between them and have them weave in and out around us. It took a lot of faith to believe his advice was true. At times there were 15 lanes of motorcycles coming straight at us as we crossed a road. Not an experience for the faint-hearted.

"One zebra crossing that sticks in my mind is the one a couple of local ladies were walking across, one pushing a pram and the other with a very young child walking beside her," I recalled. The adults were only a pace apart and yet a motorbike drove between them!

"And there was another zebra crossing where you told me to walk on your right side. Dutifully I did but thought it strange as you normally insist I'm on your left side so I'm beside your good ear and you can hear me."

"Oh yes. That was the time I told you that you were my 'bumper' protecting me should a vehicle hit us!" Douglas replied smiling at his witticism.

One-way streets are also meaningless as vehicles ignored such signs and instead went in whichever direction suited them. We had to keep our wits about us and no matter what kind of road we thought we were crossing, we looked both ways.

Traffic lights were pointless too with some traffic obeying the signals, but others not. And as for "green men" lights; in the UK they indicate it's safe to cross the road, but not in Hanoi. Naively, we thought traffic would at least slow down to let pedestrians cross the road. But no, it didn't.

Several times we stopped, just to watch motorcycles at a crossroads. The lanes were full of bikes going in different directions, and when they met at the crossroads, they continued at full speed towards each other. It made us think of the Red Arrows display team, or David and Andrew's Boys Brigade figure marching display when the diagonal files of boys passed between each other one by one in the middle of the hall without swerving. But at least these two organisations practise with each other. These bikers are relying on trust and intuition.

After these memories, the roads in Sri Lanka suddenly seemed much safer but the bus itself wasn't without danger. When George and Sylvia stood up to get off, the seat of their chair fell off and crashed onto the floor. This made us laugh but it was clearly perfectly normal as not an eye batted or turned our way.

After a light lunch of beautiful lightly battered prawns, we returned to the guest house. We did so with a great sense of anticipation. Sylvia had been told at breakfast that a fridge was going to be put in our room.

"They'll probably take one out of an upstairs room when the people check out and put it in our room," I surmised. Douglas wasn't convinced and had to be persuaded by us to buy some drinks to put in said fridge on our walk back.

The anticipation was palpable. The four of us crowded round the door, positioning ourselves in what we thought would give us the best view of the fridge, focusing our eyes on the spot where the fridge was in Sylvia and George's room. Douglas seemed to take an eternity to unlock the door and to make matters worse, opened it very slowly. Four pairs of eyes desperately peered into the darkened room. Surely our eyes were deceiving us. There wasn't a fridge where we expected to see one. Nor was there one anywhere in the bedroom.

But not to worry, there was another possibility and Douglas took the initiative saying, "I'll check the bathroom."

Off he went striding across the bedroom floor and opened the bathroom door, though he could just have looked through the large window sized opening in the wall between bedroom and bathroom. With the door opened he looked in and found what we'd all being willing him not to find – there wasn't a fridge. Our wait was to continue, and Sylvia fostered the drinks Douglas had bought, putting them in their fridge. By way of a consolation, we decided it was time for a swim in the pool but for me a cold shower first to make entry into the water less traumatic.

Jacqui and Paul joined the four of us for a game of cards after our swim. This was the first time we'd all been together, and the subject of fridges was raised.

"I've heard you had a fridge in your room when you arrived," I teased.

"Yes," Paul replied happily.

"We didn't," George added, "though we have one now."

"I think you must be gold rated guests, George and Sylvia silver rated while Douglas and I are lowly bronze as we still don't have a fridge."

"Oh, and we've got an ice-cube tray," Paul elaborated.

"What?" the four of us said in unison. "Not only a fridge but an ice-cube tray too?"

We agreed to promote them from gold to platinum rated guests. Meanwhile we would wait patiently in the hope "today" meant we would get a fridge before the end of our holiday.

Unusually, I won the game of cards. But I refused a challenge game as I'd spotted something very interesting happening at the canal. Investigation was required.

A good spectator sport followed: watching the inlet at the bottom of our garden being dredged by a small JCB digger on a floating raft. I'm sure the drivers put on a show for us. The JCB seemed to be dancing, twisting and turning while going forwards and backwards. How was this elegant movement achieved? The bucket of the digger was placed on the canal bed, the lever controls were moved up and down and the raft swung back and forth in semi-circles. It was fascinating to watch, and the operators enjoyed our attention and having photographs taken as they smiled broadly.

Sylvia and I went for a walk to check out a restaurant she and George had seen along one of the back streets. Although there was a sign saying "open", it looked decidedly shut. We wanted to find out if it was permanently closed, and if not, its opening hours.

As we were peering through the security bars, a neighbour came into view.

"Do you know if the restaurant is going to open?"

"Yes," he assured us and pointing to an open area showed us where the tables would be placed. As we continued peering, a man on a bike approached, stopped and started shouting through the gates. The owner appeared and opened the gate.

"We open 5 to 6," we were told. Thanking her very much we headed off.

"The only thing is," I said to Sylvia as we walked, "Does 5 to 6 mean 17.55, or is it only going to be open from 5 to 6 p.m., or will it open at some vague time between 5 p.m. and 6 p.m.?" Nothing like a little uncertainty in life.

Back at the guest house we found two sleeping beauties of husbands. What a life they lead.

Later in the afternoon, Sylvia and I were sitting at a table outside her room chatting and she became aware of a large box being opened and unpacked. Being a keen detective, it didn't take much for her to realise it was a fridge – it did, after all, say "Fridge" in large letters across the box. As my back was facing all these happenings, I relied on her further deduction, "This new one will be taken to one of the upstairs rooms and the small one there like ours will be brought down to your room."

All very logical as we were sure the upstairs rooms were the "posh" ones.

One of the men came up behind me and asked if they could unlock our room. Believe it or not, and despite Sylvia's predictions, I still wasn't thinking about the possibility of actually getting a fridge – hopes had been dashed too many times. Therefore, I couldn't believe it when after unlocking the door I wasn't only letting them into the room but a fridge too. Furthermore, it wasn't any old fridge. No reject from the posh rooms for us. No, we were being given the enormous, brand new fridge! Sylvia couldn't believe it either.

And more excitement was to follow. When I opened the door to the fridge, not only did we have an ice-tray, we had TWO ice-trays inside! Later over the next game of cards, we discussed the comparative fridges with the other four.

"Did you get an ice-tray?" we were asked.

"Yes, we got *two* ice-trays."

"TWO – that's not very fair."

"We also got a bunch of orchids and a box of chocolates," Douglas managed to persuade them.

"Hey, wait a minute, that's definitely not fair," was the dismayed response.

I don't know how he managed to keep a straight face when he shrugged and said, "Well it's just one of those things."

"What ranking is there above platinum?" was my final quietly spoken question.

Later that night, I had a harrowing experience. Douglas brought me back to the guest house before returning to the Main Street to meet up with George and Sylvia. I was alone in the room. Initially I didn't notice anything unusual. Suddenly I saw an intruder. An intruder from the animal kingdom and it wasn't a mosquito or any other insect. I decided I wasn't going to be brave. I left the room and went out to the reception.

"There's an animal in my room and I'm afraid. I've no idea what it is but it might climb up the wall, across the ceiling, lose its grip and come crashing down on me while I'm asleep. I don't want to waken everyone up with my screams. Can you please come to remove it?"

Milinda showed no sign of fear as he approached the room door. Before opening it though, he asked "Where is it?"

"Near the bedside table."

Having used up all my courage reserves, I let Milinda enter the room first and I slunk in behind him, trying not to cower too much. My heart was racing, the palms of my hands were sweating and droplets of sweat fell from my forehead.

Milinda had a good look at it, clearly contemplating the best approach to deal with this unwelcome visitor. But in the end, he didn't remove it!

"They're all over the place and are good for eating insects," he told me.

"But I'll scream if it falls from the ceiling onto me," I reminded him.

"Please don't worry. It won't fall," he reassured me. I took a photo to prove to the others what a terrifying experience I had while they were away enjoying themselves.

"I haven't photo-shopped this to make it look worse than it was," I forewarned them.

To my horror, rather than sympathising with me, they laughed. Had they been in my position facing this intruder would they have laughed, I thought to myself. After all, this lizard like creature was all of 2.5cm (1") long with a body that was about 0.5cm (1/4") wide. (To be honest, it looked sweet, but it would still have given me a fright if it had fallen from the ceiling onto my face during the night.

Night night, sleep tight and don't let the bed bugs bite.

PS. We gave Sylvia and George one of our ice trays. We didn't bother confessing we didn't get a bunch of orchids or a box of chocolates for many months to come.

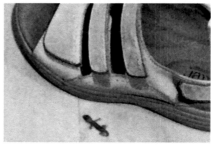

Night-time intruder

Ill, but happy caravan memories

Good afternoon dear readers – well it's afternoon here anyway. Today has not been filled with the normal array of activities and adventures. I self-certified myself to a day in the room and some bed rest. This morning I was feeling decidedly off colour. Being sick brought some relief but diarrhoea started too. A day snoozing in bed would be best for me.

I don't think I'm very ill, a bit lightheaded now. Dehydration is my self-diagnosis. A sign I'm on the mend is the distended tummy of early this morning has returned to its sylph-like self. Could the latter description be an exaggeration? Surely not! Well – yes, it is.

The time in bed made me wonder – what will I write about? I should start by saying there are distinct advantages to spending more time in the room than normal. Firstly, I'm reminded every so often of our elevated status of premium-plus guests as the fridge switches itself on and off. Secondly, I have been able to snatch some opportunities to catch up on some reading, and of course writing, in between snoozes. Finally, I'm catching up on some sleep I no doubt need.

What more could I ask for? Well there's something else: forgiveness. There's something I literally only discovered yesterday. I have a massive apology to make to son Andrew, though I feel I have an alibi: dyslexia and therefore my reading skills at times are wanting. It's all very embarrassing and has now put me in a real predicament. Let me explain:

You will recall I explained I was disappointed Andrew wasn't in favour of me wearing a tartan outfit I'd seen on a mannequin in a tourist shop on Edinburgh's Royal Mile to his wedding. I'd sent him a photo of the outfit as a joke, to which he replied, "If you don't wear this then don't bother coming to the wedding."

But I misread the reply. I completely missed the first "don't" in Andrew's message thus totally changing my interpretation and responded, "Andrew – how can you be so cruel – to your own mother! There was me thinking I'd great taste! Love you lots despite this ☺"

SORRY ANDREW!

What a predicament. He *wanted* me to wear the awful tartan outfit. I had been secretly extremely relieved by my original interpretation as I could not envisage wearing such truly hideous clothes. I don't want to upset the groom but ... oh dear, what a mess I'm in! Whatever will I do? Maybe the shop in Edinburgh will have sold out and I therefore won't be able to buy one. I suspect this is too much to hope for.

Plus because of the above misunderstanding I'd the bale of material incident in the CIB store. Was this all unnecessary? Have I indeed stocked up with enough material for a life's supply of tablecloths?

Putting this problem aside, and getting back to my self-diagnosis, I enjoyed my meal last night. However, lessons can be learned and taken from it (rightly or wrongly). The prawns were served with very thinly sliced raw vegetables. I've avoided eating salad so far. Not wanting to make a fuss and knowing Sylvia and George have been eating salad with no ill effects, I reckoned I would be OK. But in case, my illness is because of the raw vegetables, I'll not eat salad anymore.

On the other hand, perhaps it was the ice-cubes in the ginger beer mocktail. Although I've had ice-cubes before, I've decided I'll cut them out just in case ...

Perhaps, though, what caused me to be ill were the slices of fresh lime which were in the mocktail. Yes, they could have been the culprits. OK – no more fresh lime just in case ...

Or maybe it was the bunch of fresh mint leaves at the bottom of the mocktail glass. They might not have been washed in potable water. So, decision made, I'll cut out mint leaves just in case ...

I think I'll return to drinking bottles of water instead of being so "daring and adventurous" as to have a mocktail! It clearly isn't for me.

But maybe it was nothing to do with my meal or the mocktail (both of which were delicious) ... oh, the dilemmas in life ...

During my time of confinement, I found myself thinking back to how our holidays have changed over the years. We had many years of family caravanning holidays which were such fun.

Caravanning – a word which either fills you with a warm happy feeling or with anger, hostility and frustration. In my case, there are times I'm frustrated when stuck behind a caravan being towed along a country road. I don't understand drivers who seemingly ignore their car mirrors and the mile-long queue of vehicles whose occupants are anxious to get to their destinations. If only they would pull over or slow down for just a few minutes to allow the rest of us pass on the narrow twisty roads. If only they realised the wonderful feeling we get and our gratitude when such consideration is shown – until the next caravan comes into view.

This is the only negative comment I have about caravans as I have so many happy memories of our caravan holidays.

My memories are of our static caravan in Kippford in the Dumfries and Galloway region of Scotland. The caravan and the area became our second home as David and Andrew grew up.

Before the caravan, we rented a couple of cottages in the area for our annual holiday. It was on hearing about our love of the area, that May, a lovely lady in our church said we could use her caravan in Kippford. Thus, later that year we'd our first experience of caravanning as a family and we loved it.

The following year May said to us, "I'm no longer using the caravan, and neither are my family. You can have it."

"Have it?" we said in disbelief.

"Yes, and I'll leave most of the things inside too."

We managed to persuade her to take a little money for all the dishes and other things she left. All we'd to do was pay the site owners the annual site fee plus what we learned were standard "connection charges" for connecting up the services – even though they were already connected. We felt so blessed by this kindness and so began many one-and-a-half-hour drives between our house and the caravan.

Our first caravan

We'd become the very grateful owners of a 17-year-old blue and white, two bedroomed, eight berth static caravan. Many caravan sites wouldn't have allowed such an old caravan and despite showing signs of age, we loved her. The blue and white paint became chalky in the sun, coming off on hands and clothes but most years we sealed the vast area with car polish. Over the years our rubbing took the paint off exposing the shiny metal underneath.

We didn't try lighting the original gas mantle lights fearful they wouldn't be safe. Instead we happily used the against-building-regulation exposed electric wired lights and power points. We soon gave up using the Calor gas fire because of the fumes it gave off. The raised timber deck at the front of the caravan became so rotten we had to remove it. We didn't replace it as each year we wondered if the caravan would survive another winter.

There was very little, if any, insulation in the caravan structure. Thus, on cold days it was very cold inside, so we piled extra blankets and wore extra clothes in bed to keep warm. In the morning we scraped ice off the inside of the single glazed, metal framed windows. Condensation on the inside of windows was much more common than ice though and window squeegees were often put to good use.

Inside were two bedrooms, one with a narrow double bed and the other with narrow bunk beds. There was a toilet but no shower. The main living area had a small run of kitchen units, a table with bench seats which converted into a double bed, plus couches for sitting which also converted into beds.

There was an electric water heater, but we tended not to use this unless it was pouring with rain. Instead we took a yellow bucket up to the laundry room and filled it with hot water; no need then to pay for power to heat the water. Some of the neighbours called us Jack and Jill from the nursery rhyme because we "went up the hill to fetch a pale of water". Fortunately, none of us "fell and broke our crowns".

Although the distance between home and caravan was short, it was like entering a different world. The drive from our hometown took us through the rolling hillsides, passing lochs and forests to a rural destination with farm animals in the fields we passed. A beautiful drive we never tired of. One year we witnessed the awful sight of heaps of dead cows being burned on funeral pyres to prevent the spread of BSE (bovine spongiform encephalopathy). We saw country life first-hand.

The pace of life was much slower, and it was a place of relaxation we all benefitted from. At times though, the slow pace of life got frustrating, for example when we asked for things to be repaired in the caravan or on the site itself. It sometimes took literally years before our request was finally met.

We loved the caravan site. It was hilly, with a real mixture of styles and ages of caravans (some a lot older than ours) all placed in the contours of the land. There wasn't a children's play area, swimming pool, amusements or evening entertainment but this suited our type of holiday. The caravans had their own grass plot and owners could do what they wanted with this. Many owners made driveways and beautifully landscaped their plot, surrounding it all with a fence. We however didn't make many changes keeping the grass and a small flower bed at the front and back.

There was a massive advantage in not erecting a fence. The maintenance we'd to do was greatly reduced as the grass was cut for us. Fences meant all garden maintenance became the responsibility of the caravan owner. We knew some owners who came for the weekend and spent their whole time gardening before going home. But we'd a garden at home, so were happy to restrict ourselves to a couple of flower beds.

The disadvantage of not erecting a fence was "our" grass provided a shortcut to the bins and toilet block. Even when we were in the middle of playing or sitting having a meal outside folk didn't consider going another route. Fortunately, the site was generally quiet, so there wasn't a steady stream of pedestrians walking past us.

Several years after getting the caravan, we exchanged the flowers at the back for a large storage box which held golf clubs and outdoor equipment giving us more space inside.

When David and Andrew were young, I got them ready for bed before we left home on Friday evenings, bundling them into their car seats with their pyjamas on. When we arrived the sleeping beauties could easily be transferred into their beds. As they got older and joined the Boys Brigade, we collected them from there and drove straight to Kippford on Friday nights. Thus, we had the whole weekend there.

They tended to waken early in the morning, not helped by the thin curtains. I draped towels over the curtain rails to keep out the morning light, but this only slightly extended their sleeping time.

Despite repeated requests to keep quiet and not disturb their Dad who needed to catch up on sleep after his shifts, their loud whispering and giggling came straight through the thin walls between our bedrooms.

The solution was that I got up and we made a game of dressing as quietly as possible before tiptoeing to the door and pulling on our red, blue or for me khaki welly boots.

With jackets on we headed out on our adventure. Generally, we made our way to the par 3, 9-hole golf course field created in a former cow's field. Round the course we trekked, up and down the hills, through the very tall grass in the rough but never in the bunkers or on the greens.

It was always exciting when we saw rabbits or felt the hidden round form of a golf ball under our feet. To extend our outing a bit longer, we made our way to the small shop on the site which was usually open for a short while first thing in the morning. With the 10p I gave them in their little hands, they carefully chose which ten sweets they wanted in their ten-penny mix-up and left clutching the paper bag containing their precious sweets. Sweets were a treat for them. At home they knew there wasn't much point asking for them as in all likelihood the answer would have been "no". I like to think this might have had something to do with them having no fillings in their teeth despite their advancing adult years, unlike Douglas and me whose teeth are full of them. I suspect though there's a multitude of reasons why their teeth are better than ours.

"Guess how many rabbits we saw this morning," Douglas was challenged on our return. He dutifully had some guesses, with clues being given if he was too high or too low.

"Guess how many golf balls we found," was inevitably the next question.

For several years, we didn't have a television – just a radio. This was a deliberate decision mainly on my part, as I wanted us to be active and outdoors as much as possible and when indoors to spend time playing with toys or games. However, throughout one year's main summer holiday the heavens seemed to be permanently open letting escape all the rain accumulated there. I reluctantly relented, and a small portable TV was brought to the caravan to be used when weather was so inclement, we couldn't get out. However, the reception was far from good. We didn't invest in a satellite dish as others did, relying instead on an ordinary aerial fixed to the roof, so we were limited to a choice of three channels. Toys and games were therefore still on the agenda!

Just inside the entrance door was a small narrow wooden cupboard and this was where David and Andrew had their "caravan toys" – mostly small so they could have as much variety as possible. David collected little cars and yellow coloured construction vehicles while Andrew's passion was toy soldiers which he spent hours laying out ready for battle. Keeping toys at the caravan meant there was more room for us in the car as we travelled back and forth.

When they were older David and Andrew loved Beanie Babies, small soft animals and bears filled with bean-like filling. At the time it was a craze to collect them with rare ones exchanging hands for vast amounts of money. David and Andrew, however, did not become "collectors" but made up stories acting out the parts with the various Beanies they saved up to buy. Fortunately, they were more interested in buying bargains than looking for the latest character or most valuable ones. They were into quantity rather than quality.

We regularly visited a pet shop in nearby Castle Douglas to look at the animals. One day we discovered they also stocked cheap "retired" Beanies. It was here David and Andrew went to peruse, think carefully about and finally decide if any warranted being added to their increasing family. They didn't always buy; they had stringent criteria and money was too precious to spend on something which was not just right.

The Beanies, however, resided at home and were brought to and from the caravan. David and Andrew were then of an age they were expected to help with packing for trips to the caravan.

"'OK, boys," I would say, "you can take three Beanies each." I left them to choose which ones. They put them and their chosen clothes into their bags and zipped them shut.

Because I was sure I'd done a good job of raising them to do what they were told I didn't check what they had packed. It was only when I went into their tiny bedroom in the caravan, I found the ration of three Beanies had been ignored as the bottom bunk bed was covered with umpteen characters all set out for the story they were enacting.

I laughed to myself. To me it was amazing they were happy to play with these toys. I knew girls Andrew's age collected but didn't play with them and it was unlikely David's peers, being two years older, would have been interested in them.

It quickly became a joke between us, me issuing the quota allowed, them assuring me they had adhered to this, me knowing they wouldn't have done and them thinking they had won one over me as they stuffed as many as they could into their bags. I knew extra clothes washings would be required as there was no way they could bring so many

Beanies and a full quota of clothes.

I loved watching them playing with their Beanies (which are still in boxes in the loft) and was grateful they played well together with this shared interest. I know even if I mention the topic of Beanies to David nowadays, a sly little smile spreads across face as he remembers these exploits.

We're fortunate enough to have life memberships of both Historic Scotland and the National Trust for Scotland. Douglas and I bought these when I inherited money from my Grandma and my Great Aunt Mary. We're so pleased we did as every time we use them, we think of these dear relatives. There are many castles and other historic places of interest in Dumfries and Galloway. As the boys grew older, we asked them where they wanted us to take them.

"Threave Castle," was the inevitable answer.

"But you want to go there every time we're at the caravan – weekends and every school holiday. Are you not tired of going there?"

"No," was the puzzled reply. Douglas and I loved going there too so it was no hardship for us.

Threave Castle was built in 1369 by Archibald the Grim. It's a large forbidding 30 metre (98 feet) tall stone tower sitting on an island in the River Dee and was the home of the rulers of the area at the time.

Getting to the castle is an adventure. First, a three-quarters of a mile (1.2km) walk along a path through farmland, opening and shutting many wooden gates on the way. The gates' closing mechanism comprised a heavy chain in the middle of which hung a large rock. The chain was fixed between the middle of the gate and a fence post. Pushing the gate open required force because of the weight of the rock, but this weight shut the gate behind us with a loud bang. I have never seen such gate closers anywhere else and sadly they have been replaced.

At the end of the path is a jetty and most importantly a brass bell to ring. On hearing it ring, the custodians on the island know to bring the outboard-motor-driven boat back to the mainland for waiting passengers. David or Andrew (depending on whose turn it was) still rang the bell even if the boat was already ferrying others across the narrow strip of water and therefore, we could easily be seen.

On the island, we showed our very familiar membership cards and set a challenge for the boys to ask the custodians a question about the castle or surroundings.

Our familiar routine began, we climbed up the stairs in the tower, looking down through a hole in the ceiling of the prison as we passed. At some point over the years the red light illuminating the prison stopped being lit, perhaps because it made the model of the prisoner below appear even more scary than in the gloom. Down the stairs to the lower floor we went and peered over the railings into the well below. We discussed whether the water level was higher or lower than our previous visit, giving a good indication of how much rain had fallen.

A round artillery house in the defence wall surrounding the tower once contained dozens of frogs so thereafter we always hoped to see them but never did. At the harbour we looked for fish. On such a small island there was plenty to do before it was picnic time.

"It would be great if the tower roof was rebuilt," we suggested to the custodians one day. They agreed. On a subsequent visit, they told us our dream was to become a reality. We were so excited but are still waiting twenty plus years later.

When leaving, if there was no one waiting, the custodian sometimes opened the throttle and gave us an extra trip down the river instead of taking us sedately straight across to the jetty opposite. Possibly because we were well known, such trips became more frequent. We were always thrilled when we got this extra treat.

Caerlaverock Castle was another favourite especially when there were battle re-enactments taking place. David wasn't interested in guns or swords as he grew up. We put this down to the way we'd brought him up, never buying him any. Any righteous feelings we had were dashed when Andrew came into our lives. We've no idea where his love of guns and swords came from. Lacking them, Andrew ate his toast in such a way as to create a gun shape which was aimed at suitable targets in the kitchen before finally consuming it. Branches of trees and twigs became guns or swords too. He, therefore, liked the shop at this castle and by now we decided there was no point stopping him spending his money on the wooden swords he longed for or a collection of little metal models of historic soldiers.

On hot days it could become unbearably hot inside the caravan. But we'd a solution for the hot days: water pistols. David and Andrew would don their swimming trunks, fill their water pistols and chase each other round the caravan squirting merrily as they emitted squeals of delight when hit by the cool water. As the years went by, the design of water pistols changed. They got bigger; pump action was incorporated to create a powerful, pressurised jet of water. Our collection of water soakers increased. Douglas no longer required to borrow one from either David or Andrew to "check it was working" as he told them. The three of them happily pursued each other.

Invariably, I was indoors preparing the meal when all this cooling activity was going on, with every window, rooflight and door in the caravan open to help air circulate. The open window tended to be the weakness in my defences and standing at the kitchen units put me in an ideal position for a water attack. I, therefore, joined the squeals as the out of sight attackers caught me by surprise. Happy days.

As our caravan didn't have an indoor shower, we were grateful the site had a shower block we could use very close to our caravan. When David and Andrew were young though, it was too much of a hassle to try to shower them in the very small cubicles. Stored under the caravan was a large yellow baby bath, much bigger than a normal one, and big enough for several years of use.

Inevitably, the time came when using the shower was the only option. Wearing flipflops, as the shower cubicles weren't always very clean, and reducing the number of clothes being worn as there was nowhere in the cubicles to put them, we started up the hill hoping one of the two cubicles would be vacant. There was one we preferred as it was slightly bigger, the shower rose provided a better spray of water and helpfully most of the water fell in the shower tray rather than on me. Even so, the pressure of the water was low and not much water was emitted. There was a tiny triangular wooden seat in one corner of the cubicle, on which one of the boys sat while I reached over the shower tray to shower the other before they swapped positions. Once dressed in their pyjamas, I quickly had a shower myself before we returned to the caravan, me sighing with relief; the ordeal was over for another day.

When David and Andrew were old enough to shower themselves. I found myself having a shower on my own while listening to them and Douglas having a whale of a time next door in the gents' showers. Goodness knows what they were getting up to, but I didn't care.

Being at the caravan so often meant we missed going to our home church, so we set about finding a church nearby. Choosing a church is like buying a house; you can go and view umpteen houses before walking into one which immediately feels like home. We visited several churches before "feeling at home" in Castle Douglas Parish Church.

We loved the minister, the format and content of the service. The people were friendly, and importantly, David and Andrew were happy at the Sunday School. Folk in the congregation stopped us in the street on a Saturday to say they had missed us if we hadn't been at the caravan for a week or two. Yes, we felt at home there.

It was at the church we got to know the Pipe Major of Kirkcudbright[5] and District Pipe Band. He told us about the Scottish Nights every Thursday during the summer in Kirkcudbright harbour square in the shadows of MacLellan's Castle. The entertainment provided by the local Pipe Band, Brass Band and Scottish country and highland dancers was great. And of course, there was the famous tug-of-war in which ten or so strong men from the audience were enticed to pit their skill against the local Kirkcudbright team which hadn't been beaten for nearly 50 years. Generally, more than ten men took up the challenge and this increased team size was allowed.

Once the men were in position, the Kirkcudbright team was called forward and out of the audience came dozens and dozens and dozens of children – virtually every child in the audience. All took hold of the long rope laid before them and the signal was given to start pulling. The men had no chance of winning despite their concerted efforts. They were given a second chance as the teams changed ends. Again, the men were beaten, but they didn't go away empty handed as each was given a certificate to verify they had been "beaten by the Kirkudbright tug-of-war team".

One year I felt David and Andrew were reaching an age when they were likely to be getting bored of going to the caravan. I was also aware many of their friends went on holidays overseas. I did some investigating of possibilities.

"I'm wondering if you'd like to go to Euro Disney this Easter holiday instead of going to the caravan," I said to them.

With a puzzled look on their faces, their reply was, "Well if you and Dad want to."

From their point of view, Euro Disney wasn't the treat I thought it would be. They loved the caravan. And so, our caravan holidays continued, and I put any feelings of guilt behind me – I wasn't depriving them.

Finally, we sadly had to admit our original caravan had reached the end of its life. We were no longer able to repair the ever-developing leaks and the floor inside was rotting. We replaced the caravan with another second-hand one which was only about 12 years old and had a shower

5 Pronounced 'Kir-Coo-Bray".

in it. Wow!

But in 2003 we came to the sad decision we weren't getting enough use of the caravan to justify paying the increasing site fees. Douglas' shifts within Air Traffic Control together with the work he was doing as an Auxiliary Minister in the church plus David and Andrew's increasing weekend commitments meant we couldn't go as often to the caravan at weekends. However, there was a happy ending to the story. Our friend Karen and her sister Julie bought the caravan from us and kindly allowed us to have a two-week summer holiday there for the next few years.

About this time, we learned about a scheme run on a nearby caravan site – "The Spent Vicar Scheme". Two other church ministers we knew used this scheme and asked if we would like to go at the same time as their families. We applied, and Douglas was accepted as a suitable candidate. The scheme allowed ministers to rent caravans during off-season periods at reduced rates. The caravans were in the site's bronze category, but they were still newer than our caravan had been. What wonderful times we had!

In the evenings, each family took a turn to cook for the twelve of us in one of the caravans. We took crockery and cutlery to the host caravan as none were equipped for this level of catering.

After the meal, we adults banished the six children outside to play. They were of varying ages and the older ones realised if they came back, it was likely we would say it was time for bed, so they tried to keep the younger ones occupied for as long as possible.

"Go and see how many rabbits you can spot," we told them. As it was the October school holidays it was dark outside, so they happily went with their torches, in search of rabbits (of which there were many).

One night they came back suddenly, bursting into the caravan and slamming the door shut behind them. Terror was written across their faces. When we asked what was wrong, we heard the story.

"We went up the steep hill at the back of the caravan site looking for rabbits," we were told. "We started playing with our torches, flashing them on and off. We knew the signal for S.O.S. so flashed this a few times. Suddenly, we heard a loud noise and a military helicopter came over the hill! We've just run for our lives to get back here."

"From where you were and the type of torches you had there was no way the pilot of the helicopter would have seen you," Douglas tried to reassure them.

They weren't going to be easily convinced. Fortunately, Douglas had some insider knowledge, "The helicopter is part of a military exercise taking place around here. It wasn't responding to your SOS signal."

Now every time we remember that evening, we (adults anyway) can't help but laugh.

Our love for Kippford and the surrounding area continues, and we often have trips back there reliving our memories. And as we did during our family holidays, we like to do something new each time we go and it's amazing how we manage to succeed.

Since then we've been fortunate enough to have many overseas holidays, including here in Sri Lanka, which have provided us with wonderful experiences too.

Feeling a bit better, I went outside for a blether[6] with the others. When at the beach, the two ladies who sold me the dress chatted to them.

"Where other lady?" they enquired

"She's sick today."

"No eat prawns for two days. Drink coconut milk," was their advice.

"She wear new dress?" they were keen to know.

Smiles spread across their faces when Sylvia said, "Yes, she did."

Douglas tried to buy coconut milk on his way back from the beach but couldn't find a source. Fortunately, though earlier in the morning he had remembered our normal remedy and brought me a bottle of cola. I added sugar to make it flat and as I sipped it during the day, I remembered why I drink cola for medicinal purposes only. I was convinced I could feel my teeth dissolving!

Douglas and my big excitement of the day was waiting to hear from David about the sale of his house. His offer on another house in Prestwick had been accepted three days previously.

He had put his house on the market on Friday, the same day as he put in an offer for another house in Prestwick. There had been a lot of interest in his house over the weekend, He had a busy weekend showing prospective purchasers the house, knowing if his offer wasn't accepted for the new house, he would be taking it off the market. His offer was accepted on Monday, and after all the interest shown in his property, the Estate Agents decided to make today the closing date for offers, only six days after it was put on the market. I was waiting in anticipation for a phone call from David and it came mid-afternoon.

6 Blether = Scottish for "chat".

"The house is sold," he told me excitedly. "There were three offers, and all were above valuation. I've got back all the money I spent on taking it apart, fixing it and putting it back together when I bought it plus a very good profit. I'll be able to plough all the profit into doing up the new house, which as you know needs a lot done to it too."

"I'm so happy for you. It's hard to believe – within four days of us leaving the country you have bought and sold a house!" I could relax.

Douglas, George and Sylvia went out for their evening meal. I stayed put and was looked after by the great guest house staff who made me slices of dry toast whenever I asked.

Having been ill, I was concerned it would impact on my susceptibility to mosquito bites. To date I'd only been bitten once. For me, this was a brilliant result as they love my blood. I'm not sure if this was because of the vitamin B I'd been taking, the different body spray recommended or the bands I'd worn round my ankles and wrists. If it was the vitamin B there could be a problem. I'd been taking a dose every day for a couple of weeks before the holiday to build up my resistance. The colour of my urine changed to fluorescent green. But after being ill for a day, this colour was gone and possibly also the protection it offered. Time would tell.

Tuk-tuks, temples and travels

The four intrepid explorers (Douglas, Sylvia, George and I) embarked on a half day adventure, putting life and limb at risk as we went on a white-knuckle ride, walked on what was worse than burning coals and scaled rock-faces before coming face to face with sea-creatures from the deep.

The white-knuckle ride took place in two tuk-tuks in which we zig-zagged in and out of traffic (some going in the opposite direction to us). We were nearly crashed into by motorcyclists and other much larger vehicles. OK, for those with a nervous disposition, the tuk-tuk drivers were fantastic and there was nothing our drivers couldn't contend with and our knuckles weren't totally white, there were still hints of pink.

The roads were much quieter than normal, today being a Public holiday – one of the 13 Full Moon Poya days in the year. On such days, some shops and restaurants remain shut, and the sale of alcoholic beverages, meats and fish is prohibited. Every worker in Sri Lanka is entitled to a paid holiday and if an employee must work, he or she is entitled to compensation amounting to not less than one-and-a-half times the normal wage.

The tuk-tuk drivers stopped at a rice paddy field to show us this staple food and most important crop grown in Sri Lanka. The field was ready for harvesting, the plants a brown yellow colour with the stalks bowing down under the weight of the grain. The drivers picked some to show us.

Our next destination was the Aluthapola Buddhist Temple, the tuk-tuks stopped at the entrance gate where we got out.

"Take off shoes," we were instructed by a man standing at the gate.

We discarded them under a tree beside the gate and the painful long walk up the gravel drive commenced. We amused the locals as we "ouched" our way along. They strode past us with their hardened feet. But one group of locals still had their shoes on. Douglas looked around to the man at the gate (who had a distinct smile on his face, smiling at our predicament?), pointed to a group of people ahead and asked, "Why do those people still have their shoes on?"

We understood from the sign language accompanying his reply – the lady was pregnant. This was true, but there were also two men with her. We continued but heard the man shouting at the group. Protestations were returned by the shoe wearers before they finally gave in and took their shoes off – including the pregnant lady.

Apparently on normal days the place is deserted, but as it was a Poya day, Buddhists were at the temple to worship and meditate. There were many families, the children lighting coconut oil in little pottery dishes they had bought at one of the stalls lining the driveway. The sound of chanting from inside the temple echoed around outside.

Our feet, barely accustomed to walking on the rough stony path, faced their next challenge – the rocky outcrop behind the temple. We'd been told we would get a great view from the top. As we walked, the same thought passed through all our minds – we won't need a pedicure after this as any dead skin on the soles of our feet had no chance of surviving the very rough sand-paper-like, burning hot surface of the rock.

Part of the way up, we noticed a sad sight round the back of one of the small buildings – a row of broken, mainly decapitated, statues of Buddhist gods and goddesses. We were told they had come from peoples' homes, as people don't like to throw them out. I suppose it's like people not wanting to throw out Bibles and why in many homes there's a row of them on the bookshelf although only one is read.

We were glad we visited this temple despite the impact it had on our feet.

Our enthusiastic tuk-tuk drivers took us to a beach used by the locals and here too many families were having a happy holiday time in and around the water. We strangers attracted attention. Children wanted to speak to us. George was even asked, "You coming back tomorrow?"

Family fun on the beach on a Full Moon Poya day

Others wanted their photos taken; one old man hovered in the background until Sylvia spotted him. Using sign language, she asked if he wanted his photo taken too. He prepared himself, straightening his multi-coloured baseball cap, ensuring his gold chain hung evenly down his bare chest and tightening the pink, black and white striped sarong round his waist. We haven't a clue what he said but he was obviously pleased with the result when I showed him the photo I'd taken.

One of our drivers went into the water and amongst the rocks found a black spiked sea urchin. Picking it up drew the attention of children who were keen to see it. It was passed round the crowd of children who gathered, though some of the girls were not as keen as the boys to get close, cowering beyond touching distance.

"Do you see the name of the boat on the sand there?" I said pointing to a boat being used as a clothes' horse, drying piles of white clothes. "It's called *Andrew*. Photo required to send to Andrew back home."

Another happy time.

We knew dinner would be different tonight as no alcohol could be ordered.

"Don't worry," the waiter in the restaurant had told us the night before. "Bring your own alcohol, and we'll serve it to you in teapots and teacups." So off we headed for the restaurant, bottles concealed in bags.

After ordering our food, we surreptitiously asked about the alcohol.

"Just pour it into the glasses under the table yourselves," we were told.

"What about the teapot and teacups?" we asked very disappointedly.

Although he brought a teapot for us to use, we still felt hard done by and envious when we saw a tray of teapots and teacups held aloft by another waiter for his table. They received the full treatment we'd hoped for. The daft extras which make our holiday special. At least we saw the theory in action.

During the meal our thoughts were on the three-day trip the four of us were about to embark on.

"I hope it will be as good as the trip we had two years ago to see the elephants."

"Yes, this time it's whales we want to see."

"And this time we'll be very strict with the driver about when we want a toilet stop!" We all laughed remembering our first morning of that trip.

We'd left the guest house at about 9 a.m. Our driver and guide for the trip said we would have a stop at about 11.30 a.m. which seemed reasonable to us.

On the journey there was one long stretch of roadworks – an existing road was being widened and in places re-routed. Rather than doing a bit at a time, the whole stretch was dug up meaning we were driving over the orange soil for miles. This was something new since our driver made this journey four months previously. He reckoned it was in connection with the recent elections which ousted the last president despite him having managed to stop the country's war with the Tamils. He thought the new president was keen to win favour with the people by spending money on projects such as this.

11.30 a.m., our time for a break, came and went.

"When are we stopping?" we asked

"Soon," was his reply.

"When are we stopping?" was our question an hour later.

"Very soon," was his reply.

Our bladders were struggling to cope. The same question was asked several more times and received the same reply. Finally, our question was answered with a different reply, "Very, very soon."

However, as far as we were concerned the "very, very soon" timescale came and went.

"You're going to have to stop, even if it as at the side of the road," he was told, politeness having gone out the window.

Did he stop? No. Clearly this was not an option in his mind. All of us became very quiet each coping in our own way. Finally, after another half hour the car started to slow down. Before it came to a stop, all our seatbelts were off, and the car doors opened. We made a dash to the toilets the second the car stopped.

Inside the building, we yelled, "Where are the toilets?"

Anyone who had the misfortune to get in our way was quickly swept aside as our now uncrossed legs ran hot foot. Thank goodness there weren't queues at the toilets!

"No, we will not let that experience happen again," we agreed.

"I hope the accommodation is as good on this trip."

"Good? I would describe it more as one of life's experiences."

"They were ever so quaint – our mud huts."

They weren't really mud huts, but little chalets with corrugated iron roofs, stone floors and were finished inside and out with render. They were dark inside, and the lights were very dim, probably so we couldn't see the "interesting" design features and faults.

"Oh yes, we found one fault after another! Lights didn't all work. There were wires hanging from the ceiling of our bedroom with no lights attached to them and I'm not sure there was one in our shower-room. We couldn't find it anyway. The toilet roll holder was made of sticks from the forest and the tap at the sink swivelled of its own accord. The shower was literally a spout of cold water coming through the wall. The air conditioner didn't work nor did the outside lights to our chalet. Saying all that, I'm pleased we didn't reject this as a place to stay as we'd the option to do."

It was a great experience to stay there. Thankfully there were mosquito nets over the beds and mosquito coils burning in the room. I'd already been badly bitten since arriving in Sri Lanka and didn't want to get even worse.

The "mud huts" were set in large grounds with a pond, lawns and trees and a river along one side. We wandered, exploring, and quickly became aware of how peaceful it was, the sound of birds being the only sound we heard. Our nostrils picked up the familiar smell of a bonfire disposing of refuse somewhere in the vicinity. Burning plastic doesn't smell good.

"Do you remember we saw a monkey climbing a tree and sitting patiently as we filmed and photographed? Our first sighting of wildlife on the trip."

"And it was so relaxing to sit in one of the shelters with its palm leaf roof and having cuppa's and drinks brought to us."

"Especially after the traumas of the morning drive to get there!"

"It was very atmospheric when it got dark with the different coloured lights lining the path."

"Yes, they were on when we went for dinner; up the very steep flight of stairs to an upper-floor dining area. I loved how it was open to the elements with timber columns and beams supporting a thatched roof, and balustrading round the perimeter to stop us falling to the ground below! The balustrading was so rustic looking, made of tree branches complete with all their twists and kinks."

The evening meal menu was "take it or leave it", just like home. We were happy with the chicken fried rice (though I'm sure the chicken was ham) followed by watermelon or watermelon juice. Basic, but perfectly adequate.

Feelings of relaxation stopped when it was time to "shower" before bed. It was a never-to-be-forgotten experience. After adjusting my eyes to the dim lighting, I positioned myself as far away as possible from the likely trajectory of the spout of cold water above. I stretched out my arm to its maximum length and managed to find the tap. I didn't turn the tap on immediately as I needed to prepare myself for the chilly water meeting the skin on my arm. I persuaded myself there was nothing for it – I had to turn the tap. I turned it and quickly retrieved my arm and stood looking at the water. It was like water being poured out of an enormous fast flowing teapot. Yes, I was just *looking* at the water – letting it touch me was the next step.

I stretched out a foot and let the water hit a toe or two. The water wasn't just chilly or cold, it was freezing. It certainly hadn't benefited from being heated by the sun.

My normal procedure when having a shower is to stand under the warm water, get wet all over, apply soap, rinse it off and stand enjoying the feel of the water as it massages my back. This shower, however, required completely different tactics. There was no way I could step under this deluge of freezing water. Having done the toe test, I decided application of soap was best done before entering the water-zone. I'd goose pimples just thinking about what was to come.

Soap applied, the procedure of getting it off followed. First one arm, then the other. Next one leg then the other. Finally, there was no option but to do a quick body spin under the avalanche of water. Did I get acclimatised to the temperature and stay in to let the water massage my back? No, I certainly didn't! Vigorous rubbing with the towel was required to revive my body temperature and I jumped into bed to recover from the ordeal.

We all remembered our own experiences of the "shower".

"The second night's accommodation, after the elephant safari, was so different," Douglas said. "I loved it too."

"Yes, and it hadn't dawned on me it would be cold at night. I hadn't thought about the implications of Ella being high in the mountains."

Once again, the sleeping accommodation was in separate individual buildings. Our room was on the second floor of a two-storey building with our shower-room and the driver's bunk room below us. We'd brilliant views from the veranda.

"Thank goodness there were blankets in the room. To be honest, I could have done with a few more. Thank goodness too I'd brought socks to wear to try to stop my feet and ankles being bitten by the mosquitoes. I didn't need them for mosquitoes, but to keep my feet warm in bed. It was a big change from being too hot in bed even with only a sheet covering."

And there was the expedition in the afternoon to buy Ella's famous egg roti because Douglas and I hadn't heard of them before. We soon saw a sign advertising roti for sale, but when we tried to order some, were told they didn't have any. We moved on to the next similar sign, only to be told the same thing. We didn't give up and stopped at every establishment we came to with egg roti on its menu always hearing the same response. Eventually we discovered they're only made for breakfast. We were far too late. Douglas and I were left none the wiser.

But the journey wasn't wasted. We eventually managed to find a restaurant that wasn't fully booked for dinner (booking is essential in Ella as it's a popular place for backpackers) and reserved a table. We also bought a pack of cards (appropriately with pictures of elephants on them), having forgotten to bring ours.

Back at our rooms, we sat on the veranda teaching each other card games. What is it about card games that makes them seem so complicated to begin with? We wondered if we would ever remember all the rules. But by and by we did.

When we arrived at the restaurant for dinner, it appeared no table had been reserved despite us booking one. After much waving of arms by management and hurried activity by underlings they sorted a place for us.

"Do you remember the group of eight Chinese people we shared the long benches and table with? They caused the poor waiter no end of problems. I don't believe several of them had been given the wrong meal. I'm sure they just didn't like it and wanted to try something different. What a waste of food."

Our table was right at the back of the restaurant and there was a noisy generator outside, emitting smelly fumes – probably toxic we thought – which was not ideal. However, we'd a table and we were going to get some food so stayed put.

"And thank goodness you were there, Sylvia, when the lights went off and we were plunged into darkness. Or at least, thank goodness your handbag was there," I corrected. We were at the crucial point of reading the menus. The generator clearly wasn't working properly.

This is where the inventor of handbags needs to be raised onto a high pedestal. I rarely carry a handbag and when I do generally forget about it and leave it behind. Instead I prefer to rely on pockets and in situations where I can squeeze in no more, Douglas' pockets are put to good use. Sylvia's bag was hoisted upwards and placed on the table in front of her.

Because it was dark, we onlookers couldn't see what was emptied onto the table, but we heard all the sounds: bumps, thumps and metallic clanking. What could all these sounds represent? Well no self-respecting handbag is without a purse, hankies, nail file, hair comb, plasters (in case of cuts or grazes), wet wipes (for all those sticky fingers), stamps, xylophone and double base (only joking about the last two.) The emptying continued and we visualised a paper clip (might come in useful for something – you never know), sweets for tickly coughs, sweets for fresh breath, scissors, lip balm, mirror, pen, paper, diary, tweezers, bottle of water, biscuits, crisps (might get peckish, especially in a restaurant experiencing power cuts) and so on. Yes, a lady's handbag is a treasure trove.

It reminded me of a game we played at the Woman's Guild group in our church. The leader would name an item and the first person to take said item from her handbag to the front of the hall got a point for her team. I remember being totally gobsmacked at the obscure things found in some handbags.

But back to Sylvia's handbag. Finally, after much riffling, she found just what we needed – a torch. You will realise from reading this the power cut lasted a long time as the electricity hadn't come back on before we found ourselves being illuminated by the welcome torch. Aren't handbags great!

The torch was put to good use throughout the evening as the power had a habit of going off. The power cuts became so frequent we memorised what and where everything was on our plates so we could continue eating should the torch run out of power.

The drinks were an interesting experience. Sylvia's mojito cocktail was served in a very elegant glass – if you could call a jam jar elegant. George's gin was watered down. When asked if everything was OK by the waiter, the lack of a taste of gin in George's drink was mentioned. This didn't seem a problem as the glass was taken away and gin added. It was as though they expected such complaints.

The first lassi I was given was the wrong flavour and when the pineapple one I asked for was brought, it too was very watery and not very good. Not the flavoursome yoghurt drink I have grown to love in Sri Lanka.

"What about the Chinese man sitting diagonally across from you?" I was asked about.

This sparked another memory. George and I ordered the local speciality – lumpy rice. I was excited to try something new and had no idea what it would look or taste like.

My plate was placed in front of me, I picked up my cutlery to cut into one of the banana-leaf parcels.

"No eat!" the Chinese man yelled.

I looked up puzzled, and saw him standing up, yelling again, "No eat!"

I wondered what was wrong with my food, and looked down, inspecting it closely, cutlery poised.

The next thing I was aware of was the sound of the next "No eat!" getting closer. I looked up. He was leaning across the wide table towards me with a camera, head positioned over my plate. He took a photo, sat down and continued his conversation with his friends.

I could now open my banana skin parcels and found sticky rice, vegetables, meat and a hard-boiled egg inside.

Our final reminiscing about meals on the trip was thinking about breakfast the next morning.

"What a contrast – no generator fumes but pure, fresh air, sitting on our verandas listening to the birds and admiring the views."

"Yes, different sounds from those we're familiar with at the guest house. There weren't any cockerels cock-a-doodle-doodling, no church bells ringing (though I find this sound very relaxing) or chanting from the mosques."

"I loved the way breakfast was served too. Our own breakfast trays brought to us laden with food and hot and cold drinks. Blissful."

"Here's hoping our trip this time will be as good."

Time to pack for our trip south in the morning, to Mirissa, a place in Sri Lanka we hadn't been to before.

Day 1 of 2-day tour

"The first ambulance I've seen in Sri Lanka – complete with flashing lights and siren blaring," I commented. "And I've seen for the first time a policeman, white lines on a road *and* another policeman directing traffic at a chaotic road intersection."

We were in the car and had started the four-hour drive to Mirissa, a small seaside town on the south coast.

Yesterday, Milinda the owner of the guest house we'd just left, phoned and found a suitable guest house in Mirissa but wouldn't book it despite us asking him to.

"I want you to see it first," he told us

"There are loads of alternative places if you didn't like this one," he and Janaka, our driver, assured.

On arrival we were annoyed to discover the rooms hadn't been reserved and were no longer available. Milinda had booked great accommodation two years previously and we hadn't anticipated a problem.

Janaka didn't have a contingency plan after all, and the "easy task" of finding alternative accommodation was far from easy. We became very familiar with one stretch of road as we travelled back and forth several times following directions from various pedestrians and tuk-tuk drivers who suggested places to try. None had vacancies.

Finally, a tuk-tuk driver took us to his guest house. It was not what we'd hoped for and nothing like the unique and great accommodation of two years before. The rooms were extremely basic, very small and, although they had windows, the windows looked out onto a concrete wall.

"Look, it's got a fridge," Douglas said. "It's not all bad. And we've got a four-poster bed."

A four-poster bed sounds grand but let me paint a fuller picture. It was a small double bed, jammed against the walls in the corner of the room so couldn't be accessed from both sides. The big plus though were the "four posts" over which mosquito nets were draped.

To be fair, we were given an opportunity to reject the rooms, but we were tired, hungry and didn't want to spend any more time looking for accommodation. Thus, even though the room was stiflingly hot with no air-conditioning we accepted the non-negotiable and expensive night rate which excluded breakfast.

"You don't need breakfast here," Janaka told us. "You'll get breakfast on the whale watching boat in the morning."

On acceptance of the room, Douglas made a beeline for the fridge to put our water bottles in. He opened the door and made a further disappointing discovery. The fridge wasn't a fridge at all, but a small cupboard disguised to look like a fridge and being used as a bedside table.

Our aim now was to leave the disappointments of the rooms behind and get some sustenance. We headed straight for the beach which was a short walk away and found a beach restaurant. After eating we sat there for ages chatting.

"Isn't it great sitting here, and watching families having a happy time? Children are easily pleased. Give them some sand and water and they're content," I said. "Have we told you about the beach at Kippford where we had our caravan? The tide on the Solway coast goes in and out very quickly – at the speed of a galloping horse we've been told. I'm not sure if this is true but when the tide is coming in, you don't watch waves ebbing and flowing, but rather water continually creeping up the beach. It's dangerous to go onto the muddy sand, exposed when the tide goes out as the water returns so quickly."

Kippford has a shell beach. The first time we saw it we were amazed to discover it wasn't a sandy beach covered with shells. It's literally just cockle shells down to some unknown depth. When David and Andrew were young, they played at being shopkeepers carefully laying shells on their rock shop counters, categorising them into different sizes and colours. They also liked grinding shells down with handheld rocks creating another pile of produce to sell.

"The rockpools there were fun to investigate too, overturning smaller rocks in search of crabs."

"The best way of catching crabs though," Douglas continued, "was from the slipway in the village with the orange twine fishing lines we bought them."

He was right – many a time we went crabbing after checking the tide times posted in the local yachting shop to make sure there would be water and not just muddy sand banks.

Bacon rind made good bait, giving us a good excuse to have bacon rolls for lunch. We took the large yellow bucket we transported water in at the caravan site and a round blue washing-up basin, put some sea water in each before placing them at the end of the little wooden jetty ready for the crabs we caught. The orange twine was unwound, and bait attached to the hooks before being cast, the sinker weight taking the bait down to the seabed.

Oh, the excitement and anticipation when the first tug was felt on the line! Slowly the line was pulled in and as it came to the surface, the wriggling crab was spotted. The delicate operation of raising the final length of line out of the water began. Finally, exposed to the air, the crab had to be carefully transferred into the bucket or basin, depending on whether David or Andrew were landing the catch. Sighs of relief all round and heart beats could return to their normal when the mission was accomplished.

But things didn't always go according to plan. Crabs had an uncanny knack of letting go of the bait. What disappointment when they did so near the surface of the water.

One day, we were fully engrossed in our tasks at the end of the jetty. Suddenly we realised the blue basin wasn't beside our welly-clad feet. The fast-rising tide had caught us out and we hadn't noticed the basin floating away. We watched it make its way along the side of the sea wall towards the yachting marina. But the water was against the wall, so it wasn't possible to climb over and rescue it. Finally, the basin reached some plants in a small area of saltmarsh where it stopped.

Not holding much hope, we returned the next day when the tide was out, just in case our beloved blue basin was anywhere to be seen. How happy I was when we looked over the sea wall, and saw it, still on the saltmarsh. Douglas retrieved it.

"We also checked tide times when we went to Rough Island. There was a causeway linking the shell beach to the island. We couldn't go during May, June or July as this was nesting time on this island bird sanctuary," Douglas said, wanting to give a fuller picture of our times there.

Now adults, David and Andrew have shown they still love Kippford, introducing their girlfriends to the places that mean so much to them. The ultimate affirmation happened on 30 July 2016 when Andrew took Julia along the causeway to Rough Island and there asked her to marry him. And to our joy and no doubt his relief, she said, "Yes."

"Sprinklers can be fun too," I recalled thinking about our family holiday in San Francisco in 2001. We were at the start of a self-drive family holiday; an amazing holiday we wouldn't have contemplated but for the fact we won flights to America.

It was a very hot Sunday afternoon. After a lot of walking and sight-seeing we found ourselves in Golden Gate Park. The enormous park was very popular with families on Sunday afternoons but because of its size didn't feel busy.

Here David and Andrew enjoyed a highlight of their day. They spotted sprinklers watering the lawns and made a beeline for them trying to avoid getting soaked as they ran around playing with a Frisbee. I knew they actually *wanted* to get soaked and shrieks of delight could soon be heard. They had a brilliant time while Douglas and I had an opportunity to sit and relax, watching the fun. They dried out in the heat or at least they didn't let on about any discomfort the damp clothes caused on the walk back to the hotel.

David and Andrew's thoughtfulness has been apparent since they were young, though at times this has made me laugh. After San Francisco, we were in Huntington Beach, California. We hired a bodyboard. David and Andrew made friends with some other children and soon learned the technique. Douglas went to see how they were getting on, itching, I think, to have a shot too. The three of them were in the water taking turns before David and Andrew took a break from the water to work on an abandoned sandcastle, close to where I was sitting, making it huge and spectacular.

Andrew explained, "We're letting Dad have extra time with the bodyboard because he's got less life left in him than us so needs to have fun while he can." What a cheery thought from a 9-year-old!

"And there was the other sprinkler episode in London when you booked a surprise few days there for my 50th birthday in 2004," Douglas recalled.

We met Elisabeth and Kristina and their daughters, Olivia and Mabel at the bandstand in St James' Park. Elisabeth and Kristina were the first friends I made when aged five my family moved to Lenzie, on the north side of Glasgow. They lived a few houses away. Elisabeth was my age and Kristina two years older. We'd such fun as children. Given lots of freedom we got up to all sorts of exciting activities. Unfortunately for me they moved to England about five years later, but we kept in touch.

It was a roasting hot day in London, so we sat on the grass under the shade of the trees eating our picnics. I remember the delicious Victoria plums they shared with us. It was very relaxing and peaceful, away from the London busyness.

"It's raining!" I heard Kristina say in astonishment. This is not what we were expecting. "Oh no," she corrected, "it's a sprinkler on the other side of the shrubs." David and Andrew went to investigate, closely followed by the girls. Soon they were soaked to the skin. As it was about 30 degrees, we didn't mind. I even enjoyed getting my back wet.

But that wasn't the end of the day's water experiences. All four youngsters went into the fountain outside Buckingham Palace to join others already in. Just thinking about it now makes me cringe – I'm sure they shouldn't have been allowed to do this, but we let them. This is where my memory fails me. Did I pretend they were nothing to do with me? Or did I look on lovingly at my little cherubs? (well not so little – they were 14 and 12). The water in the fountain was deep enough to allow them to swim, fully clad, while onlookers watched in astonishment, taking photographs. (I'm cringing again wondering how many photograph albums they appear in?) It must be anticipated people will go into the water, as all we could smell when they came out, was chlorine disinfectant on them.

"A couple of years earlier, they paddled in the bronze fountain in the Vigeland Sculpture Park in Oslo," Douglas added.

"That's right," I said recalling the fact I liked the fountain much better than the *Monolith* sculpture we'd just walked from. It was the biggest of the 200 granite sculptures we saw in the park, a 14 metre (46 feet) high column of 121 intertwined people. It gave me the creeps when I looked at it.

"I remember what horrified them when they climbed up was the filthy water in the next level of the fountain and how much rubbish was in the water." Out of sight, out of mind.

"At least we managed to go for a proper swim later."

"Yes, but not at our hotel as the pool was closed for repair. It was good we could use another hotel's swimming pool – and ours refunded the ticket costs," I said to Douglas.

The tickets were cheaper than we'd been told, though still five times more than we paid at home. We decided we must have been paying for the view over the rooftops of the city which was definitely not something we had in dear Prestwick town.

The staff were very good on our second visit, as officially the pool wasn't open to non-residents on Sundays but seeing the boys' sad faces, they agreed to let us swim. This time we were charged the full price – ten times more than we would have paid back home.

On the way back to the hotel, Douglas said, "I'll keep this ticket and frame it."

David and Andrew's reactions were priceless and responses came thick and fast, "But you can't, Dad, you need to get the money back!"

"It cost such a lot of money!"

"Yes," Douglas teased. "That's why I'm going to frame it. It's the most expensive swim we've ever had.'

David and Andrew were horrified. I kept up the pretence; framing this was a good idea. This really alarmed them insisting we should hand the ticket in for a refund. Much to their relief, this is what we did.

"I'm now remembering the 'Scottish Shower' in the hotel spa in Madeira," I said to Douglas.

"Oh yes," he said grinning.

The swimming pool wasn't very big or warm and a couple of children were playing in it, making our preferred swimming of lengths far from easy. We opted to try the other facilities.

I'd noticed in the literature mention of a "Scottish shower". In the spa, there weren't any signs, so we weren't sure if what we experienced was the Scottish shower.

On the three surrounding walls and ceiling of the shower, were three levels of nozzles. On pressing the button, a fine mist came out of the lowest nozzles, the water being on the cool side. A while later, mist started coming out of the next level of nozzles and finally the third level too. We grew accustomed to the temperature.

"I've got the same feelings as in a slowly ascending rollercoaster. I hate it; knowing the slow ascent will be followed by a terrifying ride back down," I said to Douglas.

The "down" as far as the shower was concerned referred to the long thin nozzle above us. I was sure water would come out of this but at what temperature and force? Would it be another mist spray or a deluge of freezing water?

The water started flowing from above and when it reached us, I was pleasantly surprised – the water was warm. What a relief!

"But we'd been lulled into a false sense of security," I recalled. "Suddenly the temperature of the water turned to freezing and you grabbed me so I couldn't escape," I accused Douglas, my captor. "What an absolute horror you can be."

"It was very funny listening to you squealing – loudly," he laughed.

Does this sound like a "Scottish shower"?

Heading for "Tracey Island", Mirissa

From our relaxing position on Mirissa beach, Douglas pointed, saying, "That island over there looks just like Tracey Island from Thunderbirds. Look, people are walking to the island and along the top to the other end of the ridge. Let's do the same." He had sat long enough.

When we got there, Douglas, George and Sylvia said they weren't going to climb. They had watched people sliding on their bottoms down a steep section on the way back. I couldn't understand why the people were doing this while others were walking normally. The bottom sliders were obviously made of less stern stuff than me.

Off I set, camera in hand, up the flight of steps, passing the sign which read "private keep out, danger of rock fall". I stopped and moved to the side to give way to people who were coming back down. When I moved back onto the path, I got my first sight of what the others had obviously seen, but I had not. We'd been looking from different angles. Not only was it steep, but there was a narrow ridge of rock only 30cm (1 foot) wide, with sheer cliffs on either side. It had to be walked across.

The three below were looking up at me, watching my every move. I decided to tease them pretending I wasn't scared to make the ascent, waving happily and indicating I would be making my way up when another descending group passed me. They continued to keep their eyes fixed on me.

Once the descenders passed, I made my move. I waved again and took a couple of steps. But I turned around and indicating I wasn't going any further. I could see Douglas' lips moving,

"Thank you!" he was clearly saying though I couldn't hear him. My expedition was worth it as I got a kiss on my forehead when I reached the bottom!

Douglas and I went for a swim beside the island where several people were snorkelling. Swimming goggles on, we could see coral and fish. Not masses or the brightly coloured ones I swam with in the Bahamas many years before, but about six different kinds, mostly about 4 or 5 inches long, flat and oval. One was black, another yellow and brown striped.

Another couple signalled to me. There was something to see. I swam over but couldn't understand what they were trying to tell me except it was big. Initial looking revealed nothing, so principles of triangulation were incorporated into my searching – identifying the direction each was looking in and pinpointing the intersection point. I looked there and saw it – a turtle. And not just a 10 or 12cm (4 or 5 inch) one, but one about a metre (3 feet) long. We were swimming with a turtle in its natural environment. Amazing!

"Quick, come here," I yelled over to Douglas who was a fair distance away. I knew when he had seen it. His head suddenly rose above the water and he yelled "It's huge!"

George and Sylvia had by this time packed up our belongings, left them neatly on the beach and started walking away to find somewhere for a seat and drink in the shade. I continued in the excited yelling mode adding some frantic hand waving trying to tell them about the turtle they should come to see. Realising they hadn't understood, Douglas set off for shore, returning without them, but with his new underwater camera.

Unfortunately, a group of teenagers came on the scene and were swimming too close to the turtle so by the time Douglas arrived it had made a hasty retreat into deeper water.

I wasn't sure the photos of the turtle would have worked anyway as the water was murky due to the disturbed sand. Douglas too had doubts as the new gadget had been ultra-cheap. He took some photos of the fish instead. We were pleasantly surprised later with the results.

After all the excitement we made our way to the beach bar and joined the others.

"Is there somewhere I can change," I asked the staff.

"Yes, upstairs."

The toilet was tiny. There was no one else in the upstairs sitting area, so I said to Douglas, "It'll be easier if you just hold the towel up as a screen and I'll change out here rather than in the toilet."

Everything started fine, Douglas held the towel up, and I proceeded to remove my swimming costume. Obviously, Douglas couldn't create a complete screen round me, so I became concerned when he and the towel started moving, changing the direction he was facing.

"What on earth are you doing, Douglas?" I asked alarmed. After all, a serious operation was underway here and I felt he wasn't taking his role in the task seriously. "Please stand still!" Surely, he could concentrate on the job in hand and stay still for a short while? "It's just as well you're still hiding me from the people sitting downstairs or you'd be in deep trouble!"

"Well I've just noticed something," he said.

"What?"

"There's a CCTV camera in the corner of the ceiling over there, so I was trying to conceal you from it."

"Oh right …" I said shrinking. "That explains things. Sorry! Oh well, I'm sure they've seen worse!"

With the advantage of this insider knowledge when we reversed roles, I performed my duty of towel holder-upper perfectly.

On returning to our stiflingly hot bedroom later, Douglas realised he had lost something. Such occurrences aren't unusual when we go on holiday.

This time he had lost his FitBit, a birthday present from David, Andrew, and me. In the sauna of a bedroom, we checked and emptied the contents of all 212 pockets in his rucksack and shorts (Douglas likes things with umpteen pockets) onto the bed but no sign of it.

We remembered how George had kindly gathered all the belongings we'd left abandoned on the beach.

"I'm sure I put the FitBit and the room key into the same pocket in your shorts and put them in your rucksack, Douglas," he said. We'd found the key – we were in the room after all.

Sylvia helped with the double checking and George checked their rucksacks but to no avail. We reckoned it must have fallen out somewhere. We headed for dinner accepting it was unfortunate but something we could replace when we got home.

We'd a lovely meal in a beach restaurant, sitting in the dark under a starlit sky, with just a candle on the table for light, listening to the waves. I had a beautifully cooked tuna steak. We sat for ages, chatting. Finally, we decided to return to our saunas (bedrooms) as we'd a wakeup call at 5.15 a.m. for the whale spotting trip.

"Could we retrace our steps prior to the loss of the FitBit just in case we spot it?" I asked. By doing this I could truly put the matter to rest and accept it was lost. Off we set along the beach. George had a torch with him, and Douglas used the torch on his phone to see in the pitch black.

If we hadn't done this extra searching, we wouldn't have passed a large area of palm trees with strings of different coloured lights spiralled around their trunks which along with the nearly full moon made the trees look stunning and very atmospheric. Thus, if for no other reason our walk was worthwhile.

We looked thoroughly where Douglas had left our belongings prior to swimming with the turtle before we went to our last port of call, the beach bar – of CCTV fame.

A group of four members of staff stood in the corner with big grins spread across their faces. Had I been recognised even though on this encounter I'd my clothes on? I put this thought out of my mind.

"Has a FitBit been found?" Douglas asked.

Immediately, one of the young men said, "Ah my watch?" pointing to his wrist.

"Yes, it's like a black watch," Douglas was in the process of saying. But before he had finished the man had taken off the watch and handed it to Douglas. It was the lost FitBit.

"It was under the table," he said pointing to where we'd been sitting earlier. It must have fallen out his rucksack when he was getting his clothes to change upstairs. The men were obviously as pleased we'd come back as we were to find the FitBit, but adamantly refused to take a tip for its safe return.

Douglas took me back to our room before returning to meet up with the other two for a celebratory drink in the beach bar.

The bedroom, thankfully, had a ceiling fan which I put on full blast and had a cold shower. I left the outside door ajar hoping this would let the now cooler evening air in. I lay down on the bed, but sleep evaded me.

At low speeds the fan made a rhythmic clanking sound. At high speeds it was more like a helicopter but with a worrying grating sound. It was clearly far from being securely fixed to the ceiling and as I watched it swinging back and forth, I'd visions of it coming crashing down on top of me and slicing me into pieces. This, together with a smell of burning rubber, made me realise leaving it at high speed was rather risky and even putting my life in danger. I turned the speed down.

Once again, my body temperature rose so a second cold shower was called for, one I stayed in until I was covered in goose pimples. I made no attempt to dry myself but instead put on my nightie, letting it get wet so it would continue to keep me cool. Amazingly, I slept better than I expected.

Wonders and dangers of the sea

The next morning, the sun hadn't risen when we arrived at Mirissa Harbour, shortly after our 5.15 a.m. wakeup call, but already activity was in full swing. The fishing boats were tied up and sellers at the market were busily negotiating prices for the fish landed. Walking past them and round the top of the harbour, we were some of the first passengers to arrive at our boat.

"Where would you recommend we sit?"

"Upstairs," so upstairs we went.

We'd about an hour to wait before departure and during this time, the sun rose giving beautiful views of the very colourful brightly striped fishing boats, the red, blue, yellow, green and orange vivid against the blue sky behind them (see photo on front cover).

The crew were busy. Firstly, bottles of water and anti-sea-sickness tablets were distributed. The tablets were advertised as being one of the "included" items on the trip. While great our well-being had been thought about, I also felt this was an ominous sign. Some of those around us refused to take the tablets, despite intensive persuasion from the crew. I on the other hand also downed copious amounts of herbal tablets I'd brought with me.

Trays with cups of coffee and very gingery ginger biscuits were brought. I'd heard somewhere ginger is good for settling upset stomachs and as I get easily seasick, I munched my way through several as a further precautionary measure.

I remember being on a "submarine" once with Douglas. I only agreed to go because, being a submarine, it would go underwater so wouldn't be affected by the waves. The trouble was the submarine turned out to be a boat made to look like a yellow submarine. Yes, the windows were under the waterline, but the boat remained above it. I felt it was too late to change my mind so went aboard. When we left the shelter of the harbour, I began to feel awful. Unfortunately, there were others onboard, so we couldn't ask to return. I ended up lying down – thankful there weren't many people on board so I could stretch out along the bench seat. I felt very sick by the end of the trip, which was only half an hour long, and was so relieved to get off and breath fresh air.

Now I determinedly put various memories of being seasick behind me and focused on our whale-watching trip.

It was after 7 a.m. when we set off. The sea didn't look particularly rough, but after a short while I thought it would be better to move and stand at the front of the boat. I was feeling squeamish, despite all the precautionary measures.

I think the problem was the boat was travelling relatively slowly and as a result was going up and down on the waves rather than through them. Fortunately, it wasn't also rolling from side to side but even so the walk to the front found me being thrown about, narrowly missing collisions with other passengers.

I positioned myself at the stainless-steel railing at the front, holding on tightly trying to keep stable while keeping eyes fixed on the horizon ahead. I tried to zone out and ride the waves. However, the upper deck was set back a bit from the bow, and therefore as the boat rose up on a wave, the bow came into my line of vision, disappearing down as we crested the wave. This sight was enough to make me feel worse. I shut my eyes. So back and forth I swayed, building up muscles in my arms I've never had before.

I became aware of a young Chinese boy leaning against me. He was using me as a support. I tried ever so hard to have positive thoughts about this. He was young, and I was helping him, I reasoned. However, as Douglas knows, when I'm not feeling great, I can't cope with anyone touching me. His first lesson on this was when I was in labour with soon to be born David. The poor father-to-be was trying to be supportive and hold my hand or wipe my brow and all he got from me was, "Don't touch me!"

After a while there was no other option, I had to ask the young boy to move along a bit. He quickly slid back. A different plan of action was required as I couldn't cope with this predicament any longer.

I really wanted to lie down, but I didn't see anywhere I could do this. I certainly didn't want to go back to my original seat as even from the front of the boat where I stood, I could hear one of the men sitting in the row behind Douglas, being very noisily sick. Douglas said he hadn't heard anything like it before. I don't know how Douglas, George and Sylvia could have continued to sit there. Douglas later told me there were another four people being sick behind him. Included in this number were those who had refused to take the anti-sickness tablets. What a surprise!

I compromised and staggered back far enough to allow me to sit on one of the cushions on the deck and once more shut my eyes. I was grateful the life jacket I was wearing had a neck support as together with the railing at my back I felt secure.

I was aware of one of the crew members talking to Douglas and saying, "Ten minutes." Shortly after the same person tapped my shoulder and asked, "You OK?"

"I'm feeling a bit sick," was my understatement of the year reply.

"Blue whale near. 10 minutes."

I started to stand up, but he told me to stay put meantime, but to try to go to the front of the boat when we got close to the massive marine mammal or stand at the Captain's console next to where I was sitting. Before he left me, he spotted my iPad and said he would take photos for me with it. He was so kind. I was extremely grateful.

As instructed, at the appropriate time I stood up and quickly realised moving to the front of the boat wasn't an option. By this time, children were sitting on deck cushions all along the front railing. This gave them a great view, but I knew I wouldn't be able to reach over them to anchor myself to the railings.

However, the second option beside the Captain was ideal. There were rails to hold onto, and for most of the time no one was in front of me. I was also able to watch where the Captain was looking and steering towards which helped me spot the whales.

We saw several spouts of water coming from a whale. Whenever a spout was spotted the Captain changed direction and shot off in hot pursuit, along with several other similar vessels and yachts. It reminded me of the TV cartoon programme I watched when I was young called "Whacky Races" although in the cartoon road vehicles rather than boats raced each other.

There were lots of loud "Oo-s" and "Aah-s" especially when we caught sight of a part of a whale. After much chasing, we got a brilliant view of the whale swimming on the surface and the tail emerging before it finally dived down. There were a few other not-so-good sightings before we turned around and headed for the harbour.

My iPad was returned to me and on it was some great video footage. The crew member had stood on the ledge on the outside of the railings so had unobstructed views. I'd seen this as I hung onto the rails beside the Captain but decided it didn't matter if he dropped it overboard. I was feeling too awful to think anything could be any worse.

"It's hard to believe the blue whale's heart is the size of a small car and a human child could crawl inside its largest vein," Douglas told me later, recounting some facts he had learned from one of the crew.

"It can grow to more than the length of three buses. It's huge," he added.

The journey back to the harbour wasn't as bad as the outward journey. The boat picked up speed, so the ride was less bumpy. The outward journey had taken about 1 hour 45 minutes plus time chasing the whales, the return journey was only about an hour. During this time, Madeira cake and cold drinks were brought round. I was able to eat and enjoy some of the cake. I'd bypassed the salad rolls on the outward journey which was "breakfast".

What we hadn't expected was being entertained by the crew singing cheery local songs accompanied by a drum and small cylindrical shakers worn on their fingers. It was very relaxed and natural rather than a staged performance. There was no set "play list", instead they chatted between songs deciding what to sing next.

"I'm glad I did this trip but my whale watching days are over!" I said to Douglas when we got off the boat. (Later, even watching the video footage taken on my iPad made me feel squeamish but I'm grateful for the footage none-the-less.)

Janaka met us and we hit the road again, heading for Hikkaduwa with its long white sand beaches edged with palm trees. We all fell asleep.

"I've found a hotel at the beach which will be good for you," Janaka told us when we wakened. What a relief! We were taken to inspect it, following a member of staff through the restaurant, then outside and upstairs to the rooms. They were awful, Janaka even commented they were smelly and not suitable. I think the smell was caused by overuse of strong cleaning products. Janaka's reaction filled me with confidence. He must have alternatives, I thought. This was misguided confidence. It immediately became clear he didn't and so, the next search began.

Despite having been told many times by Sylvia we wanted to go to a guest house, not a villa or hotel, he took us to another hotel. This hotel wasn't suitable either and we were getting depressed thinking it was going to be a repeat of the previous day – trailing round looking for somewhere to stay instead of relaxing and enjoying ourselves.

"We don't want a hotel. We want a guest house. They are cheaper and more intimate," we explained again.

Finally, we felt Janaka understood and off we went down some side streets. He stopped at several properties, each time jumping out the car expectantly but invariably jumping back in quickly.

"It's full," he cheerily told us each time. We weren't feeling as cheery.

Finally, at one, the owner said he was full but asked us what our budget was. He said he would get his bike and take us to a suitable guest house. Could we allow our hopes to rise? Part of us desperately wanted to but we'd had so many disappointments.

Out came the man with his push-bike, and we found ourselves in hot pursuit down the narrow bumpy roads trying to keep up with him. He took us to a house beside a railway line, so Douglas and I felt at home because there's a railway line at the back of our garden in Scotland. (The first night in our new home, we hardly slept and thought we would never be able to get used to the sound of the trains. But by night two, we didn't even notice the trains.)

This owner's house had a newly built separate block which had two bedrooms in it and a little area outside where breakfast would be served in the morning. It was still nothing like as special as the accommodation organised for us two years previously. It wasn't cheap either, but it was clean, and we felt we could spend a couple of nights here. We were weary and hungry so accepted it.

Immediately the owner asked (translated by Janaka) what we wanted for breakfast. This wasn't what we wanted to think about. With rumbling tummies, we wanted to go for lunch. We were shown a menu (after we asked for one) which included string hoppers. Douglas and I were intrigued, and even with a verbal explanation weren't any the wiser. But throwing caution to the wind we ordered them together with the bread and jam offered. Understandably, George and Sylvia said they would choose what they wanted to eat in the morning.

This administration over, we quickly walked along the side of a railway line and crossed the single-track line at a level-crossing. We were soon at the shops, seafront hotels and restaurants with the beach beyond them.

While having lunch we decided not to dwell on the disappointment of the organisation of our accommodation but changed the subject.

"So, no more whale watching for you?" Douglas questioned me.

"No!" I exclaimed adamantly.

"It wasn't like the trip from Tai O on Ngong Ping Lantau island where we had a great experience with David and Andrew after seeing the Big Buddha and Po Lin Monastery. We all loved it."

Tai O is Hong Kong's oldest fishing village and I must admit, when we got off the bus, we wondered when the next one was to take away again. First impressions can deceive. We quickly realised how peaceful it was, so different from the hustle and bustle of Hong Kong. No multi-storey buildings, crowds or masses of traffic here.

"Just as well I saw the 'guaranteed to see dolphins' sign for the 25-minute boat tour," I said. "Yes, surprisingly I was the one to suggest a boat trip, though we took the 'guarantee' with a pinch of salt."

The boat took us up a narrow strip of water between the backs of the houses in this shanty-village-on-stilts, built over the water. Some of the buildings were made of metal sheets which for us would have been unbearably hot to live in. We felt sad seeing the very poor living conditions.

The boat turned and we were taken back to the mooring. We were bewildered. What about the 25-minute trip? What about the dolphins we were "guaranteed" to see? It turned out we hadn't been conned. Our captain jumped off and onto another boat to lead a fishing expedition while a new captain came aboard.

Out into the bay we sped, the throttle of the boat fully opened. It was wonderfully refreshing to have the cooling breeze in our faces. Soon an amazing sight of dolphins came into view ahead of us. They were jumping out of the water in their natural surroundings with no feeding to entice them to come near us. We drew up alongside them and followed them until they finally disappeared. It was fantastic.

"Thank goodness we stopped at Tai O and didn't immediately board another bus to the train back to Kowloon."

Our trip on a catamaran in Madeira in 2009, also with David and Andrew, was brilliant too. When the dolphins were first spotted, there was great excitement onboard. We moved to the front of the catamaran and onto the netting which stretched between the two hulls. Dolphins swam under us, just in front of us and in fact, all around us. On one occasion, I saw a line of five dolphins jumping out of the water at the same time. It was also great seeing the very young ones – they looked so cute. There were about fifty dolphins in the group, and the crewman thought this was probably a different group from the day before, because there weren't any whales accompanying them.

"You weren't so keen on the snorkelling off the catamaran though," Douglas reminded me.

"No, it brought back memories of my first dive in the Holy Loch in Scotland. It was at the end of a diving course which had been in a swimming pool. The course was great, and I really enjoyed my six weeks of tuition. But to be awarded the certificate I'd to complete a dive in open water, thus the trip to the Holy Loch.

It was a freezing cold day, and the group all put on wet suits. I found I was hardly able to walk to the water's edge because of the full quota of lead weights for saltwater round my waist plus the weight of the oxygen cylinder.

However, into the water I walked, not very elegantly because of the flippers, and lowered myself into the water. I knew the water would be cold. The wetsuit made it feel slightly less so, but the still exposed patches of my face felt as though they turned to ice.

As we all progressed into the still shallow water our flippers churned up the sand beneath us. When I was fully submerged, I couldn't see a thing in front of me, but reckoned everyone in the group (who were all men) must be ahead of me. I therefore started to kick furiously to catch up with them.

I felt I was never going to catch them, and suddenly felt a tug on my leg. I surfaced because I still couldn't see anything underwater and discovered it was one of the instructors. I'd been heading out into the middle of the loch, in completely the wrong direction.

I got such a fright and found I couldn't breathe properly. I ended up having to lie on my back and be towed back to shore by the instructor. When I was a youngster, I took lifesaving lessons in a local swimming pool where I learned how to tow and resuscitate others, but never expected decades later to be the one being saved. Thus, ended diving for me – in Scotland anyway. Maybe I'll have another go somewhere where the water is warmer and clearer."

"OK, what about a happier memory now, our swim with dolphins in Australia," Douglas said.

"Oh, that is something I'll never forget."

There were only 22 of us on the boat which normally took 30-40 people on this trip, so we'd plenty of room to spread out as we tried to get our wetsuits on. We helped each other: pulling, pushing and squee-zing in the various parts of our anatomies which no longer matched the "perfect" figures the wetsuits were designed for. Mission accomplished it was time for a hot cuppa and ginger biscuits.

Off the boat set, after we were offered one further preventative measure – a tub containing something to smell, which we were assured would stop seasickness in its tracks. We decided to wait to see how I got on before forking out the $10 price tag.

We were told about the procedures to follow when dolphins were spotted. We were split into four groups; each member was given a coloured belt to wear over their wet suits. Two groups would go into the water at a time and in preparation for our launch, the two assigned groups were to sit on the steps at the stern. Once given the order we were to go down a metal ladder, push off as quickly as possible and grab hold of the belt of the person in front of us, forming a line behind our group leader. The leader had a yellow hand-held motorised *diver propulsion vehicle/scooter* which would pull us through the water.

A few dolphins were spotted soon after we left the harbour and the first two groups went into the water. It was good to watch them demonstrating. The dolphins, however, weren't for hanging around, so our group didn't go into the water. The skipper headed off in another direction searching for another family group of dolphins. He had no idea where or if he would find the dolphins as they are wild and as in Homg

Kong aren't fed by the crew to attract them.

After a while, we were told, "Get ready," so down onto the steps our group went where snorkels and masks were positioned. Soon the order came from the skipper above us, "Right guys: go, go, go!"

There was no going back now. It was an anxious time, between getting into the water, managing to link up with the person in front and waiting for Douglas to grab hold of my belt behind me at which point I could relax. I saw three dolphins very close to us, but they disappeared so quickly Douglas didn't see them.

We heard the instruction from our leader, "Heads up," which meant look up and get back onto the boat.

A few reminders and pieces of advice made our next times in the water much easier. We'd to keep our legs and free arm still and rely on being pulled along – there was no need to do any swimming. Also, the water wasn't cold. It was 23 degrees, so any anxiousness caused by memories of my diving experience in the Holy Loch were forgotten. The wet suits kept us on top of the water. We didn't need to hold our breath as we weren't under the surface of the water. The priority was to get into the water as quickly as possible, grab hold of the belt in front and keep looking down to see all the amazing action around us.

"On our second time in the water, you were told to go behind the leader, weren't you Douglas?"

"Yes, and I saw dolphins too which was great."

"Plus, there was the signalling I devised to help you look in the right direction. With the hand holding onto your belt I prodded right if you were to look right and left if you were to look left when I saw dolphins. Ingenious."

"Yes, but if you recall, it wasn't as ingenious as you thought."

"OK, I admit, it would have been better if I'd devised the plan before we were in the water and explained the code. Plus, I hadn't appreciated the thick wetsuit meant you didn't feel any of my prodding anyway! I remember you looked awful when you came out the water on that occasion, your face very grey."

"Yes, I'd swallowed a lot of sea water. Fortunately, the extra tuition about head positioning so the water wouldn't go down the snorkel sorted that problem."

Our third time in the water was brilliant, indescribable really. There were lots of dolphins – so close – swimming beside and under us. Some were so close we couldn't see the full length of them. They were amazing to watch. Sometimes two swam beside each other, as though they were doing synchronised swimming. When they turned over we could see their white undersides. Some had scars – something I'd only ever seen on TV documentaries. I could hear their clicking and whistling, though it was too quiet for Douglas to hear. I was so pleased this time was special for Douglas too.

During our next few times in the water, we learned just to relax and really take in the marvellous experience we were having.

"And wasn't the massive tray of fruit we could eat when we finished each swim so refreshing. The chopped-up melon, watermelon, oranges and grapes got rid of any saltiness in our mouths. And our last sightings of the dolphins were as the boat sped back to the harbour creating a massive wash behind us. This was the only time the dolphins followed us. They love surfing in the waves created by boats. It was great to watch them jumping out of the water and Douglas got some fantastic photographs."

A happy memory to end on.

Feeling refreshed after lunch George, Sylvia, Douglas and I were looking forward to our next activity. We'd asked Janaka to take us to a turtle sanctuary.

On the way back to the guest house I'd a notion to fit in one extra thing: a wee shot of bodysurfing. We only had 15 minutes to spare. Quickly paying the agreed rate (less than the cost of an ice cream back home for an hour) I set off purposefully. With board in hand and safety strap round my wrist, I was ready to go.

I took my lead from others who were already in the water assuming they were standing in a good place waiting for the waves. In my excitement I was able to completely ignore the contrast between air and water temperatures. as there was no time to acclimatise,

Douglas was on the beach, my mini iPad in his hand, poised ready to get the fantastic action pictures I anticipated of me riding endlessly on top of the white capped waves.

Quickly, I was riding my first wave and it was great. However, I immediately realised this was beginners' luck as I didn't manage to time the next few waves correctly.

When I got my timing correct, the waves took me right in to the edge of the water and on one occasion I crashed into Douglas' feet as he videoed. I'd absolutely no control over what I was doing.

I was so relieved I'd kept my t-shirt on to prevent sun burning. It transpired the sun wasn't the problem. I discovered it's not at all sensible to go body surfing in a bikini. When I came to a stop at the water's edge I had to pause before I stood up. During this time, I remained underwater rearranging my bikini to ensure I was decent when I stood up as the pressure of water had a habit of changing its position – the bottoms went down, and the top up!

Although I only had a short time in the water, it was such fun. I ended up with a battle scar though. I think if I'd had tuition before going into the water, I would have been told to keep my elbows on the board. But I didn't and in the shallow water my elbow scraped along the gritty sand and it got badly grazed. But it was an injury I was proud to show off.

Now fast forward a few minutes: we're back at the guest house room getting ready to go out again.

It's been a while since I've featured Douglas and the theme of losing things. But I'm about to rectify this. Douglas realised he had left his sandals behind at our previous accommodation. This was a pity as although it's not a problem to buy sandals here, none of them had enclosed toes. Open toed sandals, he has discovered, are not suitable for his design of feet; his second toe is significantly longer than his big toe. As a result, if wearing open toed sandals, he always stubs his second toe and I hear him saying, "ouch" or words to that effect.

I explained the predicament of the left-behind-sandals to Janaka and asked if he could contact the owner to see if they had been found and could be posted back to our guest house where we would return to in few days. Instead Janaka said he would drive back tomorrow after he dropped us off in Galle where we were going for the day. This was very kind of him.

We set off in the car once more heading for the Sea Turtle Hatchery. Based on our previous experiences, we were concerned about Janaka's ability to get us there, but he appeared confident.

Things were looking good – for a short while anyway. But stops began. The window was rolled down, he exchanged words with pedestrians and tuk-tuk drivers (note the plurals as this happened several times). He didn't know where he was going, and we realised those he asked didn't know either. We were directed this way and that, doing many a U-turn in the process. When we finally arrived at the Urawatta Sea Turtle Hatchery (near the Urawatta Bridge on Galle Road, Urawatta) we knew we'd already driven passed it – at least once. A brightly painted wall mural welcomed us to this conservation project.

The hatchery wasn't at all what I expected. It was small and thankfully not commercialised or a tourist hotspot. This meant we'd a very relaxed private tour.

First, the owner showed us the sand bed where he put the turtle eggs to hatch. He buys the eggs for the sanctuary and they take 47 days to hatch. I was amazed at the precision of the timescale!

Sitting on the sandy ground was a series of rectangular concrete tanks with blue painted sides. These were the turtles' homes after hatching. Each had a corrugated roof canopy providing shade for the turtles and as the hot sun's rays beat down, we were grateful for the shade too. The first tank contained the one-day old turtles.

"Don't they grow quickly!" I observed as we walked from tank to tank seeing where they moved to as they got older and bigger.

"Some of the turtles have been rescued from the sea and brought here for us to look after," the owner told us as we looked in another tank. "They've been injured, some because they were caught in fishing nets. This one," he said pointing, "has a damaged leg but the worst thing is it can't sink. It has swallowed plastic bags which had air in them, so the turtle is now buoyant." It was so sad to hear about the needless suffering caused by humans.

"Will we see turtles being released into the sea?" I asked.

"No. We are not like the big commercialised turtle farms set up for tourists. I don't do daily releases."

I was disappointed but didn't feel so bad when he explained other tricks used elsewhere.

"They feed the turtles after they're released to make sure they don't swim away which they would normally do. The females shouldn't make their first return journey until they're 20 years old when they come back to lay their first eggs." More messing with nature.

We weren't at the sanctuary for long, but it was interesting, and the owner insisted on us holding one of the turtles. I felt a bit uncomfortable about this, as until now our tour had been about looking after the turtles in as natural a way as possible. Perhaps the ones he gave us to hold won't be released.

Back in the car we remembered when we were last in Sri Lanka seeing many pictures, canvases, postcards, wooden carvings etc. of the stick fishermen. Vertical poles are driven into the sandy seabed. Each has a cross member attached to it. In the pictures the old fishermen are seen perched on the cross member, hunkered down, wearing hats and sarongs with a simple wooden fishing rod in hand. We understood this was a traditional way of fishing along the south coast where we now were.

"Can you take us to see stick fishermen?" we asked Janaka.

"Yes, but as soon as you get out of a car to take photos, the fishermen jump down and ask for money."

"So, they're not really fishing?"

"No, it's just a tourist attraction now. All they want is your money. One tourist who went to take a photo was dragged into the water, a hat put on his head, he was lifted onto the pole and a fishing rod put in his hand. To begin with he thought it good fun and caught some tiny fish. Twenty minutes later he was getting fed up. Eventually he was taken down and told to pay 6000 rupees." (Approximately £33). "He only had 3000 rupees. The men were not happy and followed him back to his tuk-tuk shouting for more money. As they drove off, the 'fishermen' shouted saying they hoped his plane would crash." How awful we thought.

As we drove, we saw some of the poles, but not just a few as are seen in paintings, but dozens and dozens of them in a large group. Not the romantic imagery in our minds. Some "fishermen" were on poles, but they weren't even dressed in the traditional clothes but instead were wearing jeans and t-shirts with not a traditional hat in sight. So instead of photos, we'll hold in our minds the sunset paintings of the crouching fishermen balanced on poles, fishing rod in hand.

We did make another stop though. This was to see the Tsunami Honganji Vihara, just off Bentota-Galle Road at Hikkaduwa town. Here there's an 18 metre (60 feet) tall statue of Buddha on a little island in a lake close to the road. The statue is looking out to the Indian Ocean, its right arm bent at the elbow and palm facing the ocean. Sadly, it was erected to commemorate the many thousands of lives lost when the 2004 Boxing Day tsunami struck. The estimated number of those who perished ranges from 1,700 to over 2,000. An accurate number will never be known.

What makes it more poignant is the statue's height. It's the same height as the second of the four waves which came over the land. Standing on the roadside looking at the ocean, it was impossible to imagine such a height of wave.

Most of those who perished were in a train travelling on the line close to the shore. Others climbed onto the roof of the train after the first wave struck or hid behind the train thinking it would protect them. Instead, the train was found about 100 metres (330 feet) away from the track, the wave having lifted it up and dropped it in this new location as its power weakened.

Remembering the awful tragedy made me think of the impact it had on Andrew. He was eleven at the time and felt he had to do something to help the survivors. He decided to do a sponsored run and opted to do a 6-mile run, twice round a 3-mile route he knew.

As Andrew was going to be running on his own, I said I would go with him to keep him company. There was one proviso – I wasn't going to run, as I knew there was no way I would be able to keep up with him. I wouldn't be able to run one mile let alone six. I would cycle.

I remember the Sunday afternoon well. The weather was awful. The wind was blowing a gale. Cycling was very difficult along the seafront promenade section. Many a time the force of the wind nearly brought me to a standstill.

By the end of the first circuit I was exhausted. "I'm sure people would understand if you only did three miles," I suggested.

This thought hadn't crossed his mind. "You can go home, and I'll meet you there."

This wasn't something I could bring myself to do and round the route we both went again. There wasn't any possibility I was really keeping him company as I couldn't even speak. All my energy was required to keep breathing and turning the pedals. I'm sure few words of encouragement passed my lips. He was the one who was encouraging me by his perseverance!

By the time I got home, my legs were like jelly. He, on the other hand, took it all in his stride. He was fit and a good runner, but this was by far the furthest he had ever run. I was very proud he had wanted to help those whose lives had been destroyed. He didn't just think about it, he did something about it. He raised well over £700 in sponsorship from friends and family, people in our church and his school which was marvellous.

Our evening in Sri Lanka was finished as ever with a meal, this time sitting at a table on the beach, with petrol burning lanterns adding to the atmosphere. A good way to end our thought-provoking day and dispelling our earlier disappointments.

Tsunami Honganji Vihara. The statue of Buddha is the same height
as the second of four waves over the land in 2004 Boxing Day tsunami

Lost and Found

Hoppers and string hoppers for breakfast

George and Sylvia's request to wait until the morning to choose their breakfast choices was either ignored or lost in translation. Hoppers, string hoppers and curry sauce was brought to the table for all of us.

The mystery for Douglas and me was solved. String hoppers are steam-cooked rice noodles. The hoppers are like very thin crepes made from fermented batter. We put the string hoppers into the crepe-like hoppers, added curry sauce, wrapped them up and ate them like fajitas.

Breakfast over, we organised ourselves for our outing to Galle.

"Have you contacted the guest house we came from yesterday to see if they had found Douglas' sandals?" I asked Janaka as we were loading the car. "It would save you driving all the way back if they aren't there anymore."

He quickly started checking his phone, scrolling through a huge list of calls trying to locate the required phone number. Finally, he admitted he didn't have the phone number so would just drive back.

Unexpectedly I heard Sylvia behind me saying, "Douglas – you've got your sandals on!"

And sure enough, Douglas was walking towards us looking rather shamefaced, wearing his "lost" sandals. He had found them in one of his bags which was under some papers in our room. He was very embarrassed about the whole incident and particularly his lack of searching skills, but he gave us a laugh and a happy end to this story.

Our outing to Galle, started with a half hour drive from Hikkaduwa. Once there we were dropped off at the fort. The initial fort was built in 1588 by the Portuguese on a small rocky peninsula. The Dutch started extensive fortification work in 1649. Now it's a UNESCO World Heritage Site.

The fort wasn't as I expected. Overlooking the sea were ruins of the fortifications and living quarters for the garrison. But this wasn't the whole fort. Instead the "fort" included the whole historic walled town of Galle we had just driven into.

We climbed up to a large grassy area in the middle of the ruins. Here some men were playing football, and on many occasions, Sylvia seemed to be right in the middle of the action as the football came whizzing past her at very close quarters, to the delight of the players.

"Do you think they're using you as target practice?" I asked her.

Round a corner we found another group of men who were engrossed in a gentler pursuit – yoga. Engrossed though they were, they noticed us and wanted us to join in. We decided to take the easier option of smiling, saying hello and walking by. If they were anything like the football players, they would also have taken great delight at our expense when they saw our hopeless yoga skills.

From the top of the fort wall we overlooked a large sports ground and saw the beginnings of a school sports day unfolding. Round the sports track were large brightly coloured gazebos providing competitors and spectators with shade from the hot sun's rays.

Hundreds of girls in white uniforms were there. All schools we've seen in Sri Lanka have white cotton uniforms. I have no idea how parents keep them gleaming white. In local buses we've seen children at the end of a school day, their uniforms no longer gleaming. This is not surprising with the dusty roads and similarly dusty playgrounds surrounding the school buildings. And yet at the beginning of the next day the uniforms are immaculate again.

On our travels we've passed several sports grounds holding similar events. Despite this we hadn't seen a single race taking place. We pinned our hopes on this changing today.

We were entertained as we listened to the seemingly never-ending loudspeaker announcements. An English translation followed each announcement which allowed us to identify the arrival and names of all the dignitaries for the day.

It wasn't just the announcements that took ages – everything seemed slow. We saw groups of girls standing holding flags before eventually, other girls marched in formation towards them.

Finally, we gave up hope of ever seeing a race and left the girls behind. Still listening to the announcements, we went for a long walk around the fort walls. At least we walked for as long as we could cope with in the heat – which on reflection wasn't very long. The streets below beckoned us.

The town was completely different from any of the other towns we've visited in Sri Lanka. The narrow roads contained what we regard as normal shops and restaurants rather than the open fronted shops or stalls we'd become accustomed to. Generally, the shops were selling better quality goods than elsewhere with the bonus that they were cheaper than in the UK.

Top of our agenda was a cuppa though and we thankfully found a suitable café. We didn't rush to leave, partly because the service was slow, but also because it was a pleasant place to sit and cool down.

A family came in, Mum, Dad and their three children. We couldn't help noticing the lack of communication between the parents and children. Mobile phones were the parents' priority. The children didn't talk to each other either. They sat looking miserable. I felt it was sad and am sorry to say this lack of communication between parents and children seems to be increasingly the norm in the UK too. In contrast and as ever, we didn't sit in silence!

"Wasn't it good you found your sandals, Douglas?" I said.

"Yes," and after a pause he added, "I'm concerned you're now going to recount other holiday lost property stories."

"Well, that's a thought. They could be spread out throughout the day. I could even include some about me."

"Mm, I suppose so."

OK, I'll set the scene of tale number one; it's April 2000 and we're with David and Andrew in New York, after we'd been moved from the terribly small room in the hotel with insufficient beds to a more appropriate one.

We'd a great day sightseeing, doing a lot of walking but using public transport too because it was raining and therefore made good use of our Metro Cards. There had been far more showers than we expected and by the time we were ready to go back to the hotel we were wet.

We arrived at a bus stop where Douglas made the discovery; the Metro cards were no longer in his pocket. They had fallen out, so we couldn't get on the bus. Tired though we were, we decided to walk. The rain started again but we traipsed on, passing the mainly stationary traffic in the inevitable New York traffic jam, with horns being constantly blasted by frustrated drivers.

At one point we heard the siren of an emergency vehicle. We kept looking round to check on its progress, only to discover it wasn't making any progress. We were amazed no vehicles moved out of the way to let it pass.

Looking back on it, I can't remember why we didn't just buy more Metro tickets and get the bus. Perhaps we thought the hotel was closer or we would walk to the next bus stop while the traffic was stationary and as nothing moved much, we kept walking to the following bus stop. I remember thinking we should get one of the many taxis but realised this was pointless as we were walking faster than they were driving. I also remember feeling exhausted and realising David (aged 10) and Andrew (aged 8) were fantastic, coping far better than I did on this unanticipated walk.

We ended up walking all the way back to the hotel and calculated we'd walked seven miles that day. Having walked this distance, much of it through the rain, I think we'd an excuse for feeling tired.

"Now tell us a tale about *you* losing something, Margaret."

"Yes, it's only fair I tell you about one of my mishaps. This one took place in beautiful Saalbach-Hinterglemm in Austria which we visited with friends Chris and Dave. We were on a walking holiday and what an amazing holiday it turned out to be. Everything, including the weather, was fantastic. We'd come equipped with all our waterproofs and yet it was t-shirt and shorts we wore. The sun shone, the sky was blue, the mountains were magnificent with a multitude of different varieties of wildflowers poking up through the grass covered slopes.

Before getting in the cable car at the beginning of our second day, I went to the toilet and while there devised a plan to make sure I always gathered together all my belongings before leaving a toilet, restaurant or wherever I was. It was simple really, count what I took in with me and count before I left. In this case I had three items – rucksack, walking pole and iPad. It was much easier to count to three than to remember the individual items, I reasoned. If I didn't get to number three in my counting before leaving, I knew there was something missing and I could work out what I'd forgotten. Simple. I was pleased I was now going to be much more organized.

Our 5-day pass for the cable cars allowed us onto the now familiar mode of transport which took us to the top of the mountain to start our walk. It was an even hotter day than previous ones and when we got out of the cable car, we found the views were even clearer than on a previous day we'd been here. Until now I'd decided I wouldn't take any photos at the beginning of the walk but on seeing these views I changed my mind.

Realisation struck – I didn't have my iPad. I immediately knew exactly where it was – in the toilet at the bottom of the mountain. My plan of action to be ultra-organised and count to ensure I didn't leave anything behind had failed. Having counted when I went to the toilet, I'd forgotten to count again before I left!

The cable car we'd come up in was just about to leave so I jumped back in and headed down the mountain. As the door shut, I remembered Douglas had my cable car pass.

"Never mind," I thought to myself. "I'm sure the staff at the bottom will understand and let me back on to return to the others."

The cable car stopped at a mid-station. It was here I suddenly thought; perhaps I hadn't left the iPad in the toilet at all but in the pod we'd travelled up in. I jumped out of the pod I was in and checked the one behind, knowing it was the one we'd ascended in. But the iPad wasn't there. There was an attendant on the platform, so I told him I'd left the iPad in the toilet below and asked if he could contact the bottom station to let them know.

On arrival at the bottom station I explained about my loss. The attendant told me it was in the ticket office waiting for me. I also explained about my ticket.

"Your husband is coming down in the next cable car. Don't go back up. Wait here for him," I was instructed.

Sure enough, my iPad was at the ticket office. What I thought was very clever and what I hadn't thought about was the lady asked me to input my unlocking code to prove it was my iPad. Proof given, off I set, now with all three of my numbered possessions.

Douglas, having realised I didn't have my lift pass spoke to the attendant at the top. He didn't speak English, so Douglas did a great job of putting together some German accompanied by actions:

"*Meine Frau ist,*"[7] he said pointing to bottom of mountain.

"*Ich,*"[8] he continued, holding up my pass.

The attendant understood him perfectly and replied in German. Douglas had to say to him, "*Ich nicht spreche kein Deutsch.*"[9]

The attendant looked confused. Douglas had given the impression he was a fluent speaker. (I was very impressed when he told me his part of the tale.) With a tone of urgency, the attendant made it clear Douglas had to take the lift pass for me. Thus, he and I had a reunion at the bottom and immediately made our return journey to meet Chris and Dave again, having unexpectedly got extra value for money from our cable car passes.

"So yes, I lose things too."

Reminiscing finished for the time being, rested, and revived by sustenance, it was time to wander round the streets in Galle. We found a great museum – The Historical Mansion Art Gallery, Museum & Arcade in Leyn Baan Street. It was a bit like the Burrell collection in Glasgow, Scotland. This museum only contained one man's collection too and, in this case, it was Abdul Gaffer the owner of a gem quarry.

---

[7] My wife is

[8] I

[9] I don't speak German

Prior to it becoming a museum, the colonial Dutch house now displaying the collection, was a ruin. We were shown photos which confirmed the enormous amount of renovation work undertaken.

Our guide here spoke excellent English and was very proud of Sri Lanka's links with the UK, pointing out all sorts of items made in the UK or associated with it, like Queen Victoria memorabilia and newspaper records of our present Queen's visit to Sri Lanka in 1954 (Douglas' year of birth).

"What is this?" the guide asked showing us a shallow rimmed bowl with a hole in the rim. We hadn't seen one before.

"Can you give us a clue?"

"It was made by Wedgwood."

We were still none the wiser. Another clue might have been a cork for the hole was missing but even with this piece of vital information, I'm not sure we would have been able to say what it was.

"We give in," we all agreed. "What is this dish?"

"It's a child's feeding bowl. The bowl is double skinned. Hot water was poured into the hole and the cork inserted, to keep the food in the bowl warm for longer."

We also saw demonstrations of lace making and gem polishing, both demonstrators anxious to have their photos taken as they worked.

Cultural education over, we went shopping and were pleased to see a Barefoot store. Sylvia and I had been to another branch in Colombo two years previously while George and Douglas went on a fishing trip. We loved the simple designs of the products and their bright colours. This time I bought some wooden trivets shaped like elephants to replace mis-matching cork table mats I've used for the last 30 years.

We met up with Janaka again and put our purchases in the car.

"We're very hot and thirsty," we told him. "Where would you recommend we go for a drink?"

"I know somewhere. I will drive you there."

"But we don't want to get lost again," one of us said.

"There might not be anywhere to park when we get there," another added.

"How far away is this place?"

"Five minutes," he said.

"Five minutes' walking?"

"Yes."

"Not five minutes in the car?" I was determined to ensure he fully understood.

"Yes, five minutes' walking."

Off we set with Janaka leading the way. Five minutes came and went.

"How much further?" one of us enquired.

"Next place," was the reply. "Next place" in our understanding, came and went.

"How much further?" we repeated, and we heard the same reply.

This question and answer session repeated several more times until we finally reached our destination.

"Next place" was not a description any of us recognised as being appropriate for the distance travelled. "Next block" wouldn't even have been appropriate. Nor was the "five minutes" accurate. Janaka was teased by us about the meaning in Sri Lanka of "five minutes" and "next place". Lots of big smiles were returned by him to this teasing. We couldn't ever get cross with Janaka. Frustrated? Yes, this was more likely.

We were all disappointed with the place – once again a large hotel, this one geared up to deal with coach parties coming for meals and not the likes of our small group. We felt out of place and an inconvenience to the staff as they scurried past to deal with the large groups needing fed. However, we finally got the cold drinks we wanted.

I think Janaka must have felt bad about misleading us about how far we had to walk in the sweltering heat because after he finished his drink he disappeared and when we came out of the hotel, he was waiting with the car.

"Now I will take you to a beach so you can go swimming," he told us.

We arrived at the entrance to White Jungle Beach.

"Look at the descriptions and spelling on the sign," I said, pointing. "Happyness Freedom Beach, and there's a party here every 'Wednes Day'." We couldn't help but smile.

To get to the beach in the secluded bay we walked down a steep path through the jungle. The sandy beach itself wasn't big but there were a couple of beach cafés. A swim in the sea provided very welcome cool refreshment. What was sad though was seeing rubbish on the beach and it was difficult to find somewhere to sit where heaps of rubbish under the trees weren't visible. None the less, we'd a relaxing time, seated at rickety tables under the canopy of the shady open-sided sitting area of the ramshackle snack bar.

"I've kept you in suspense long enough," I said to the others. "It's time to tell another lost property tale. This one took place when Douglas and I were nearing the end a tour of Kangaroo Island in Australia. We were about to get into the minibus which would take us to the ferry to return us to the mainland."

"Can I get the external battery pack as my iPad is running low on power?" I'd asked Douglas.

He got his rucksack out from amongst the luggage and brought it into the minibus. The logical place for the battery pack would have been in the front pocket along with his various cables, but it wasn't there. One by one he looked in each of the many other rucksack pockets without success. He moved onto the various compartments and pockets in his camera case then the numerous ones in his hiking trousers. No luck.

He checked the rucksack again this time more thoroughly, so all sorts of clothes and other paraphernalia were tossed up in the air as his head got more buried inside the bag. He still didn't find the illusive battery pack.

I suddenly thought about my mini rucksack. Maybe Douglas didn't have the battery pack at all! I started looking, hoping on one hand it was there, but knowing if it was, I'd be extremely embarrassed. I didn't have it and Douglas was now convinced he had left it at the hotel. There was one last place to check – my big rucksack in the luggage compartment of the minibus. The minibus stopped at a café and I retrieved said rucksack.

"Here's the phone number of the hotel," I said giving it to Douglas. "While I'm checking my rucksack, you could phone to see if we left it in our room. If so, you could ask them to post it on to us. We've still got another three weeks in Australia after all."

I didn't find the battery pack. Douglas was having trouble phoning.

"Check my rucksack again," he instructed me while he waited to get through to the hotel.

Finally, I heard him speaking to the receptionist and just as she was saying nothing had been found, I put my hand on something in his rucksack and pulled it out. "Is this the battery pack?" I asked.

"Yes," was the relieved reply from a very humiliated Douglas. "How could I have missed it?" There's no answer to some questions.

We arrived at the ferry terminal. As I walked away from the minibus heading for the ferry, I heard the driver calling my name. I turned round and saw him holding aloft my big rucksack which I'd completely forgotten about, leaving it in the luggage compartment of the minibus.

Douglas reckons our score was one each that day.

"All's well that ends well, and I think we'd better head back to Janaka now," Douglas said. Was he avoiding more tales?

I wasn't looking forward to climbing back up the path to the car. First, there were 124 steps (totally accurate as I counted them on the way down. Yes accurate, unlike the number of pockets I stated were in Douglas' rucksack and shorts when we were looking for his lost Fitbit. He corrected me, so I feel it's only right I include an erratum while it's on my mind. He told me there weren't 212 pockets in his rucksack and shorts – only 159.)

Step climbing completed, there was a steep path ahead. Much of the path was smooth as it was paved with flat stones and rocks. Even this smooth section wasn't straightforward, though, as there were protruding roots and rocks to negotiate. I'd prepared myself for the long haul and focused on each step rather than thinking too much about how much further we'd to climb, mindfulness in action. To my surprise, either the mindfulness worked, or my perception on the way down was wrong as we arrived at the top much sooner than I expected. It wasn't too bad a climb after all.

"Can you drive us back to the guest house so we can have a shower and bring us back to Galle for our evening meal?" we asked Janaka.

"No problem," was his happy, accommodating reply.

"We want to go to a small restaurant to eat."

"No problem."

Later, back in Galle, where did he take us? The same large coach-party hotel he had taken us to earlier in the day for a drink. We couldn't believe it and he seemed surprised to learn we didn't want to eat there!

Off we set on our own in search of a suitable restaurant. None we tried sold alcohol and the others fancied a drink with their meals. Perhaps this was why Janaka took us to the hotel, but he didn't explain this.

Finally, we found a restaurant where we ate in lovely surroundings – in a courtyard with lights on the trees. Unfortunately, the surroundings didn't mean a perfect meal as Sylvia's chicken was very over-cooked and tough.

"Have we time for one last lost and found story?" I enquired.

"Absolutely," was the reply.

Douglas and I were on a special holiday in South Africa, to celebrate me finishing working as a Quantity Surveying lecturer. For a couple of nights, we stayed in Stellenbosch before joining up with a group at a

Safari Park.

At Stellenbosch we went to the Botanic Gardens, a short walk away from the hotel. It was so peaceful as few folks were about so early in the morning, most arriving as we left.

Douglas realised something had dropped out of his pocket. I'm not saying what it was because in my daily email home there was a typing error and all recipients were left wondering what was lost. This immediately caused concern, but I was oblivious to this until the next day when I saw their emails to me.

"What fell out of Douglas' pocket?" they wanted to know. "Was it his wallet, credit card holder or passport?"

Back to the story. Despite retracing our steps, we didn't find the missing item. We decided we would return the next day to see if anyone had found it.

The next morning, we busied ourselves packing suitcases as we were leaving Stellenbosch later.

"Where's the bag of clothes for washing?" I asked Douglas.

"I've been wondering the same thing. We must have left it in the last hotel. Hopefully the clothes will find a good home."

"Gives us an excuse to go back to Vietnam so you can get another t-shirt with the picture of the crazy motorcyclists; the one with the caption 'Hanoi traffic'."

On the way to the Botanic Gardens after breakfast, the church was open. We decided to go in as it had been closed when we were on a walking tour of the town the previous day. I visualised a great photo: with the front door in the foreground, I would capture the stained-glass window at the far end of the church. Knowing the best photo would be produced with my iPad I opened my bag to get it but discovered it wasn't there. Oh no! I knew I'd taken a photo at breakfast time of a squirrel for my friend Jill who loves them so felt sure I must have left it on the table in the dining room. I decided it was best to return rapidly to the hotel and hopefully get it. My run was worthwhile as sure enough I'd left it on the table. I was so relieved. One lost item found.

When we got to the Botanic Gardens, we went straight to the shop to ask about our missing item and yes it had been found. More relief. What was it? A wallet, credit card holder or passport? Nothing as dramatic thank goodness. Instead, Douglas was reunited with his favourite hat.

Back at the hotel, we finished packing our cases and Douglas was making a final check of the wardrobes when low and behold he came across our missing bag of washing. He had taken it out of his case when we arrived but forgotten where he had put it.

It's always good finding things but the tale doesn't end there.

We'd a few hours to have a final wander round the town, buy some last souvenirs, have a bite to eat and importantly buy another memory card for the camcorder as I didn't want to run out when in the game reserve. At 1 p.m., a minibus arrived to take us back to Cape Town for the flight to Johannesburg during which I finished reading the book *Mandela: my prisoner, my friend*. What a great read it was.

After disembarking we waited ages for our cases. Passengers were getting irate – some even putting their heads through the rubber strip "curtain" the cases come though on the conveyor belt, shouting at the baggage handlers on the other side. Our two cases were the first to appear!

We stayed overnight in an hotel at the airport and on returning to our room after our meal, I discovered I'd left the battery charger and one of the batteries for the camcorder in the last hotel. I'd decided to top up the last battery before we checked out so it would be all systems go when we arrived at the safari park. I forgot to unplug it. So much for buying an extra memory card.

I phoned the hotel and tour company. The hotel said they would check with staff in the morning. The tour company said someone was following us from the hotel to the same game reserve and would be able to bring it if it was found. I wasn't hopeful and decided I would just have to take less video footage using the other batteries I had with me.

The next day, no charger arrived.

We'd a great time at the game reserve and at the end were taken by minibus back to Johannesburg Airport. There, a man stood with a sign which read "Mr and Mrs Moore". In his hand was an envelope. It contained the left-behind battery charger and battery for my camcorder. How wonderful and unexpected! Having been without them, I'd opted to record less footage than normal, but the bonus was less editing when I got home.

"Enough blethering. It's time to ask Janaka to drive us back to Hikkaduwa."

"Our final request of the day, Janaka: Can you let us off at the other end of Hikkaduwa so we can walk and see a bit more of the town?"

"No problem." We'd heard this response before.

Just to be on the safe side, I asked one more question, "How far is it to the guest house?"

"1.5km," was the answer.

"No problem," we replied laughing.

Off we set and after a while we walked down onto the beach as we wanted to go to a beach bar. We walked, expecting to see the beach bars strung out along the coast when we rounded the corner.

"OK, not this corner," we found ourselves saying, "but we'll see them around the next corner."

Similarly reassuring each other at several subsequent corners, we were faced with a problem: round the next bend the tide was fully in. We cut back up into the grounds of a hotel intending to walk round the perimeter until we could get back onto the beach. We were promptly met by a security man asking, "Can I help? This is a private hotel."

Despite our concerns he assured us it was possible to continue round on the shore and even recommended a restaurant.

Off we set again, by now in the pitch darkness. George's four-year-old £1 torch was running out of battery life and Douglas' phone was in a similar low battery predicament. Me being me assured everyone it would be fine even without torches. Where was their sense of adventure? On we plodded, until even I had to admit defeat.

We returned to the posh hotel and walked purposefully through the grounds and into the hotel intending to walk through and out the other side onto the Main Street. Much to our relief we weren't spotted by the security guard. It would have been embarrassing if we'd met him again especially as we hadn't managed to agree on a concocted tale to explain why we were there again.

Once inside the enormous hotel, it was far from obvious which way to go. There was a distinct lack of signs for trespassers like us. We managed to avoid being questioned by the members of staff we passed. Politely saying "hello" to them, I felt I was James Bond on a secret mission. Only the dramatic background music was missing.

We spotted a couple who we hoped were heading for the front door and started following them. They led us into a car park. Were we at the front of the hotel, I wondered? I didn't take time to look around me, focusing instead on making my way over to the security gate they were heading for: the security gate which separated us from freedom. Thoughts went through my mind; "Will we be required to show a hotel room key-card to get out? What would James Bond do in this situation?"

The couple reached the gate first – which they would do as they were ahead of us. I saw a security man leaving the sentry box and walking towards them. What would happen now? Would a torch be shone in their faces to check their identity against a hotel database? Would they be interrogated?

My heart was pounding as I looked on. Should we stop to see what happened or continue onwards?

The gate began to slowly open, and it was very slow. Would it be fully open by the time we got there allowing us just to walk through while the security guard's attention was focused on the other couple, just like in a Bond film? Bond, I was sure would implement the "walk straight through" approach.

The other couple passed the security guards successfully. We kept walking and said a confident "thank you" to the security guard as we walked under the still open barrier. We'd made it – our mission had been accomplished – we were free at last!

Why I thought we needed key-cards to exit the premises is beyond me. Perhaps weariness and a desire to reach our destination was making my imagination run riot.

We found our way back onto the beach and eventually after a long walk found a suitable bar. However, even this wasn't straightforward. George and Douglas like to have bottles of the local *Lion* beer for two reasons – it tastes better (apparently) and is cheaper than buying the smaller cans. We tried several establishments, but they only sold cans. Sylvia on the other hand fancied a cocktail. She asked in one place if they served cocktails and was met with a positive response followed by the names of two different cocktails, the names of which evade me, so I'll call them X and Y. She asked if they had a list of other cocktails she could look at and this time was met with a rude attitude, the barman saying, "I told you lady; you can have X or Y."

We didn't buy any drinks here but finally found an alternative relaxing bar.

"I thought you said it was a 1.5km walk back to the guest house," we teased Janaka when we got back at the guest house.

"It was. I checked on the way back," he defended himself.

"How much was it exactly?

"1.8km ... well a bit over 2km," he corrected.

It seemed much longer than 2km (1.25 miles) but we were hot, thirsty and hadn't a clue where you were. Plus, I'm sure we added significantly to the distance by walking along the beach instead of staying on the road.

"Tomorrow can you drive back to Negombo via Bentota beach?" we asked Janaka. George and Sylvia had been there before and loved it.

"That's not possible," he replied. We were taken aback, expecting, "no problem" to be his reply. "It will take six or seven hours to drive back that route."

"Is there anywhere else we could stop on the way back?"

"No."

"Final, final request of the day, Janaka. Can you tell the owner we want our breakfast at 8 a.m. George and Sylvia want egg sandwiches: Douglas and I want egg roti."

"No problem."

Fort at Galle

St Valentine's Day "Strumpling"

The final morning of our tour.

"Happy Valentine's Day," we greeted each other at the breakfast table.

George and Sylvia had gone to the outside table well before 8 a.m., not because they wanted their breakfast, but to enjoy the early morning sounds of nature. However, breakfast food was immediately brought, and not just for them but for us too. In Sri Lanka we're prepared for things being late, as everyone is so relaxed, but we're not prepared for things being early. George and Sylvia covered our plates to try to keep the food warm.

The egg sandwich Sylvia and George ordered was an omelette. The eggs tasted normal, not like the strangely flavoured ones back in Negombo. Our egg roti was very filling and looked like two thick square potato scones with stuffing in the middle. We couldn't work out what the stuffing was, but it was very tasty.

"No red roses for you and me from the owner like we got two years ago," I said to Sylvia. "Or passion fruit with our buffalo curd. These little things made our last holiday in Sri Lanka special."

I can still remember the Valentine's card I received. On the front of the card were four pictures – one in each corner: top left was an olive, top right a sheep, bottom left a fairy and bottom right a lit match.

I had to decode the message the pictures portrayed. I considered them carefully but admitted I required assistance from the senior detective at the table (a.k.a. Douglas). Finally, I decoded the message:

"I love" (from the picture of the olive)

"you" (the sheep was in fact an ewe)

"very" (represented by a fairy)

"much" (from the picture of a match).

It was like the crossword Douglas and I do in the "*i*" newspaper. The answers to the first two clues across, link together to make another word or phrase. For example – if the answer to 1 across is TEND and the answer to 2 across is HOLLERS, the new phrase created by joining the two is TEN DOLLARS.

This example is straightforward. Others however are dependent on pronunciation and our Scottish accents don't help solve the puzzle. Douglas, being good at mimicking other accents, pronounces the words with a south of England accent which we've found is often required to solve the conundrum.

I guessed the Valentine's card was from Douglas. I'd an extra clue for this; he had signed the card.

Getting back to this year's Valentine's Day, Janaka caught us by surprise after breakfast, suggesting he could take us back to Galle for the morning before starting on the main journey of the day.

"No thanks," we replied. "We've seen all we want to see in Galle. We're now content to return to Negombo."

Later, I learned it would only have added 45 minutes to our journey to go via Bentota – much less than the journey time Janaka suggested. This and some time on the beach would have been equivalent to revisiting Galle. We were disappointed.

On the drive back, we stopped at the same service station we'd stopped at on day one of our tour. "We've got here very quickly," I said, puzzled.

"But remember, we've just come from Hikkaduwa, not Marissa where we drove to originally. Marissa's much further away," Douglas enlightened me.

"Och¹⁰ yes, of course. Plus, we spent such a long time looking for somewhere to stay in Marissa, so the journey seemed longer. We're going to get back to Negombo even sooner than I'd anticipated."

Back in the car, I noticed a couple of interesting instructions to drivers on the freeway/expressway/motorway:

"Do not drive backwards on the expressway"

"Do not enter the expressway when drunken"

Breaking these common-sense rules doesn't bear thinking about!

We passed Colombo and were nearly back at Negombo when Janaka drove along a small section of coastal road we hadn't been on before.

He stopped at a beach and suggested we could go for a swim here instead of Bentota where we'd hoped to go.

"There's a lot of rubbish on the beach though," he said, something we'd already noticed. By now he knew we didn't like seeing rubbish on the otherwise beautiful beaches.

"Just take us back to the guest house, please."

I think he'd realised he should have taken us Bentota. George had been watching the speedometer as we drove along the freeway and noticed he was driving much more slowly than on the way south. We all felt he was trying to delay our arrival back. Milinda was clearly surprised to see us when we arrived back and said he wasn't expecting us for another few hours. We hadn't expected to be back so soon either. We'd paid for a four-day trip, after all.

A quiet afternoon at our familiar beach followed and as always, a tasty dinner. During this evening meal we chatted as normal, this time recounting Valentine's Day experiences.

---

¹⁰ a little Scottish word that can be used in various situations. Here a translation would be "Oh"

In 2015 our friend Iain who lived not far from us in Scotland had introduced us to the delights of Sri Lanka and was with us. Having been before he was a great guide. He suggested a tour of the markets so into a two-seater tuk-tuk the three of us squeezed.

We drove along the road beside the canal, away from the busy and noisy Sea Street. However, the relative peace and quiet (the sound our tuk-tuk engine made was far from quiet) didn't last for long because we turned onto Sea Street for a photo stop: to take pictures of the very colourful Sri Singama Kali Amman Kovil Hindu temple. The gates to the temple were locked so we couldn't venture in. Most of the photos also featured buses and other vehicles as they sped past us. But suddenly there was a break in the traffic and for a moment or two all was quiet, and we could even hear some birds chirping. It was literally only a few seconds before normality resumed.

Our first market of the day was the large fish market. To get to it we walked through a small fruit and vegetable market. The sound of people shouting, along with loud music filled our ears making for a happy excited atmosphere. Varieties of fruit and vegetable we hadn't seen met our eyes.

The fish market was huge. We couldn't believe how many new varieties of fish and other sea creatures we saw on the numerous stalls.

Some stalls were large, while others consisted merely of a small quantity of fish on a couple of small square boards lying on the ground with a lady squatting behind them. Other ladies stood with an even smaller pile of fish at their feet. With such large quantities available at the main stalls, I wondered if the ladies would sell their fish any more easily in this large market than those we'd seen in the streets at night or in the small fish market on the beach near our guest house.

Some of the larger fish were about a metre (3 feet) long and once purchased were simply held by the gills and dragged along the ground behind the purchaser.

There was a row of chopping tables and benches with men behind them wielding large cleavers for anyone wanting their fish filleted. The chopping tables were sections of tree trunks about 60cm (2 feet) in diameter and a metre (3 feet) high. Once prepared, the fish was transferred onto the wooden bench made of odds and ends of planks of wood.

Some stalls were in a large hangar, others were outside under the beating sun; so different from what we're familiar with – fish on ice in refrigerated cabinets.

The sun was ideal for the fish laid out for drying. There were many long rows each comprising small strips of hessian on which the tiny fish were laid.

"It's amazing birds don't come to eat the fish in such a wide, open area," I remarked. "Do you remember the day a seagull happily swooped down and took a burger off the barbecue in our garden when I was standing right beside it? I got such a fright."

We saw the reason for the small strips of hessian. When the fish had dried sufficiently, two people each took an end of the strip and lifted it up. The fish fell into the centre of the hessian and were tipped into a large waiting basket ready to be taken into the market for selling. The basket had a handle on each side. A pole put through the handles allowed two men to raise the pole onto their shoulders and carry the basket inside. The tiny fish were put into large cardboard boxes and two lads put their full upper body weight onto pieces of cardboard on top of the fish to compact as many as possible into the box before the box was closed.

We felt we'd experienced all aspects of buying, selling and preparation of the fish in this, a real working market.

"Where are we going to now?" I enquired as we got back into the tuk-tuk.

Dried fish being loaded into a basket at the Fish Market

"A market beside the railway station. It sells material, clothes and all sorts of household items."

The market was still being set up and what a palaver it looked. Enormous tarpaulins were hoisted to create a covering for the stalls and the passageway between them. As we walked it was like taking part in an adult version of a parachute game. Sometimes the hoisting was followed by the tarpaulins falling back down on us. We survived uninjured. Thankfully, we'd arrived before the "roof" was completed as whilst providing shade, I'm sure it would become unbearably hot under the tarpaulin.

"We might see unusual gifts for David and Andrew. Keep your eyes peeled," Douglas said.

We spotted and chose simple hand-made ladles made from coconut shells with a length of wood added for the handle. We couldn't wait to see their reaction. We also bought Douglas' mum a hand-held floor brush made of coconut hair. We like buying locally made things rather than traditional "tourist" gifts.

"And now to the fruit market," we were told.

The carefully placed fruit and vegetables made a colourful display. We saw whole stocks of the tiny, chubby bananas we so enjoy at breakfast in the guest house, sometimes served with delicious buffalo curd. Spices in hessian sacks were also beautifully presented to entice buyers.

"Take a photo of him," a lady stallholder indicated to Douglas using hand signals to explain what she wanted. She was pointing to another stallholder, an elderly gentleman, next to her. He was delighted.

"Would you like your photo taken?" I asked her, using more hand signals. She too was clearly pleased when Douglas showed her the photo taken.

Aren't digital cameras great? We can see the results instantaneously. Not like when I was young, and it was a spool of film, allowing 24 photographs to be taken during the holiday (or 36 if the more expensive spool could be afforded). Sometimes an extra photo could be squeezed in depending on how the film had been loaded into the camera and this felt like a great bonus. But when the winder on the camera indicated you had taken far more than this, it was worrying. In all likelihood the film hadn't been loaded properly in the camera and wasn't taking any photographs. What disappointment followed. Great shots seen through the viewfinder didn't come to fruition.

Then, once back from holiday the film was carefully wound back into the spool, removed from the camera and posted to the lab for developing. The anticipation mounted until the envelope with the printed photographs dropped through the letterbox. Nervous expectation followed as the envelope was opened and the contents looked at, slowly, one at a time, each shot having been photographed only once. And yes, there were times of disappointment, but the good photographs were precious and carefully put into photograph albums.

Enough reminiscing and back to the fruit market. We made another purchase – a watermelon to enjoy while sitting on the veranda of the guest house. Iain pointed to one. We hadn't a clue what the lady was saying in her reply and explanation. She picked up and replaced various ones, comparing sizes and colours before finally weighing one and telling us its price. We assume she was selecting the best one for us. Off we set back to the guest house sharing our limited space in the tuk-tuk with a large watermelon.

"We'd another tuk-tuk ride in the afternoon, didn't we Douglas? This time just the two of us. We went to *The Grand* tearoom. We sampled the fantastic cakes, milk shakes and tea Jacqui and Paul had told us about. It was so inexpensive; a speciality tea, an ice cream milkshake, blueberry cheesecake plus almond and pear cake cost the equivalent of one cup of coffee back home. Brilliant!"

"And despite all this mid-afternoon eating, we had room for an evening meal," Douglas recalled. Well, we were on holiday after all. The end of a happy Valentine's Day two years earlier.

While we were chatting, Sylvia took us all by surprise, incorporating into her conversation the word "strumpling".

"What did you say? Strumpling?" we enquired.

"Yes," Sylvia replied.

"There's no such word."

"Yes, there is."

"What does it mean?"

"I don't know what it means but I bet there is such a word."

Thus, the gauntlet was laid down and I picked it up. I would check to see if there was such a word.

Places of worship and ATM

Another quiet day down at the beach. While lying on the sun lounger as the welcome gentle breeze blew and the palm branches rustled on the trees around us, I couldn't help but smile when an incident during our last Sri Lankan holiday came to mind.

Sitting in the shade of an onshore catamaran at the beach

We were on a half-day tour with a tuk-tuk driver as our guide. He took us to see Risen Christ Church, Kadolkale, a lovely big modern church. It's set in large grounds and on the left-hand side was a large stone cliff face with a cave grotto in the middle. Douglas, however, discovered the stone cliff and cave were made of fiberglass and close-up didn't look as realistic.

On top of the square tower of the church is a statue of Jesus with one hand raised. The church itself was very bright and airy and there were paintings on the walls both inside and out. All round the walls of the Church were open doors to allow both people and air to circulate; hot weather had been taken account of when designing this building and we welcomed the cooler temperature inside.

It was Sunday and we weren't there at the time of a full church service, but a baptism service for four very young babies was taking place at the front of the sanctuary. It was very moving to watch, even though we couldn't understand what was being said.

But it wasn't just what was happening inside the church that was interesting. Picture the scene we witnessed outside:

The pitched roof of the building extended beyond the line of the external wall creating an overhang of say four metres (about 13 feet) providing shade for the marble walkway below. The roof was supported by columns and horizontal beams with a triangular void between the top of the beam and the underside of the roof.

A group of three teenage lads were enjoying themselves throwing flip-flops up in the air towards the beam. They were trying to knock another flip-flop off the beam. It was balanced half on and half off, four metres above their heads. A cheer went up when the flip-flop was hit but their delight evaporated when they realised it had been knocked completely *onto* the beam rather than falling to the ground. With it no longer visible from below, hitting it again was no longer an option. I thought of the poor youngster who was going to have to walk home with only one flip-flop and explain to his parents what had happened to the other.

The smallest of the trio was instructed to go and off he ran, smiling broadly towards us. Soon he returned with a very long and wobbly aluminium ladder. The lad who had been doing most of the throwing scrambled up the rickety ladder. Was he the guilty party who got the flip-flop stuck up there in the first place, or was it his flip-flop he was trying to retrieve? I was relieved when two of the others went and held the bottom of the ladder.

On reaching the top of the ladder, the climber was still well below the beam. He stood on the top rung and then beyond this onto the top of the ladder legs from where he was able to pull himself onto the beam. Once there, he scrambled along the narrow beam, knocking down not one but three flip-flops and a collection of other objects which had found a resting place there. Goodness knows how long they had been there.

Back onto the top of the ladder he got and climbed down, obviously not having been in the least bit scared by the height or possible dangers he faced during the escapade. He smiled infectiously, appearing happy to have me as an audience, recording the exploits on my video camera. I got the impression this wasn't a new game for them.

This made me think of other holiday experiences in places of worship. We like to go to a church on Sundays when on holiday. This wasn't possible in Sri Lanka, but we enjoyed the sound of singing coming from a church as we ate our early breakfast beside the canal. We were sure all the windows and doors were open, and the sound was further amplified by a loudspeaker. Similarly, we heard the Muslim calls to prayer throughout the day, beginning around 5 a.m.

We like to find out about other religions and visit their places of worship, experiencing the different sights, sounds and smells. In one temple Douglas and I went to in Hong Kong, so much incense was burning the building was full of smoke. We weren't in long before tears were streaming down my face. Reluctantly I admitted defeat and went back outside, having seen little of what lay within.

One Sunday in 2001 when on our family self-drive holiday down the west coast of America, we went to a church service, in the Crystal Cathedral in Orange County, California. I didn't know what to expect but was amazed by the huge, tall glass and steel structures we saw as we approached. The enormous carpark was like going to a supermarket but on a much bigger scale than I'd seen before. The cathedral sat 3,000 people along with 1,000 singers and musicians. Our home church accommodates about 300, so for us this was massive.

"We're too late. Look at all the people pouring out of the building," I said.

"Let's see if we can get in to have a look inside while we're here," Douglas suggested.

"I can hear singing," I said hopefully.

A section of glazing the whole height of the cathedral was open for ventilation and this is where the sound of singing came from. Inside a Spanish service had just started, one of several services during the day. Not being Spanish speakers, we opted to sit in the balcony and watch.

Having spotted a sign, Douglas said, "We can get headsets to listen to an English translation." He disappeared and soon returned with the requisite equipment.

We watched a huge screen where camera footage of the people taking part in the service was projected. This was brilliant as from where we sat, they looked tiny in this huge building. During hymn singing, not only did the choir appear on the screen, but also the words of the song. Even though we hadn't a clue what the words meant, I thought we did a pretty good job at singing with the congregation.

There was one special highlight which made the whole experience especially meaningful for me. One of the hymns sung as a solo was, "My Jesus, My Saviour", one of my favourites. What was wonderful was she first sang in English and then in Spanish when everyone joined in. It was really moving singing this song I knew so well but normally sing many miles away in the UK.

The headset translation did not work well for us. It was delayed, the tone used by the lady doing the translation was without expression (unlike the preacher) and there was a lot of background noise. It sounded as though the translator was in the creche with lots of young boisterous children around her.

When the preacher started to give the sermon, we found it even more difficult to follow. At times he raised his voice for emphasis and along with the many confirming "Amens" from the congregation as he spoke, we couldn't hear what the translator was saying. We listened for a short while but decided to slip out leaving the other worshippers behind.

A marvellous experience.

On another family holiday, this time in Toronto, Canada, we were very warmly welcomed when we went to a church service there.

There were only about 35 people in the congregation, so we swelled their number substantially. We felt at home during the first part of the service, but the guest preacher began to speak and what he said was far from what we expected.

"I was very close to standing up and leading you all out," Douglas said to us after the service.

"It was strange hearing someone so blatantly discrediting the Bible, saying he didn't believe it was the inspired word of God and we could interpret it any way we wanted," I said. "But I kept expecting him to tell us he was only joking, or this was someone else's point of view – not his own. But he didn't. He seemed to be on his soapbox having a right good rant. I was relieved when he suddenly said, 'Right that's enough' and we sang the final hymn."

By the end of the sermon, I wondered why he didn't find a new profession as the Bible has such a central role to the Christian faith.

After the service, we got the impression the rest of the congregation were feeling just as uncomfortable and one man even said apologetically, "This is not our normal type of preacher."

It certainly gave the four of us plenty to discuss afterwards.

But what about experiences of other religions? Well twice when in Hong Kong after lecturing trips, I've been to see the Big Buddha and Po Lin Monastery. The journey alone was an adventure. On the first excursion in 2006 Douglas, David, Andrew and I made our way to Tung Chung MTR station, left the station at exit B where Bus 23 then took us to Ngong Ping Village, the home of the Big Buddha. The bus journey included steep 1:8 hills. Fortunately, we were in an air-conditioned bus for the hour-long journey, as it was a hot and humid day.

"Wow, look over there!" I exclaimed as I suddenly saw the bronze Big Buddha from the bus, sitting above the treeline on top of a mountain in the distance. It's well named – it's big – huge actually: 34 metres tall (111 feet).

We hadn't been to a Buddhist Temple before so didn't know what to expect and as I'd refused to go to Religious Education classes at school as my mum was the one and only RE teacher in the school, I found my lack of knowledge of Buddhism a handicap.

It wasn't what we expected. Much of the area around the Buddha statue was like a tourist attraction selling souvenirs. We expected to see monks rather than shops, but there wasn't one monk to be seen.

We did expect to climb lots of steps as we'd seen them in pictures and climb the 260 or so we did, grateful for the free bottle of water received with our entry ticket. It was good to stop often for a breather, have a gulp of water and sprinkle some water down the backs of our necks to cool down.

The following year, again after lecturing, my sister Clare and lecturing colleague Lin used a different means of transport, The Ngong Ping Cable Car, to get to the Big Buddha. The big mistake we made was not buying our tickets for the cable car in advance. At Tung Chung we joined a long queue instead of the fast-track option. We were in the queue for far longer than the 25 minute cable car journey.

We climbed the steps to see the Buddha first, to get the physical exertions over and done with. Clare was worried she wouldn't manage to get up the stairs, but as pacemaker she had Lin and I running up behind her exhausted.

Once back down the stairs and in the monastery area the burning incense made for a very smoky atmosphere. We didn't see any sacksful of prayers being burned as I'd seen the year before, but we saw a monk this time!

There was now a bigger tourist "village" with shops, eating places, and a couple of new *Experience* shows.

In the first show, donned with headphones we moved through various rooms learning about Siddhartha Gautama and why he started Buddhism. One room surprised us as it had a vibrating floor representing a herd of running elephants.

When we came out, we noticed the sky turning very dark, and crowds of people running towards the cable car. We decided not to follow but wait to see the second of the shows. As we waited, the heavens opened, and thunder clapped. We filled our time dotting in and out of shops, getting wet in the process, but it was warm rain.

We each received a HK$20 voucher to spend in the shops when we bought our tickets. I assume this was instead of the bottle of water and ice cream voucher we were given last year. Clare didn't want anything and gave me her voucher. I used the two towards the cost of a cerise polo shirt with a Hong Kong logo which I fell in love with.

"The cable car is now closed due to bad weather," we heard announced.

"Never mind. The rain will stop while we're in the second show."

It was a large-screen, surround-sound, cartoon about monkeys. The moral of the tale told was "it's better to give than to receive." We found it amusing – the cartoon I mean, not the moral of tale. We're big kids at heart.

Outside it was still raining heavily, and the cable car still not operating. Finally, it restarted. The queue though was now massive.

"Let's have a cuppa. The queue will shrink as we drink."

Instead, we watched the queue get progressively longer. After learning the queue represented a 40-minute wait, we decided we'd better join it. Impressively it took exactly 40 minutes for us to reach a cable car. Back to Kowloon we returned.

Some years later, Douglas and I were staying with his cousin Glenn his wife Helen and son Alex, in Kirribilli (a suburb of Sydney, Australia). It was a wonderful walk to church for the Sunday service, walking under the Sydney Harbour Bridge with great views of the Sydney Opera House on the other side of the river. The sun was shining, the sky was blue, and we couldn't resist taking a detour into a little bay to take a photograph featuring both the Bridge and the Opera House. This was our undoing as far as getting to church on time was concerned and we arrived at Christ Church Lavender Bay a couple of minutes late. The choir had just started singing their introit. We sat down and got ourselves into a worshipping frame of mind. But something very different happened. Something we hadn't experienced in a service before.

A man got up and stood at one of the lecterns. This wasn't unusual. It was what he said that for us was.

"We're going to be doing something that only happens once a year."

"How amazing we're here on such a special day!" I thought. I couldn't believe how fortunate we were. So many things on our tour of Australia have turned out to be better than expected and here we were about to add to their number. This on top of the information Helen had told me at breakfast time, "Sometimes there are home-made cakes with the after-service cuppa instead of biscuits," and I'd spotted cake on the way into church. We'd arrived in Sydney on the correct weekend!

But back to the annual event I mentioned. It turned out to be a fire drill. We've never had a fire drill in any church we've been in. For me, born in 1961, and Douglas in 1954, this is a great many years. Maybe we should think about introducing them in our church back home.

Fire drill started, we all went outside into the sunshine and chatted to people on the lawn in a happy social gathering. Our evacuation of the building had been timed and apparently, we achieved a very acceptable time and were allowed back into church.

It was an Anglican church and coming from a Presbyterian church back home we found the format of worship different to what we're familiar with. We don't have a Book of Common Prayer, as was the case here, setting out what is to be read and said by those leading and those attending the service. In the Presbyterian church each minister determines the format and content, and generally there's much less participation from the congregation. It was refreshing to know much of the service and prayers said would be said in all Anglican churches around the world either at the same time as us or at least during a 24-hour period.

After the service, we enjoyed the home baking, and everyone was keen to tell us all about their family connections with Scotland. We felt at home.

Later in the same holiday we stayed with my cousin Lorna, her husband Dallas, daughter Sarah and grandson Charlie, in Bungendore (a town 36km east of Canberra).

"Would you like to go to an outdoors Harvest Thanksgiving service?" Lorna asked.

"Absolutely. Outdoors will be a first for us, as will having Harvest Thanksgiving in March. We'll now go to two Harvest Thanksgivings this year as back home ours will be in October."

When we arrived at St Philip's Bungendore Anglican Church, the garden surrounding the church building was set up for the service. Harvest produce brought by church members was displayed on bales of hay. Other bales and chairs were ready for people to sit on. One bale of hay though was already occupied – by a happy smiling scarecrow. The coffee stall was also ready and naturally we couldn't help but notice the fantastic homemade baking waiting to be consumed after the service. A trestle table with a selection of clothes, straw and other bits and pieces confused us. We couldn't figure out what these were for.

We soon discovered it's not just Scotland where weather can impact on outdoor plans. In Bungendore the problem wasn't rain or snow but strong winds. Even though the winds were warm (again something we're not normally familiar with in Scotland) the outdoors service was hurriedly changed from the garden into the church along with the bales of hay and other key items.

"Why are we moving indoors?" we asked. "After all the wind is warm."

"Because the strength of the wind could cause tree branches to break off and cause injury to anyone in the wrong place at the wrong time."

Many trees around Australia have dead branches, killed by forest fires. The trees re-grow new branches around the dead ones, but the dead branches can be very dangerous. I will always remember one fact we learned on a tour earlier in the holiday; in Australia more deaths are caused when dead branches break and fall onto passers-by than are caused by shark attacks in the surrounding oceans of this massive country. It seemed hard to believe but it explained why the risk was taken seriously at the church.

Inside the picturesque, old, traditional styled stone church we participated in a happy, informal service and it was good to see the children being involved too. At the close of the service, we headed outside where we chose our standing positions well away from the dangers of the trees to enjoy the aforementioned cuppa and baking including wonderful freshly baked scones.

We also discovered what the trestle table with clothes on it was for. The children busied themselves, making two more scarecrows by stuffing the clothes with straw. The new scarecrows joined the already complete one but not immediately. We were amused as we watched the children decide the two new scarecrows should go through a marriage ceremony first.

Everyone was friendly and we learned about relatives who had moved to Australia from Scotland or their experiences of going to Scotland on holiday. Everyone's so proud of their heritage.

Next, Lorna took us to the monthly craft market held in Bungendore and we enjoyed having a wander there before meeting up with Dallas and Lorna's friend and colleague Emily for another coffee (we declined an offer of more baking) at Bungendore Wood Works Gallery. The Gallery contained an extensive array of beautiful items for sale, all attractively displayed and showing the skills of the Australian wood workers who crafted them. Some items were practical while others decorative, but all exhibited the smoothness, natural colours and grains of the wood which always attract us.

As we were sitting chatting, there was a power cut followed by the sound of sirens. The whole atmosphere of the café changed. Hot strong winds not only increase the likelihood of falling branches but also dramatically raise the risk of forest fires. Outside the sky was grey. Was it dust whipped up by the winds or was it smoke?

Dallas went outside to check. There were two fire engines, and fire fighters on the street but no sign of smoke or fire nearby. The power cut was affecting the whole town.

The café was emptying, and Dallas said we should go home. Just before we left, Douglas and I chose carved wooden salad tongs as a souvenir and managed to buy, paying with cash as the electronic tills weren't working. We learned there were areas in Australia on high alert for fires but not Bungendore – then anyway.

Douglas and I went home with Dallas in his car. As usual we drove into the driveway, but the garage door didn't open automatically. We hadn't thought about this impact of the power cut. Plus, the garage was the only means of access into the house for us, via a door inside as we didn't have keys for any of the other external doors. Dallas ended up breaking into his own home – a great photo opportunity for me.

Accessing the Internet on mobile phones confirmed our fears; there were forest fires. However, we were not in immediate danger.

The power seemed to be off for ages, but it was purely because time was passing slowly as we sat quietly and thought about the implications of the forest fires on so many other families. We were fortunate. Our power came back on after only an hour.

We stayed indoors for the rest of the afternoon with all the windows shut to keep out the dust blowing in the wind.

When the winds subsided, we sat outside and enjoyed a family meal of great Steak Diane. Dallas cooked on the barbeque while Lorna and I were in the kitchen. Lorna demonstrated something I hadn't seen before: an Australian microwave clay potato pot which cooked the potatoes to perfection.

And thus, another Sunday ended, a more sombre one than usual. The afternoon had given us a tiny glimpse of what it was like to live in an area where forest fires are a danger and the devastation they cause. About 70 homes had been destroyed that day.

My thoughts returned to our current beach surroundings and how fortunate we were to have been to Sri Lanka not once but twice.

Douglas and I returned to our room to deposit our beach accoutrements before heading to the shops. I wanted to take a pair of earrings back to the jeweller who had made them two years previously. I got the earrings and a necklace made to replace a necklace stolen when our house was burgled when we were in Hong Kong. I'm not someone who wears a lot of jewellery, but I really liked the necklace and it was useful if I was getting dressed-up for an evening event. I knew I wouldn't be able to buy a replacement back home so got one made, drawing the design and choosing the stones I wanted. The earrings were an upsell by the jeweller. This year I wanted him to change the backs of the earrings as the stems were too thick for the holes in my ears. He was happy to do this, and earrings left we went to the cash machine to withdraw money.

The cash machine Douglas used on a previous occasion had a long queue at it, so we opted to go to another on the opposite side of the hotel entrance. No queue there. Great. After all, it was very hot and not ideal for standing with the sun beating down on us.

Douglas opened the door and I followed him into the ATM cubicle, but as there was no air conditioning as I'd hoped, I went back outside and waited. Shortly afterwards he too came out.

"The ATM has swallowed my card before giving me any money," he told me.

This was far from ideal.

"Will my card for this account stop working too, do you think?" We hoped not as this was the account our money was in to pay for our room at the guest house, cash being preferred to credit cards.

As we were discussing what to do, a local man approached us.

"Have you lost a card in the ATM?" he asked.

We confirmed our predicament.

"That's the ATM for my bank. Use my phone and tell them what has happened." He passed his phone to Douglas.

"There was a sign on the door last week warning people with foreign cards not to use the machine because there was a problem with it," he told me while Douglas was on the phone. "The best thing to do is go to the bank in the town centre first thing in the morning before the machines are emptied. I know you told me you have another card with you, but tell them you don't, and they should get your card back for you."

This was very reassuring, but when Douglas came off the phone, he told us a different story, giving no hope of getting the card back. We said farewell to the very helpful man.

"I shouldn't have used that machine."

"How were you to know the machine was broken? I would have done the same thing; there was a long queue at the other one. Anyway, we've used several different machines around town and haven't had any problems."

"My phone's stopped working so we can't even contact our bank."

"It's OK, we'll get things sorted," I tried to reassure.

Back at the guest house, fellow holidaymaker Paul came to the rescue. He told us to use his phone and we learned from our bank the card had been "declined", the most likely reason being a faulty cash machine. It wouldn't affect my card we were relieved to learn. We were financially secure for the rest of the holiday.

A few hours later at our next meal with George and Sylvia I was able to reveal the outcome of my research into the meaning of "strumpling". (Wonder if I can describe myself as an etymologist? It sounds good).

The definition of strumpling is – a meaningless word used in place of any word(s) in a sentence. Especially good to use in place of profanity. "What the strumpling is going on around here?"

(www.urbandictionary.com)

Now, ever to go above and beyond the bounds of duty, I'd also looked up the meaning of "scrumpling" as this is what I initially thought Sylvia had said. This too had a definition:

Scrumpling, Scrumplings

1: bits of marijuana stashed around the house for later smoking when the normal supply has run dry.

2: bits of marijuana left on a table, book, etc when rolling a joint, to be gathered up for smoking (www.urbandictionary.com)

I think Sylvia is going to stick with "strumpling" as her new word!

Cash and discount cards

Our first task of the morning was to enquire about the debit card swallowed by the ATM. Douglas and I took a tuk-tuk the few miles to the bank. Although we'd been reassured my card would work, we felt it best to report the gobbled-up one. We didn't build our hopes up of getting the card back, but just in case, went equipped with his passport, plus details of his blood group, name of great, great grandfather's dog, the date and time (to the second) when the bank card originally dropped through our letterbox at home, fingerprints etc etc; you know, all the usual information required now-a-days to prove identity.

Inside the large air-conditioned bank was a long chicane which Douglas entered, ready to speak to a teller when he eventually reached the front of the queue. I, in the meantime, went investigating, looking for a customer service desk. I didn't find one, but up a few stairs from the main banking floor was a girl sitting at a desk.

"Yes, I can help," she said. I called Douglas over and she invited us to sit down opposite her. After hearing our problem, she got up, went to a desk behind her and spoke to an older lady. Standing, I could see the beautiful sari the young girl had on. She looked amazing.

We'd plenty of time to people watch. No one seemed busy or in any hurry. First the two ladies talked for a while, then the older one disappeared somewhere leaving the younger one to answer the phone for her. It rang often, but she didn't appear to take any messages to pass on. The older lady returned and stood beside her desk where she was joined by one and later a second man. The four chatted, seemingly with no inclination to work.

The younger lady finally sat down again and started asking us questions. Initially, I thought these related to the lost card, but I soon realised she was just chatting. Eventually, the older lady came and said a man was coming to see us, but I couldn't make out what else she included in the explanation. We thanked her profusely.

After a further wait a man came who I took to be, though perhaps was not, the bank manager. We were expecting to be interrogated but instead he said he would take us back to the ATM at the hotel. We couldn't believe it!

"Do you think we'll join him in a large, chauffeur-driven limo?" I asked Douglas as this was the only way I could imagine this man travelling. Once outside the front door, he was surrounded by other men; plain clothed security I surmised. Very impressive, I thought.

But no limo for us; he told us to get a tuk-tuk. He would meet us at the hotel. Oh well – nothing like dreaming. Before we parted, I asked one of the men to make sure the tuk-tuk driver knew where to take us and establish the fare, the latter being common practice. We set off and arrived at the infamous ATM ahead of the bank manager.

Instead of a limo, he arrived in a large 4x4 land cruiser. I decided he must be one of the directors of the bank as another two important looking gentlemen got out of the car, more clearly looking around as bodyguards do.

The three of them plus the driver lined up in formation – two in front, two behind and on the command marched forward into the hotel, going directly to the reception desk. Here the bank boss was treated like royalty with bowing, curtsying and handshakes from those at reception. One member of reception staff scurried away, returned and presented him with a key on a velvet cushion held in outstretched arms as her head bowed low. (OK I got carried away with this description, but she gave him the key.)

The four, remaining in formation, about turned and made their way to a door, which was unlocked and opened allowing all four to pass through. The door shut behind them and we were left waiting expectantly, wondering what was happening. Suddenly, out they emerged, the boss holding a *handful* of different bank cards.

Nothing was said as Douglas held open his passport and I showed him my bank card for the same account. The passport was looked at briefly before the boss instructed one of his sidekicks to photograph it. This done, the handover presentation of the card took place. They were happy to have a posed photo taken by me of this but declined Douglas' offer of a cup of tea as a thank you from us. The boss apologised for our inconvenience and said there was something wrong with the machine. Later we used the card to buy something in a shop to check it was working and it was fine – thank goodness!

We took a local bus back into the town centre as I wanted to buy some more material (for the wedding outfit as I had some inspirational

132

thoughts) and some small hand towels. Also, Sylvia had developed an ear infection and we said we would get her some drops from a pharmacy.

We found an excellent café with a very enthusiastic owner who was delighted we wanted to try some local cakes. We chose a coconut filled crepe and a slice of coconut cake, which looked like a spiced fruit cake. I saw pictures on the back wall of different cold drinks and went to choose one.

"What is wood apple?" I had to ask.

"It a little bit sour," the man warned me. "But I put ice cream in. Then it will be good for you."

The mention of ice cream sold it to me. On tasting the wood apple drink, I found "sour", even a "little bit sour", to a Sri Lankan is far from sour to our taste buds. It tasted *ultra*-sweet to me. The juice itself was brown in colour and thick like a smoothie but rough in texture. I enjoyed it but wouldn't rush to buy another – even with ice cream. It was too sweet for me.

Douglas in café: Coffee, wood apple drink with ice cream, coconut cake and coconut crepes

"It's great we got the card back," I said to Douglas. "What is it about us and cards on holiday?"

"What, like during our family holiday in Girona, Spain you mean?"

"Well, now you come to mention it," I said smiling, realising he had read my train of thought. He has often been reminded of our holiday there in 2003 and how we along with David and Andrew survived for *days* on biscuits and crisps. Let me explain.

We were on a short break and quickly discovered very few places accepted credit cards. We didn't expect to have to use cash for meals or train tickets for a daytrip to Barcelona, things we would automatically pay using credit cards at home or on other overseas holidays. As a result, we were quickly using up the cash we had with us and we had not seen any cash machines anywhere. As a last resort we went to the train station, where thankfully, an ATM was found.

Douglas inserted his card and tapped in his pin, but the card was spewed back out. He tried once more, and the same thing happened. Not wanting to risk trying again in case the card was withheld, we went into the adjacent bank. The lady there was very pleasant and eventually we understood what she was telling us – Douglas' bank card had expired a few weeks previously.

"I've brought the old card instead of the replacement one," he said woefully. In those days, we only used this debit card when on holiday and I didn't take any with me. We therefore couldn't get any money but somehow had to get through the rest of our holiday. Needless to say, Douglas was very annoyed with himself.

We headed back to the hop-on hop-off tour bus we'd a day ticket for. Our destination was the *Montjuïc* Cable Car which would take us up to the castle. We were entitled to a discount because we were on the bus tour, but unfortunately, yet again, it was cash only to buy the tickets so more of our dwindling money supply was used up – most of it actually. We lived dangerously!

The cable car ride was brilliant. We got great views of the city and were amazed when through a feat of engineering the cable car changed direction, having been transferred onto a different cable inside a little building. Suddenly we were travelling at right angles to our original direction of travel.

After a bit more sightseeing, we realised if we rushed, we would be able to catch a soon departing train. Douglas checked his wallet and with a little cash was able to buy one packet of crisps and one bottle of water at a small shop on the platform to keep us going till we got back to Girona. We were all hungry, so it wasn't much, but we were all aware of our cash predicament. Possibly not wanting their Dad to feel even worse, both boys agreed, "These are the best crisps we've tasted in our lives."

We were also pleased to remember some sweets we'd taken from a large bowl in the hotel reception as we left in the morning. Thankfully we hadn't eaten them earlier.

Unfortunately, the very busy train was delayed and didn't arrive back at Girona until 10 p.m. by which time the supermarket we knew took credit cards was shut, as was the restaurant in the hotel. So, in our room we survived on biscuits, crisps and sweets we'd bought previously for our flight home.

For the rest of our holiday we had to survive with no cash. This became like a game and rather than being a disaster, was fun. My memory of surviving penniless extended over a period of three days during which we survived by eating crisps and biscuits. And this is the story David, Andrew and I told everyone for many years – and reminded Douglas of.

However, one day I reread my diary and discovered fuller information.

The day after our trip to Barcelona our money spinning was put into practice. We'd a great day. Not our usual sightseeing, as we'd no money for entrance fees. Instead we spent the morning wandering round Girona seeing things we hadn't noticed before. Importantly we found three potential restaurants where credit cards were accepted for evening meals.

In the afternoon we lazed around the hotel enjoying the swimming pool. We'd filled up our stomachs well at breakfast time, so a top-up of more crisps and biscuits kept us going until the daily afternoon supply of drinks and cakes were available in the hotel reception area.

In the evening we went to the first restaurant we'd seen earlier but it was shut. Heading for our second choice, we saw a fourth possible restaurant and went in, sat down and asked for an English menu. The man explained he wouldn't be preparing food from the menu until 7 p.m., though he could make us pizza or salad. We decided to continue our journey to original option number two.

This served tapas. At the time, tapas were something we weren't familiar with and we didn't want to take a risk, so we went to the final place we'd seen in the morning.

This finally, was "just right". (as in *Goldilocks and the Three Bears* when Goldilocks eventually found the porridge was "just right" and she ate it all up.). Here, we had a meal and paid with our credit card. Success! Well, except for the initial disappointment when we discovered the restaurant didn't serve paella. One of the things on our "to do list" was to try paella.

I realise you will be wondering why the lack of paella was so disappointing; after all, as I mentioned earlier, in my mind we'd other days left of our holiday. Plenty of time to find a suitable restaurant. However, on re-reading my diary it revealed we flew home the following morning!

So now the truth is out, and I admit in writing; Douglas' memory is more accurate than mine; he always denied my recounting of the tale, though I think my original unwittingly exaggerated version sounds better.

"Yes, that was an extreme experience of cards not working," I admitted. "But there have been a few others we could have done without. Do you remember the restaurant in Hong Kong when I was lecturing there in 2015? The restaurant overlooked the harbour, and we watched all the well-lit boats passing by the multitude of illuminated skyscrapers on the opposite bank. The skyline was wonderful. The meal was good too and fortunately we were in a small section in the restaurant, slightly remote from the main area where a noisy certificate presentation to businesspeople was taking place. It was impossible to ignore all the loud, enthusiastic announcements and cheering.

We were pleased when we finished our meal and asked for the bill, ready to make a hasty retreat into the more acceptable very noisy street outside!

The bill arrived, and I handed over my credit card to pay. It's strange to remember it was normal to let staff take credit cards away for processing, rather than them bringing a card-reader to the table. We waited for ages to get our receipt and the credit card back. Eventually a manager came to our table and asked us to go with him to the till. There was a problem we were told; not what we wanted to hear.

We watched as the credit card was inserted into the machine but rejected. We couldn't understand as the card had been used earlier in the day without difficulty.

A debit card was fished out of my purse and similarly put into the machine. Although the pin was accepted there was a delay in the procedure and after a minute it cancelled the transaction and we tried again. Thankfully after three attempts, the money was taken from my account, I was given my card and we left, relieved.

When I phoned the bank from our hotel, we were assured everything was fine and there must be something wrong in the restaurant. We didn't risk going back there to eat!"

"Can I finish with a couple of holiday memories from my childhood?" I requested.

"Yes. That'll be safe as it can't involve slagging me!" Douglas replied.

I remember when I was young, we didn't have oodles of money. We always had happy family holidays in Scotland.

One of my few early memories happened when I was very young. We were staying in Tarbert, a village on the banks of Loch Fyne in Scotland. In the bedroom was a very big free-standing wardrobe, the likes of which I'd not seen before. It had to be investigated. I opened the door and stepped in. It wasn't at all like *The Lion, the Witch and the Wardrobe* where the children found wonderful things inside. The wardrobe unbalanced and down it fell with me in it. I don't remember anything else except it being quickly lifted back up and I got out, none the worse from my ordeal.

What I remember more vividly because I was older were the journeys home from holiday, when literally all the unspent pennies were collected and carefully counted. We even checked all the nooks and crannies in the car and emptied our pockets in case there were one or two extras we'd forgotten about (unlikely though this was). Would there be enough money for us to get some fish suppers[11] to share when we got home, or only pokes[12] of chips? To tell you the truth, it didn't matter if it was only chips as this was a treat for us. And thus, we would arrive home penniless and happy.

"Right – enough chit chatting, we've a mission to complete. You're wanting to buy more material," Douglas reminded me.

Yes, I wanted more material. I'd been thinking about the outfit I planned to have made for Julia and Andrew's wedding and thought a seamstress might like to make an outfit with panels of different colours. I wanted her to have options. If the material wasn't used, I would make even more tablecloths, or perhaps napkins – or even placemats. Plenty of options.

Douglas and I chose the material. It was cut from the bales, folded up and a hand-written note detailed the cost.

"You like a discount card?" I was asked.

"Yes please," I said, never being one to turn down a bargain. It was a simple procedure. On a small slip of paper, I wrote my name and address, signed and dated it. This was attached to the fabric along with the handwritten bill which we took to the tills on the ground floor.

---

[11] In Scotland, at the chip shop, we don't ask for fish and chips, we ask for a fish supper, meaning we want chips as well as fish. A 'single fish' is asked for if we only want fish. Similarly, a haggis supper would be haggis with chips or a sausage supper would be sausage and chips.

[12] In Scotland, a poke of chips is a bag of chips, the bag formed by folding a large sheet of newspaper, though now new white paper is generally used.

All of this you will be relieved to hear happened without incident. I'm not sure whether the staff recognised us, but if they did, were very good at pretending they didn't. I suppose they were just pleased to survive the ordeal of serving me again!

When we went down the two flights of stairs to the checkout, the girl removed the signed slip of paper and I noticed her turning to the checkout assistant beside her. She said something and smiled. She handed me my new discount card and in anticipation I waited to find out how much discount I would receive. The girl at the till had difficulty processing the fabric costs, cancelling it a couple of times and starting over again. She finally put through the hand towels we were also buying and waited for assistance.

I held up the discount card to ensure she hadn't forgotten to include the discount amongst all the cancelling. This was met with smiles and nods. Finally, everything was sorted, Douglas paid with a credit card and we were given the receipt. I noticed the amount on the credit card receipt was 100 rupees *more* than the cost of our purchases. Clearly, we hadn't received the discount.

I asked why we were paying extra, pointing at the figures on the receipt. She in turn pointed to the figures. Our lack of ability to speak Sri Lankan meant we weren't getting anywhere.

By this time there was a man standing behind us who became our interpreter. After more questions and answers an explanation finally emerged. We'd paid 100 rupees for the discount card and discounts would start when we next made a purchase!

"So, our new 'discount' card resulted in us paying more for our purchases," Douglas laughed. Fortunately, 100 rupees is hardly anything – less than the cost of a small bag of crisps in the UK so we didn't leave the shop poverty-stricken.

As expert users of public transport we took a bus back. While making our way to the guest house after getting off the packed bus, we met Sylvia, George, Jacqui and Paul who were all going for lunch. We joined them after dumping our purchases in our room and lifting in the pile of clean laundry left outside our door. It's such a treat to have our clothes laundered by the maid and at a very reasonable price; not something I'd contemplate when staying in hotels.

"We've now got a discount card for the CIB store, so please borrow it if you're going shopping there," I told the others.

After a satisfying lunch George, Sylvia, Douglas and I found ourselves investigating other possible trips we could go on. We decided to use a travel agent and enquired about a couple of nights in the Maldives but discovered this wouldn't work.

In the months leading up to our holiday in Sri Lanka, our flight times had been changed several times. We ended up with longer stops in Dubai making the overall journey time longer. George and Sylvia had been delayed even longer. We now discovered the reason. The runway at Colombo Airport was closed on a long-term basis during the day to allow maintenance to be carried out.

This closure also affected flights to the Maldives. The flight would depart late in the evening and on arrival we would have to sit in the airport for six hours. Then in the morning we would be taken by boat to our island hotel. We reckoned this unfortunately made the trip unviable.

Other tour options were suggested, and we discussed these over our evening meal on the beach. Boy, what a hard life we lead!

Holiday activities

I needed time to catch up with writing and photo/video editing so stayed at the guest house. Douglas stayed for much of the time too, before going to the beach for a swim and lunch with George and Sylvia. When I joined them later in the afternoon, we booked our next tour. We were going to be travelling in style, spread out in a minibus rather than squashed in a car. We accepted the travel agent's advice and combined two separate trips we had thought of with an overnight stay in Trincomalee.

Feeling pleased with ourselves, we set off for our evening meal, going to Coconut Lodge restaurant which had become our favourite. The chef was brilliant at cooking recipes from around the world, all to an exceptionally high standard.

I wanted something plain to eat but was a bit hesitant about ordering Spaghetti Napolitano because pasta in another restaurant was undercooked. However, I needn't have worried.

"The tomato sauce is delicious. I wouldn't get better in Italy!" I told the others. "I would love to watch the chef making it so I could get some tips."

Sylvia tried to entice George into showing us how to fold napkins, but he was shy to show off his talents which until then we hadn't even known about. As we were the only customers, when the waiter asked if we wanted anything else, I asked, "Can you show us how to fold a napkin?"

A masterclass in napkin folding followed, bringing back memories of the *Generation Game* on television in which couples competed against each other to complete challenges. I always remember one in which contestants had to fold a quilt cover set so it fitted neatly into the packet ready for a shop display. It proved to be an impossibility for them.

During our masterclass, we'd to be quick to keep up with the speed of the demonstration. Fortunately, the waiter had the knack of being able to both demonstrate and fix our errors at the same time. No sooner had we finished one design and sat back to admire our efforts than with a flick of the wrist he had undone his napkin and launched immediately into another design.

Some of our efforts looked like the demonstration model, others required a lot of imagination. I'm not convinced anyone would have recognised our "chickens". We must have made 10 different designs and I almost immediately forgot how to do any of them! Thank goodness for the Internet.

"That was so much fun," I said. "Simple pleasures! When David and Andrew were young, they were happy with just sand and water and if there are stones to throw into the sea and shells to find, even better. Great sandcastles were built, with defensive motes for the incoming tide to fill. There would be squeals of horror and instructions yelled to delay the sandcastle slipping below the ever-rising water. But nature always won.

"We enjoyed packing a picnic, loading the car with buckets and spades, picnic blankets, swimwear, bats, balls and frisbees. In the caravan these were stored in a hidden storage compartment under the sofa seat cushion. Unsurprisingly, in Scotland we also took a windbreak as even on sunny days the wind could be blowing. There wasn't much room left for us to get into the car!"

"It's always good to try new things on holiday too," I continued. "One I remember was in 2001 when we were in San Francisco's Golden Gate Park, USA, at the start of our family touring holiday."

We'd seen posters advertising pedal vehicles called Surreys for hire.

"They look fun," I said to Douglas. After all, the pictures in the posters showed happy smiling people, waving to passers-by as they pedalled. Obviously, everyone was having a great time. Yes, this would be a great experience for us, I persuaded Douglas.

We didn't know which type of Surrey to hire as there were many options, but the man recommended one for two pedalling adults with space between us for David while Andrew was to sit in the large luggage basket at the front. Some might think he was relegated to third class travel, but he had a private compartment normally reserved for first class travel with great unobstructed views to boot!

David and Andrew were given crash helmets to wear.

"Why have the boys been given helmets?" I joked with Douglas as we set off. "Do you think the man doesn't trust our cycling skills? Or is the reason we haven't been given helmets to wear because our lives are less valuable than the younger generation?"

I soon discovered what I thought looked like fun didn't live up to my expectations. The Surrey had no gears and was very hard to pedal. To make matters worse, the side I was pedalling seemed to be at a different gearing to Douglas' side. This meant at higher speeds, my pedals just spun round with my little short legs trying desperately to keep up. Effectively I was contributing nothing to our efforts. The four of us ended up getting off and pushing! Not the happy family experience portrayed on all the advertising posters.

We mentioned our problems to the man when we returned, and he gave us a credit note. We would have preferred a refund as we didn't expect to be able to use the voucher. He assured us the company had various centres in other cities, so we would be able to use the voucher at some point during the remainder of our touring holiday.

As it turned out plans changed, and we returned to San Francisco for the last few days of our holiday, so we went back to the Golden Gate Park.

After the trauma with the Surreys, we hired a three wheeled go-cart and a Fliker for David and Andrew. Douglas and I were happy to spectate.

We'd never seen a Fliker and it was years later before we saw any in our hometown. It looked like a three wheeled scooter with two platforms in a "v" shape, one for each foot. They didn't manage to master the wobbling-of-bottom technique required to get it moving but enjoyed themselves regardless using their own methods.

Our bad experience relating to hiring vehicles unfortunately continued with the go-cart. David had a mishap – or at least his jacket did. He had taken it off and put it on the back of the seat not realising one of the sleeves was hanging over the side. It caught in the chain and the sleeve was ripped to shreds. Fortunately, it was his jacket and not him.

To add salt to the wound, as I was struggling to remove the jacket from the chain, the sprinkler on the lawn beside us switched on full force and being in its line of fire I ended up with a soaking wet bottom. It could have been worse. I could have been soaked all over, but this was bad enough!

To recover from the ordeals, we bought coffee and popcorn and sat on a bench beside the lake. Unfortunately for me, but much to the delight of the pigeons, some of the popcorn spilled. To put it mildly, I'm not a fan of pigeons and hate them coming near me. But the pigeons had one thing on their mind – the popcorn feast lying before them.

With the pigeons coming closer I sprang into action and tried to kick the popcorn away. This sudden movement frightened the pigeons and much flapping of wings followed, the downdraft moving the popcorn closer rather than further away as I intended. The pigeons were in hot pursuit of the popcorn now round my ankles.

"Do something!" I pleaded with my loving family as the pigeons reached me. Unlike me, they were extremely amused by my ordeal and were too busy laughing to help me. A decision was made – I was off and soon disappeared over the horizon.

"A happier memory, involving David and Andrew and crafts, sticks in my mind," I said as I looked at the array of napkins in front of us. In Oslo, Norway in 2002 we went to *Norsk Farmasihistorisk* Museum – a Norwegian open-air Folk Museum. We had fun wandering round the streets of the Old Town and the rural farm buildings, popping in and out of some of the 160 or so reconstructed buildings.

During this time, we came across a house in which was a children's craft table. I won't ever forget the red apples David and Andrew made. They joined another couple of boys standing at a big old wooden kitchen table on which were round plastic washing up bowls containing warm soapy water. Each boy was given a large lump of unspun wool, about 15cm (6") in diameter, which they put in the soapy water squeezing it till it sucked up plenty of water. Lifting it out of the water, they squeezed it again expelling water and forming it into a ball shape – or should I say an apple shape. Next, they were given some red dyed unspun wool. They put a layer of this round the ball while ensuring it retained its apple shape.

I have a photo of David and Andrew looking very serious as they concentrated on completing the next task – cutting out leaf shapes from a sheet of green felt. A piece of brown wool was knotted at one end and the other end threaded through the eye of a needle before the needle was pushed through the middle of the apple. The wool was pulled tight to form the indentation found at the bottom of apples and finally the needle was passed through the carefully cut leaf shapes. The wool was tied off with a loop, so it could be hung up.

Off we went clutching two newly made and still wet wool apples which took days to fully dry. They were great mementos of the holiday especially as David and Andrew hadn't seen any souvenirs they wanted to buy.

"What about the snooker tournament in Madeira in 2012 with David and Andrew?" Douglas prompted.

"Oh yes, I ended up doing very well," I recalled.

On our first night, we had a game in the hotel after our evening meal in a nearby restaurant. We formed two teams – Douglas and I against the "Junior Moores" team.

I knew the theory, but the cue had other ideas. Although I was in Douglas' team, I was effectively in the Junior Moores team as they gained many points from my numerous foul shots.

Douglas (as our team score was down to him alone) beat the Junior Moores with nearly double their score. Before you get the impression Douglas will be making an appearance in the Snooker World Championship at the Crucible, England, I must mention he didn't pot more than two (or was it three) balls at any one time at the table. The game, you will understand, therefore took a long time to complete. Meanwhile I looked longingly at the table tennis table next to us, which unfortunately was in use.

David potted the last black which pleased them, and a rematch was organised as the Junior Moores were determined to win one game.

The next evening, we had a wonderful "steak on the stone" for dinner. As the roasting hot stone was brought to the table and placed in front of us, the steak continued to sizzle and cook. We decided ourselves how much more cooking we wanted before moving the succulent meat onto our plates, to join the piles of vegetables.

On returning to the hotel, tiredness drew me to bed, while the others had another game of snooker. Apparently, the scores were made up mostly of foul strokes and for a long time the highest break was one point! Things were not improving.

"You did really well at snooker last night, Mum," I was told the next morning. "You were third out of the four of us."

"But I didn't play," I reminded them.

"We decided halfway through the game we would award all the points from foul strokes to you."

"So, I might have won if you'd 'included' me right from the start of the game?"

In the following night's snooker challenge, after starting well and leading for a while, I slipped back to third place. Not a bad result as again, I hadn't been near the snooker table. This "foul stroke scoring" suited me fine though my game was deteriorating as I'd been awarded points from the beginning of the game this time and yet I still finished third. I'd hoped for a silver medal position – at least.

David did well – leading for most of the game but lost his nerve and slipped back to second place. Andrew played so badly he waited behind afterwards for half an hour of practising.

The next night I improved and came second (in absentia) but was given strict instructions: I had to play in person on our final night in case I won without lifting a cue or striking a ball.

Our last game of snooker was a very close match. As instructed, I really played and this time we played as individuals.

The tension mounted with Douglas and Andrew neck and neck. The final black ball would determine the winner. Douglas missed, and finally the honour went to Andrew. Douglas was second and David and I were joint third. If we'd been playing as our teams, the Junior Moores would have won – their ambition of beating Douglas and I (well Douglas really) would have been achieved.

If I'd not been playing, and relied on the foul stroke scoring method, I would have won this match. Snooker is not our strong point!

"I really enjoyed a couple of Levada walks in Madeira, or at least enjoyed them *most* of the time," Douglas continued.

We went on our first guided Levada walk, following a section of one of the many mini irrigation channels transporting water around the island as they zig-zag down the mountains. We were told about the rota which sets out the times when adjacent landowners can draw water for their land and crops and for how long.

There were six others on the walk with us. We often stopped as we walked and Antonio, the guide, explained about the different plants we saw.

Andrew and David tended to walk at the front of the group with Antonio, having long conversations and debates with him. Antonio suggested Renaldo was the best footballer in the world. Andrew didn't agree and a friendly argument ensued.

Varied topics of conversation followed. Andrew's question about the President of Madeira set off a tirade of swearing from Antonio, so we guessed he didn't like the President and blamed him for a corrupt regime uncovered during an economic crisis.

Later a question and answer session followed, Andrew asking the questions, Antonio providing the answers. I quietly listened in the background:

"Do you have a family?"

"No, I live with my mother."

"Have you been married?"

"Women cause too many problems I have found." This response needed clarification:

"Have you been married in the past?"

"Yes many, many times."

"How many times – three or four?"

"No – many, many times."

"Five or six times?"

"No – many, many times."

"Too many times to remember?"

"Yes."

I tried to return my dropped jaw to its normal position as I reasoned; perhaps he was referring to his number of girlfriends he had had over the years rather than marriages. But perhaps not! This type of banter went on between the three of them for much of the two-hour walk.

The walk was brilliant with stunning scenery; mountains all around us, terraced for growing vegetables and every once in a while, we came across a house. The walk in the heart of nature was quiet and peaceful.

At one point in the walk, Antonio stepped up onto the concrete Levada channel along which the water flows to talk to us. We all turned to face him, with the valley and mountains beyond at our backs.

When he finished the explanation, he stepped forward off the concrete and back onto the path. Disaster struck. As Antonio stepped forward Andrew stepped back to make room for him on the narrow path.

Immediately Andrew disappeared from sight over the edge of a high cliff. Our hearts missed a beat. Antonio leapt into action in the process accidently punching David in the face sending his prescription sunglasses flying over the cliff. Never have we been so grateful to thorny bramble[13] bushes on any walk. Without their profuse growth from small crevices in the sheer cliff face, Andrew would have fallen to the valley floor far below. Instead he was trapped perilously.

David and Antonio were just able to reach Andrew's outstretched arms and pulled. Andrew kicked at the bramble bushes whose thorns had embedded themselves in his legs and clothes. It all happened so quickly we didn't really have time to think. Andrew was fine, though very embarrassed and covered in scratches. David's glasses were seen no more.

Only a few yards further along the path our minds went into overdrive. Here things could have turned out very differently. Here, the same sheer cliff was free of vegetation. And we realised we couldn't see the bottom of the cliff; it was so sheer and far below us.

Antonio at the end of the walk, gave Andrew a big hug saying, "Thank the Lord you are with us and I am not in jail." We fully concurred with this prayer of thanksgiving.

Perhaps surprisingly, the experience did not put us off going on a second Levada walk, a longer, four-hour walk. Instead of a minibus, a taxi came to the hotel at 8.50 a.m. to transport us to the starting point.

This was our first experience on the island of a taxi driver who didn't speak much English. Every so often he tried to tell us something – often with imitating sounds accompanied with hand gestures, usually with both hands at the same time, steering wheel forgotten about.

The car was a bit of a wreck and not a Mercedes as nearly all the taxis we'd seen. Andrew said it made him embarrassed as it was a British built car. As David opened a door the handle nearly came off. In the absence of air conditioning, the driver kept his front window open. We quickly learned to hold our breath for as long as possible in the many tunnels we went through as traffic exhaust fumes poured into the car. The combination of the fume filled tunnels and the twisty roads going up the mountain, made me wish I'd taken a travel pill.

"I'm sure I heard the driver saying there was a 'big problem' with the car," I said to the others.

Douglas asked him, "Is there a problem with the clutch?"

13 Bramble: Scottish for "blackberry".

"Yes."

Great, we thought sarcastically. Here we were in a dangerous car on mountainous, twisty roads.

"Maybe the problem is he hasn't passed his driving test," Andrew quietly suggested to me. "Every time we're going up one of these very steep hills, he stays in fourth gear until he nearly stalls then jumps into first gear."

Andrew was right about the gears and each time it happened the car lurched forward and we were sent flying towards the windscreen. Thankfully the restraining power of our seatbelts saved us.

The other problem with the car was although the back seat was able to seat three people, it wasn't suitable for three adults. I was sitting in the middle. Down the back of my "seat" was a narrow very hard band which separated me from the two other seats. I felt my spine rolling back and forth over this as we swerved round the tight corners and felt sure all the knobbly bits down my spine were being bruised black and blue.

Somehow, we arrived safe and sound at the rendezvous point. Our adrenaline levels returned to normal as we enjoyed munching juicy peaches while waiting for our guide and the rest of the group to arrive.

When one minibus arrived, who should get out but Antonio – our guide on the last tour. On seeing Andrew – he shouted, "See you Jimmy," with a Scottish accent, and came over and shook our hands, pleased to see us again.

Antonio disappeared into a shop then reappeared with a massive roll and coffee announcing it was his breakfast. He told us a minibus had broken down and another had to go back to get the passengers.

"You could have had longer in bed," I said to David and Andrew.

"You're not the only one thinking this," Andrew replied.

Although this gave us time to enjoy the fantastic views of the mountains, it was chilly as we stood waiting. We were in the shade and at an altitude of 1,100 metres (3,600 feet). We were assured we would heat up as we walked.

At last we began. There were 28 in our group, including Antonio and another guide. One guide walked at the front and the other referred to as "the sweeper" hurried along any slow walkers at the back. Many other groups were doing the same walk, some in the opposite direction.

We set off downhill in very different surroundings to the last Levada walk. This walk was mainly through woodland, with open areas every now and then where we could see the impressive mountains across the valley, the Levadas we'd already walked beside and those ahead of us.

Initially the path was wide and smooth and wasn't beside a Levada. At times the rough path was partially paved with rocks forming steppingstones. When we got to and followed the route of the Levada, the path in places was very narrow – 45cm (18 inches) wide, sometimes with a fence on the side opposite the Levada wall. At other times instead of a protective fence there was a shear drop just as we had experienced on our last Levada walk. Care and attention were required.

We walked at a good pace for us although others might have found it too quick, passing many waterfalls and springs coming out of the rocks. The water in the Levada was icy cold and unexpectedly at one point we saw small trout, about the length of my hand, swimming in water in the U-shaped concrete Levada channel.

When we stopped for lunch two hours later, we didn't feel tired as we had done at the end of our first Levada walk. This time we had been mainly shaded by the trees rather than walking in the heat of the day.

Our picnic was eaten as we sat on rocks with high horse-shoe shaped cliffs partially surrounding us, water cascading impressively from the top. During rainy seasons, the rocks we were sitting on disappeared becoming part of the riverbed.

Many other groups were also having their lunch break here. We were given strict instructions that this was a 30-minute stop.

As we were in the middle of nowhere, there were no toilets, but we were directed down a path where there were suitable bushes for us to hide behind. When I went down the path, I came across a person who had just broken his ankle.

"It will take 'many, many' (Antonio liked this phrase) hours to rescue him."

I could understand why. He would have to be stretchered out – no possibility of helicopter rescue here.

We set off again, Antonio waiting behind as "sweeper" as there were a few folks who hadn't come to the departure point on time.

After the next stop and another head count, the re-united group set off again. A viewing point at a break in the forest followed and we could see the surrounding mountains once more. It was here I learned we'd passed another person with a broken ankle. I hadn't even noticed, concentrating too hard on watching my own footing!

The first of the rescuers came running very quickly towards and passed us, with a massive pack on his back. He must have been very fit. Later, a second rescuer similarly passed us.

Antonio did another head count before we pressed on.

Six more rescuers passed as we walked, this time they were carrying two empty stretchers. How they were going to get the stretchers back along some of these narrow paths I don't know – a very difficult task.

We walked on and finally arrived at an 800 metre (875 yard) long tunnel. We were issued with torches to use as we walked through the darkness. Antonio counted again and found four people were missing. He counted again. The other guide counted. They conferred and agreed our group size was only 24 instead of 28. We'd lost four of our group.

It was hard to believe we could be four people short. Our heads had been counted so many times. However, the paths had been very busy with different groups. I thought about the previous head count on a wide bridge and wondered if I'd heard someone who Antonio had counted as being in our group indicating she wasn't with us. As she wasn't speaking in English, I couldn't be sure what she was saying and because the group was so big, I couldn't have told you whether she was someone in our group or not.

The fact remained – we were four people short and Antonio said, "This is why I told you all to keep together!" To put it mildly, he wasn't happy, and no wonder. It must have been awful for him – I know how nervous I became when helping on school trips in case any of my six charges disappeared.

We waited a while in the hope the four missing people caught up. Then the other guide began retracing our route hoping, I'm sure, he didn't find them with broken ankles or worse.

After some more waiting, Antonio instructed, "Go on through the tunnel on your own. After fifteen minutes you will be at the end of the walk. The café is there, and your minibuses will be there too."

Off we set, now guideless and were relieved when we saw minibuses ahead. We hadn't got lost!

Our taxi driver said he could take us to the hotel immediately, or we could go to the café first as per the tour itinerary. We opted for the former, though this meant we didn't unravel the mystery of the four lost trekkers.

It was a 50-minute, mostly downhill drive back to the hotel. The car and driver thankfully coped better than on the uphill roads of the morning.

With a few hand signals and a couple of "whooshes" from the driver, we learned a tree had fallen across the road. The massive trunk and branches had already been cut up and enough moved to allow the traffic to pass.

"How often are trees blown down?" Douglas asked.

"Yes – 1 o'clock," the driver replied. We'd visions of trees falling every day at 1 o'clock just like the 1 o'clock gun fired every day at Edinburgh Castle, Scotland.

Other holiday exploits take a lot of planning. Inadvertently, Douglas and I booked a holiday which clashed with the Ayrshire Fiddle Orchestra's (AFO) local summer concert. I was extremely upset when I discovered the mistake. We would miss what I knew would be a special event prior to the orchestra embarking on their bi-annual overseas tour. They were going to America and Canada. David is the Musical Director and the orchestra sounded fantastic in their newly released CD.

I discussed the possibility of changing the dates of our holiday, but deep down knew this wasn't an option. David and Leah[14] were very understanding when I told them, Leah telling me I'd a lifetime of AFO concerts ahead of me so missing one wasn't a problem.

Despite all their assurances I still felt bad. I devised a plan. One of their concerts was to be in Toronto. I'd always wanted to see the orchestra play on one of the overseas tours but like nearly all parents hadn't. I thought about my cousin George and his wife, Bunty, who lived near Toronto and wondered if I could stay with them. They quickly agreed. We would keep my trip a secret and surprise David and Leah on the night.

David had been in AFO since he was eleven when, having reached the required ability as a fiddle[15] player, he was invited to join. I remember those early days well. I felt dreadful as I took him to the Saturday rehearsals knowing most of the music was too difficult for him. A lot of traditional Scottish fiddle music is played at a very fast pace. With so many notes on the page I struggled to read it so knew how hard it was for him.

The large stage in Ayr Town Hall, has wide steep steps rising from the back of both sides. At his first concert nine months later, he was perched on the highest step. I saw him concentrating intensely on the music. He

---

[14] At the time of writing, David and Leah were due to marry on 25 July 2020. Due to Covid-19, they will now marry on 24 July 2021.

[15] Fiddle = Scottish for a violin. The orchestra plays mainly traditional Scottish music.

and the other young players had been told not to worry if they couldn't play all the notes; they were to make sure their bows were going up and down at the same time as the others in the orchestra. He had mastered this, and I could tell from his finger movements he was really playing some of the slow airs. Parts of the fast reels though required finger miming. From these early days there was no looking back. As the years passed and he improved, he moved down from the dizzy heights of the steps and onto the stage, then closer and closer to the front.

He studied music at the Royal Conservatoire of Scotland in Glasgow. Now as the Musical Director of AFO, he's the conductor and writes and arranges music for the orchestra to play at their many concerts both in the UK and around the world.

The lead up to my departure to Toronto was very strange. I was so intent on making sure I didn't say anything to David and Leah about the planned trip I effectively obliterated it from my mind, to the extent I didn't tell people who should have known I was going away for a week. Douglas fortunately had been told!

On the day of the concert, George, Bunty and I drove from their home in St Catharines to Toronto. The roads were busy and half an hour before reaching our destination, I suddenly saw a bus in the slow-moving traffic. It would be just like the thing if the two AFO coaches travelled the same road and ever observant David spotted me.

There was only one thing for it – I had to hide. I put on the only thing I had with me, my cerise pink cagoule and pulled the hood over my face. Sorted, I thought.

The trouble was, it was a hot day and with the cagoule on, it was like being in a sauna. I didn't fancy arriving with soaking wet clothes. With an enormous struggle while keeping the hood over my face and my seat belt on I managed to extricate my wet arms from the sleeves they had stuck themselves to.

We finally arrived at St John's Presbyterian Church on Broadview Avenue. There were tell-tale traffic cones outside the building, but no buses so I felt sure they hadn't arrived. We parked in a side street. George and Bunty went to investigate, with strict instructions only to speak to Euan or Kathleen, the other touring orchestra directors. They were the only ones who knew I was coming. I remained in the car covered by my camouflaging cerise cagoule – waiting.

"The orchestra hasn't arrived. They've been held up in traffic," they reported back. "I've sworn the people to secrecy. They've recommended a café we can go to, then you'll be hidden in the church."

"I'll leave my grey backpack in the car as I know David would recognise it. He and Andrew tease me about it."

"Your grey backpack – but it's your cerise cagoule which stands out like a sore thumb!"

Bunty was right so George was stripped of his jacket. Off we set, me sweltering with not one but two jackets on.

We found the café, had something to eat and after two attempts, hot rather than luke-warm coffee.

"It's time to get you hidden in the church," Bunty said. But as we approached, we saw the buses had arrived. This complicated things as the young players and adult helpers were swarming around, enjoying the barbecue prepared for them.

"I'll hide behind this bush while you go ahead to check things out," I said to Bunty. George was instructed to further conceal me.

The signal came and by the hand gestures we knew we were to move quickly to the front door of the church. Once inside there was confusion. The lady we spoke to tried to direct us to the best seats but eventually she understood I was not to be seen. George and Bunty sat down in the middle of the front pew and I on a seat behind a screen at the back of the church. I could see David setting out the chairs for the players at the front of the church. He didn't recognise George and Bunty. George's blue jacket with its hood was excellent camouflage as no one approached me. Either that or they often saw people sitting crouched down and trying to look inconspicuous whilst looking very conspicuous ... and suspicious.

"I think it would be best if you saw David before the concert rather than surprising him during it as planned," Euan advised. "It's been a difficult day for the orchestra. The travelling took three hours more than expected. There hasn't been time to go to the hotel as intended. Instead we've come straight to the church and as if that's not enough, some youngsters are suffering from heat exhaustion. I think David is likely to burst into tears if you appear during the concert."

Shortly after, Kathleen came and said, "Follow me."

I was taken into the halls at the back of the church where David was waiting. He'd been told someone special wanted to see him privately. He thought it strange George and Bunty would make such a request. I revealed myself – and yes, David cried as we held each other in a long hug. He had no idea I would be there, so all the secrecy had worked.

When I saw Leah, she exclaimed, "I knew you'd come!" A woman's intuition. "I said to David you and Douglas would make the trip after missing the summer concert, but he said 'no' because you'd be looking after our wee dog Bella."

Douglas would have loved to have come too, but he couldn't take any more time off his church duties.

There was no air-conditioning in the church, and it was far too hot for our Scottish orchestra members who were all wearing their colourful but warm kilt outfits. A decision was made during a short break; the orchestra would move outside and the remainder of the concert was performed on the lawn.

Outside, the orchestra rose to another level, reinvigorated by the cooler atmosphere. David announced I was there and the next piece of music he conducted was *Inisheer* – one of his own arrangements for the orchestra and a favourite of mine. As ever I felt prickles going up the back of my neck – a sign the music spoke to my heart.

At the end of the concert I was amazed by the number of people who asked David to have a photograph taken with him. He told me this was normal, but this time no one had asked to have their programme signed. Bunty and I rectified this, and he professionally opened our programmes to the page with his photo and dutifully added his signature.

I also got a memento – one of the many posters from outside advertising the event. It has the photo of David leaping in mid-air while conducting. And can I see the side of Andrew's head playing the percussion as he used to do? I've decided it is.

"So, the end of my last tale for tonight," I concluded. "Memories of happy holiday activities to end another happy evening with our great napkin folding waiter."

Napkin folding masterclass

Five go fishing topped off with lashings of ice cream

Preparing for launch: Douglas' long legs are an advantage

Douglas, George and Sylvia joined Jacqui and Paul on a fishing trip. I avoided another trip on the ocean wave and opted to be the official photographer, adjudicator and awarder of prizes. We agreed on four prizes to be awarded to the person who caught the:

- most fish
- biggest fish
- smallest fish
- most varieties of fish.

Rising early, we walked to the beach, arriving at the appointed place at 7 a.m. We were met by the barefooted, t-shirt, shorts and baseball-cap clad owner of a simple fibreglass boat with an outboard motor. Like the other boats on the beach it was uniquely decorated with colourful geometric painting. Most were painted with primary colours but this one was blue, turquoise, white and mustard. A couple of plank seats spanned between the boat's port and starboard, with cushions to provide comfort for the passengers' posteriors.

After putting on lifejackets, the task was to launch the boat. All the men pushed the boat to turn it, so the bow faced the sea. Another broadly smiling boat owner with magnificent white teeth joined the men to help push it forward, over the 60cm (24") high vertical sand cliff created by the tide, and beyond into the blue waters below. Douglas forgot about the sand precipice and as he walked the sand collapsed under his feet, sending him crashing downwards much to everyone's amusement; a very different reaction to Andrew's real cliff-fall experience.

Once the boat was partly in the water, the five fishers clambered in. The outboard motor was tested and with a final push from the other boat owner they were off. Or at least that was the plan. They didn't get very far – only a few metres – before the engine cut out. There were anxious moments as the motor started then stopped several times before they finally picked up speed and headed for the fishing grounds.

Having taken some photos of the proceedings, my next task was to buy prizes. As I feared, the shops along the Main Street were shut.

"When do the shops open?" I asked a policeman.

"9 a.m." The same time they were due to return.

However, as I walked back to the guest house to get something to eat, I discovered a shop due to open at 8 a.m. Perfect.

There wasn't much to choose from in the shop as I wanted prizes with a "fishy" theme, but I found four little fish ornaments: three glass and one wooden. I also bought a wooden spoon so all five participants would be prize-winners. With my adjudicator's hat on I decided each participant could receive only one prize.

I arrived back at the beach at 8.45 a.m. taking more photos as I walked along. I quickly discovered the landmarks I'd taken note of to identify the original launch site and returning point had changed. The large catamaran with "Welcome to Sri Lanka 2017" sail was nowhere in sight, and the men who had been pulling in the enormously long multi coloured fishing nets were gone. I saw the sand cliff was still there so walked towards it, stopping to chat to various locals along the way, answering the usual three questions. "Where you from?" "How long you stay here?" "Been here before?" I declined all the offers of boat trips and items to buy.

Realising I wasn't entirely sure where the boat launched from, I showed some photos of the fishing boat and catamaran I'd taken earlier. The responses I got all indicated I was in the right area, so I settled myself to watch for their return. It was a like the whale watching trip except rather than watching for a whale surfacing, I was watching for a small boat with an outboard motor. Several times I saw a boat approaching and walked towards it. Each time it was the wrong boat.

As 9 a.m. came and went, I wasn't concerned. This was Sri Lanka after all, and things don't always keep to our time scales. Also, one of the men I spoke to said, "Sometimes they a bit late."

Perhaps, I thought, the fishing was so good they were being given extra time. Or perhaps the fishing wasn't good at the original site, so they had gone elsewhere.

Seeing nothing approaching, I went for a walk to the breakwater and collected shells, every so often casting my eyes seaward. I started walking back and was thrilled to see another boat come into sight. This was them! So I thought anyway, until I saw the boat had only two people onboard.

I looked again at the photos with the breakwater and took other photos to judge whether I was in the right area. Everything looked right.

10 a.m. came and went. I was now decidedly worried. Had the dodgy outboard motor failed? Were they bobbing around somewhere in the middle of the ocean? Should I go back to the guest house and report them missing?

I walked back towards the road trying again to notice something to confirm I was in the right place, but nothing brought back memories. I hadn't been paying attention as we walked to the beach together. I remembered Jacqui mentioning the name of a hotel they stayed in once – "Silver Sands" and asked for directions to this.

"No not here. Way along beach," I was told, so my memory of the name of the hotel was wrong I reasoned.

Finally, I decided there was nothing more I could do. I should return to the guest house. On my way back, I saw a man I'd seen earlier sitting in a little hut. As with everyone else I met, he called me, and I looked up ready with my reply of "no thank you" to whatever boat trip he offered. I saw the expected broad smiling face but also was met by the unexpected sight of his deliberately exposed private parts. On top of now feeling very worried about the others, this was the last thing I needed. What kind of area had I found myself in? Was I going to be OK walking back to the guest house? This year there had been some incidents involving tourists as they made their way to and from the guest house, usually being grabbed by passing motor cyclists. Douglas didn't like me walking on my own and here I was – on my own.

I quickly passed and got to the road and started walking towards the turn-off for the guest house. Even after walking for a while, I didn't recognise any of my surrounding. I walked on and on, still without recognition. I'd really messed up.

Eventually familiarity returned, and I was pleased to find the required turn-off. I walked up this road and soon George came into view. He was looking for me, and Douglas was heading in another direction along the alternative road we often walked. They were worried about me.

I started running to catch Douglas. When I turned a corner, I saw him in the distance. Several times, I stopped running, cupped my hands round my mouth and shouted his name, hoping he would hear me. He didn't. I hoped he would look round and spot me before he turned onto the main road, but he didn't. On I ran, getting hotter and hotter and finally caught up with him, breathless. By now my face was like a beetroot. I was so relieved to catch him, knowing he would be as worried about me as I had been about him. I had no idea how I got so lost on the beach.

Back to the guest house we headed and, on the way, met George who had wisely decided not to let me out of his sight again.

Once reunited I heard about the fishing trip. Unfortunately, it wasn't nearly as good as a similar trip Douglas and George had been on two years previously. This time the water was choppy, they couldn't see any fish swimming in the coral and only one fish was caught, by Jacqui, much to her surprise. The boat owner had caught some unusual creatures, but overall it was a disappointing trip.

And so, to the presentation of prizes. Officially, Jacqui won all categories except the wooden spoon. However, we decided to award prizes for other categories:

1. **For catching a fish** – Jacqui

2. **The bravest person** was awarded to Paul who had turned distinctly green in the choppy water. (Thank goodness I didn't go.)

3. **The wettest person** award went to Sylvia whose position in the boat ensured she got a good soaking when the boat tossed and turned as it ploughed through the waves.

4. **The person who broke the wooden bench on the boat** was

awarded to George, though to be fair, Douglas apparently had a part to play in this too.

5. The wooden spoon was awarded to Douglas not for any specific reason other than I'd decided everyone had to receive a prize.

In the afternoon, Douglas and I went for a walk to find out how I'd managed to end up in the wrong part of the beach. It wasn't a difficult mystery to solve. On returning to the beach with the prizes I turned right instead of left! I have no idea how I managed to make such a mistake, especially as this route was completely different, taking me through the beach fish market. The breakwater I walked to, looked the same but was further along the coast. No wonder I didn't see the boats I expected. My own daftness continues to surprise me.

As we'd a late breakfast none of us wanted lunch, but instead went for a coffee – I suppose like an afternoon tea, without all the cakes or tea.

"I need to have an ice cream after all the trauma of this morning," I informed the others. After some debate, they agreed to stick to coffee as planned. Mind you, to each coffee glass was added a liqueur and topped off with ice cream!

"I love ice cream," I remarked.

"We've noticed," I heard three voices reply in unison.

"I don't love *all* ice cream though. Given a choice, I wouldn't select chocolate flavour, and I wouldn't bother again with the bright green coloured, green-tea flavour I was tempted to try in Hong Kong."

"Douglas, do you remember taking David, Andrew and me to an ice cream shop in Huntington Beach, California where you got food poisoning many years before?" I asked.

"Let's get the facts straight. It wasn't that particular shop, but one in the same chain in another town," he corrected.

"OK, but it was just as well we didn't see the ice cream before we ordered it, or we might have had second thoughts. We ordered small cones and were so relieved we hadn't asked for large ones. The small ones were *huge*."

"Do you want them dipped?" we were asked.

"I'll have chocolate please," Andrew said.

"Cherry for me," Douglas added while I opted for butterscotch dip and David kept his plain.

Dipping took place but as the lady had her back to us, we didn't see anything until she turned round, cones in hands. She must have seen our jaws drop. We were gob-smacked!

The cherry dip was the brightest red you can imagine, and the butterscotch, fluorescent orange. I wondered what chemicals created such vibrancy with only the chocolate appearing as anticipated. Although the colours were off-putting, not eating the ice creams was out of the question as far as I was concerned and fortunately, they tasted much better than they looked! Best of all, we didn't get food poisoning as Douglas had done all those years before.

Several years later when in Tobermory, Canada, with David and Andrew, we were again surprised by the ice cream we were served.

Douglas and I decided to share a 3-scoop tub, while David and Andrew felt they could only manage a single scoop each. They had eaten a huge breakfast.

"Can we have a 3-scoop and two single scoop tubs please?" I asked.

The lad behind the counter looked at me blankly.

Douglas realised the problem, and corrected my terminology, "Can we have a 3-scoop dish and two single scoop dishes please?"

The 3-scoop "dish" (which looked exactly like our tubs) was prepared first and single scoop ones that followed looked no smaller.

"Are these single scoop dishes?" I asked, thinking he had misunderstood.

"Yea," he assured me.

Astonished, we took our purchases outside. "This is more like four scoops of ice cream!" David said as he ate from his single scoop dish. He was right. Although we made every effort, none of us could finish what we'd bought. One single scoop dish between the four of us would have been enough and we felt very wasteful throwing the leftovers in the bin.

"This reminds me of one of the host families I stayed with in Canada when touring with Ayrshire Fiddle Orchestra," Andrew said. "They took me to an ice cream shop, and I got something I hadn't had before, a half-litre tub of ice cream. Each in the host family ordered one litre portions which they happily ate. I couldn't believe anyone could eat so much ice cream. while I struggled to get through half the quantity! I finished it though as I didn't want to appear rude by leaving any."

Where has my love for ice cream come from? I don't know, but I remember my first knickerbocker glory and what a treat it was. I was thirteen years old and on a family holiday in Gullane, a seaside town on the Firth of Forth in Scotland. I remember family times on the beautiful sandy beach, sheltered by windbreaks we erected between the sand dunes. It seemed a very long walk over dunes to get to the beach. On the first day of our holiday my youngest sister Clare's glasses couldn't be found when she returned from a swim in the sea. She needed to wear them all the time. I remember digging and digging in the fine sand trying to find them and feeling downcast when I didn't succeed. I wonder if they resurfaced or if they've sunk deeper and deeper during the many years since the fateful day.

As always Mum took me, and sisters Jean and Sheila, out individually for a treat during our holiday. Clare and her twin sister Jennifer were only three at the time and sadly I don't remember their treats.

My treat on this holiday was to go to a café – an old-fashioned traditional café with square tables covered with red and white checked tablecloths. We sat on rickety wooden chairs. I could choose any ice cream sundae from the menu. I hadn't had a sundae before and when the knickerbocker glory in its tall tapered glass along with a long-handled spoon arrived at our table I'm sure my eyes must have popped out of my head. In the glass were layers of tinned fruit, scoops of ice cream and strawberry sauce, finished off with swirling cream rising well above the top rim of the glass. Additional strawberry sauce on the cream dripped down the outside of the glass. Finally, a red maraschino cherry had been carefully positioned on the very top of the cream. And so, the eating began.

"I wonder if any of the ice cream in these tales was 'real ice cream'," Douglas contemplated. "I suspect much of it was 'industrial'."

Douglas and I learned about this difference when we were on a package tour holiday to Lake Garda, Italy. It was our first holiday without David and Andrew. We left home with a very strange feeling – something just didn't seem right. However, we consoled ourselves as we acknowledged how very fortunate we'd been to have had them on holiday with us for so many years. They were by then 20 and 18 years old after all.

"Alessandro, our tour guide, made the holiday," I recalled. "Right from the moment we met him at the airport we were entertained by his non-stop talking. One of our day trips included a stop in Verona. During our free time, we went to Juliet's balcony, from Shakespeare's famous *Romeo and Juliet* play. Although Verona was the setting for the tragedy, Alessandro told us the balcony was a hoax created when tourists started coming to Verona in the 19th century asking to see it."

"Don't go inside Arena di Verona (the Roman Amphitheatre)," Alessandro advised. "Just look at the outside. Too much restoration inside and no longer authentic looking. Better to go to the Coliseum in Rome."

Thus, the Coliseum has been added to our bucket list.

His advice wasn't all negative though and we saw some amazing buildings and of course there was ice cream.

"You want ice cream? Only one shop you should go," Alessandro had told us before we got off the coach. "Go to ice cream shop near Arena di Verona. It's *real* ice cream, not industrial," he told us, emphasising "real". How he tut-tutted "industrial" ice cream. "Industrial ice cream is heaped high in plastic containers, so customers are tempted by colours. Real ice cream is made in small quantities and kept in steel containers with lids so you can't see. It's made with fruit only when it's in season. Fig ice cream is only available one week in the year."

There was no way we would return to the coach before sampling the "real" ice cream. In the shop, as we'd been told, was a row of stainless-steel lids hiding the contents of the containers. Only a list of varieties influenced our choice which is just as well as otherwise Douglas may not have chosen his favourite mint chocolate chip. When his ice cream was handed over, we couldn't believe the brightness of green colour; it was on a par with the red and orange ice creams in California. It was so refreshingly good to eat though. We'd discovered how much we rely on our eyes when choosing tasty treats.

"Have you ever refused ice cream?" I was asked.

"Yes, believe it or not. Before going on a tour in India, I'd been advised not to eat any, as there was no guarantee about how sterile the ingredients were, when it was made or how well frozen the ice cream was kept before reaching us. Trying to avoid an upset stomach, I followed this advice to the letter meaning I said "No thank you" when offered the final course of our dinner on the train between Kalka and Delhi. It made me realise how much I was missing ice cream though."

And yet, I even cancelled an order of ice cream during an Icelandic break.

We'd been on a tour to see the Gullfoss Waterfall and other amazing sights on the island and got back to the hotel at 7 p.m., much later than we normally ate. David and Andrew were aged 10 and 8 at the time and were tired so we opted to eat in the hotel rather than getting a taxi into town. I wasn't wanting a big meal so opted for soup followed by ice cream.

The soup however came with a basketful of lovely rolls – the kind once started eating, it's hard to stop, and I didn't stop. David's meal included a delicious side salad which he didn't want so I ate this too. As a result, I was full so cancelled my ice cream order.

I watched as David and Andrew tucked into their ice creams. I was proud of myself resisting the temptation to have a taste. After all I was full, I told myself.

But when they put their spoons down, defeated by the large quantity served. I had to review the situation. After all, it's terrible to waste good food and it would be awful if the staff at the hotel thought David and Andrew hadn't enjoyed their deserts. Added to that, I hadn't eaten for a few minutes so perhaps a little space had made itself available in my stomach – a "left-over ice cream" size of space.

So yes, I have cancelled an order for ice cream but in the end wasn't deprived of my love for the sweet, cold delight and in truth, this was my second ice cream of the day. In the afternoon while on the tour we stopped at a gift shop and tearoom. While most others on the tour sampled the cakes, which gave the place it's nickname, "Yummy Cake Town", our family indulged in enormous ice cream cones.

"Enough chatting about ice cream," Douglas said. "We've unfinished business to attend to."

He was right. We returned to the jeweller for my earrings.

"Please take a seat," the jeweller said, moving the seats to let us sit down. We recognised this as a prelude to a sales pitch.

"Just two or three minutes," he said and disappeared into the adjoining grocery shop.

The two or three minutes came and went, and we were left in solitary confinement for what seemed like an eternity wondering how we would avoid being persuaded to buy jewellery we didn't want when he returned. He took so long, I thought he must have gone to get the earrings from whoever was carrying out the repair.

Eventually he returned, opened a drawer behind him and picked up a box, opened it and low and behold, there were my earrings. I've no idea what he was doing when he abandoned us.

Sitting in trepidation we answered the normal introductory niceties. Douglas took the initiative and as soon as possible asked, "How much do the repairs cost?"

Silence followed and we waited, anticipating the sales pitch of "very good prices" for necklaces etc. Suspense built as the silence continued. He started to gently tilt his head from side to side, contemplating.

Finally, he spoke. "No charge."

Still we waited for the catch.

"Tell your friends about this shop," he concluded. No sales pitch.

We were stunned but managed to quickly rise from our seats, shake his hand, thank him profusely, accept his apology for keeping us waiting and left the shop delighted.

Later, I recalled a final sobering ice cream tale from Australia. My cousin Lorna and her husband Dallas took us on a wonderful day trip which included Tidbinbilla Nature Reserve.

In a fenced off section of the reserve we saw koalas. They were being reintroduced to the area as all the koalas had been killed in a bush fire in 2003.

We met a couple who were very pleased to tell us about a snake they had seen not far from where we were. They showed us a photo of it, Dallas identifying it as a Tiger Snake. They asked if it was dangerous or poisonous and Dallas made it very clear to them – it was. He later told us they must have been far too close to the snake to have been able to take such a photograph.

A short while later, we met them again. They told us they were too scared to stay any longer in case of another snake encounter. So, while we didn't personally see a Tiger Snake, our claim to fame was we saw a photo of one taken just a short distance away.

When we went to the lakes nearby, we were on the lookout for another animal – a platypus. We knew they were immensely shy creatures and were pleased very few people were around who like us might scare them away. As we walked, I found myself seeing all sorts of ideal places where, if I was a platypus, I would have been hiding. On reaching each, I was disappointed. The conclusion I drew from this: I clearly don't think like a platypus!

Yes, I was disappointed not to see a platypus, but I knew it was highly unlikely. In the 17 years Lorna and Dallas had been living in Australia, Dallas had only once seen one – the previous year when Lorna's brother Hugh visited from Scotland.

So why have I been writing about all this wildlife in a chapter about ice cream? Well, as we walked round the reserve there were other things to see too. There were wise sayings and one related to ice cream which was clearly of interest to me. There was a row of posts next to the path. On each post was a card and on each card was one of the following lines to explain the importance of rocks in relation to ice cream. Here is what

I read:
- No rocks, no ice cream
- No rocks means no minerals
- No minerals, no productive soils
- No soil, no grasses
- No grasses? No cows
- No cows, no milk
- No milk, no ice cream
- No ice cream?

End of quote.
What a thought-provoking message for all ice cream lovers!

Wildlife, weather and a manicure

in-between

Unusually the Sri Lankan morning sky was overcast but this brought the advantage of a cooler start to the day. Over breakfast we were treated to more wildlife sightings in the canal. A large monitor lizard swam very close by before climbing up onto the bank opposite.

A floating island of palm branches moved towards us on the slowly flowing water. On it, two birds stood like statues. A perfect photo built in my mind. Once the floating island came closer, I would capture this along with a white bird with a fish in its beak standing on the opposite bank, plus the hump of the lizard which had returned to the water. I lined the photo shot up and was about a second away from perfection when away soared the birds from their floating transport followed by the bird with its fish. What patience nature photographers must have. I'm sure they would have been more sensible than me, taking multiple photos as opposed to waiting as I did for "perfection" but ending up with nothing.

"Another photo missed," I said sadly to Douglas. "Just like when we were on the lagoon boat trip with George and Sylvia last time we were here."

A local fisherman was standing in his traditional long narrow wooden boat working with his net. I video recorded him meticulously pulling in the net and removing the few small fish he'd caught. He slowly prepared his net for reuse but as this was taking ages, I stopped recording. Then I saw a marvellous sight. He threw his round fishing net upwards. It spun through the air before landing in a perfect circle on the water's surface. If only I'd kept filming. Fortunately, the "footage" remains in my memory. So many other missed shots are lost forever.

Sometimes on holiday I treat myself to a manicure. Unfortunately, the outcomes thus far have ranged from disastrous and painful, to not quite so disastrous. Some would say I'm a glutton for punishment, but Sylvia and I planned to go for a pedicure and manicure at the end of our holiday. I was hoping things would be different this time. However, my nails had grown so much I couldn't wait any longer.

After a morning at the beach, when we watched a chipmunk running nimbly up and down the coconut palms and across the parasols, I decided to try a nail salon on the Main Street. But most definitely *not* the one where Sylvia and I had a pedicure two years previously. There we'd suffered torture never again to be repeated. Douglas and I passed the torture chamber the previous night and saw a group of tourists looking at the price list and both of us turned to them and said, "No – don't go there!" They looked a bit bemused but hopefully got the message.

The alternative salon Douglas and I went into was welcomingly cooled by air-conditioning. This was an immediate plus compared to the afore-mentioned horror chamber where we longed for some to cool our fevered brows.

"Can I have a manicure but no nail varnish, please?" I enquired in this new salon.

"Yes," I was delighted to hear.

"How long will it take?" Douglas asked.

"15 minutes." I was surprised to hear how quick she was going to be.

"I'll go for a walk and meet you back here," Douglas said.

"Why not stay here in the cool. The sofa looks comfortable and it's very hot outside now," I suggested.

"Good idea," he said on reflection.

I was shown where to sit, and the procedure began. Hands bathed in a glass bowl of water with a luxurious pale orange additive. So far so good. The filing began.

"I like my nails short," I explained.

She filed my first thumb.

"It OK?" she asked showing me the thumb.

"No, shorter please."

A second and third time the same question was asked, and I gave the same reply, pointing and trying to show her how long I wanted the nails to be. I wanted to take over the filing to demonstrate but suddenly I had an inspirational thought. "Douglas, can you come and show her the length of your nails?"

But showing her his nails didn't have the desired effect.

"You want manicure too?"

"No!" was the horrified reply and it took me all my powers of persuasion to stop him running out of the salon. Communication was clearly an issue.

She left her seat and returned with nail clippers. Good idea I thought, though was surprised she didn't get gardening shears instead as I felt my nails were so long.

I let her continue without interruption, clipping, filing, cuticle tidying up and buffing, all the while looking at her beautifully manicured nails. She sat back and asked once again, "It OK?"

I suspected things were not OK, but not wanting to judge unfairly I thought it best to put my glasses on to ensure I wasn't seeing things. Suffice to say, glasses didn't solve the problem. My nails, in no way, shape or form remotely resembled the beautifully manicured nails on her hands. Mine were all different lengths, some curved, others straight and cuticles little improved. Yes, I appreciate I'd presented her with a challenge, but I thought it would be very satisfying for her to achieve the transformation I expected. There was no one else in the salon waiting so there was no pressure on her time.

The pointing out of necessary improvements began. She happily did the renovation work asked for but any sense of pampering I'd hoped for was well and truly lost when I felt I'd become her teacher. Even Douglas couldn't believe what he was hearing me request as it was all basic common sense. Anyway, by the end of it, my nails looked better than when I entered the salon. They were no longer annoying me as they certainly had done in their previous long state.

"You should have asked her where she got her nails done and gone there," George wisely said when I recounted the tale later. I'm still longing for perfect, immaculately manicured fingernails. Perhaps a new venue on another holiday will find my dream realised.

"Here's the discount card back for CIB we borrowed," Jacqui said when she and Paul came to join us for a game of cards. I was so pleased she had borrowed it, but disappointment followed when she dropped a bombshell.

"But it's not a discount card. It's a points card."

"I wonder if I will receive statements of the points accumulated?" I joked. (PS: at time of publication, no such notification has been received and I have resigned myself to visualising all the points floating around unclaimed somewhere in the IT ether or some computer system in Sri Lanka.)

It was nearly dark and suddenly we became aware of a noise overhead. It was fruit bats communicating with each other as they flew. They were enormous – bigger than crows. I tried to take photos as they appeared in the patches of sky between the silhouettes of the trees but misjudged when to "click" leading to another wildlife photographic hiccup.

My last successful photo of the day was more straightforward as the subjects didn't move. Kapok or ceiba trees grew in the guest house garden, from which seed pods dangled at different stages of maturity. The pods over time turn brown, ultimately bursting open revealing silky kapok fibres inside. My focus was on these open pods, revealing to me the origin of the buoyant kapok filling which I'd previously heard of but known nothing about.

"It's been very hot today, not at all what we expected at breakfast time."

And so, a relaxing conversation began, interspersed with us debating whose turn it was to deal the next hand of cards.

"I heard on the radio a list of things differentiating us UK citizens from others around the world," I began. "We supposedly apologise far more often than other people. I know I'm guilty of this."

"Mum," David once said to me. "Did you just say 'sorry' to the cupboard?"

"Oh yes, so I did. Well I bumped into it, so it deserved an apology."

Another differentiation identified is our ability and need to queue and our annoyance with anyone who doesn't do likewise. But top of the list is our ability to bring the topic of weather into just about every conversation. I suppose it's a neutral, inoffensive topic easily spoken about even with strangers. It's easy to say, "Hello, lovely day," or "Hi. It's good it's stopped raining" or "Good morning. What a windy day – good for the washing though. I love hanging washing outside and watching it blow and oh the delight of bringing it back indoors, dry and smelling fresh."

We found ourselves comparing experiences of holidaying in caravans. Sometimes it was so hot inside we sat outside late into the evening hoping it would cool down. Only once did we come home from the caravan earlier than planned because we'd seen enough rain for one holiday. Most of the time we adapted to weather and no matter what had a great time.

But it's not just in Bonnie[16] Scotland where it rains a lot at times. On one occasion when in Hong Kong lecturing, there was constant heavy rain, way beyond anything I'd experienced there before. I could have done with having wellington boots with me, but instead I had sandals. The pavements and roads were like rivers and my sandals were lined with a material which didn't dry out overnight. The lecturing schedule was so tight there was no opportunity to nip out and buy more appropriate footwear. In the mornings, I dreaded putting my feet into these wet articles. With constantly wet feet I couldn't help but think how awful it must have been for the poor soldiers who got trench foot during World War One.

Douglas on the other hand, on an earlier trip to Hong Kong had to deal with different weather – a scorching hot day in Macau. He, David and Andrew had gone there one day while I was working, and the younger generation couldn't believe the sight of Douglas' shirt.

"You know how in cowboy films the cowboys' shirts have sweaty patches not just underarm, but front and back too? Well, Dad looked *exactly* like that," they told me later.

"One place we expected rain but got wind instead was in Reykjavik," Douglas said.

"Yes, in the morning although the sun was shining, it was zero degrees with a very cold wind blowing. We walked to Hallgrímskirkja Church where we sheltered inside the bright interior, admiring the three differently sized organs and the beautiful stained-glass windows. We were disappointed not to have the challenge of climbing the stairs in the tower but instead had to use the lift to reach the roof where the views of Reykjavik were amazing. The wind was howling through the many openings in the structure, so we quickly took some photos before heading back down.

Back at the hotel we boarded a minibus driven by our guide on the

16 Bonnie is Scottish for "beautiful" or "attractive".

Golden Circle tour. As we travelled, we admired the fantastic scenery – the flat plains contrasting with the rugged mountain formations. The sun shone, and everything looked great. We saw Mount Heckler, the volcano which had erupted only two months previously. The now solidified lava formed a black line through the snow.

We realised the wind was strengthening. The driver slowed to a crawl because the minibus was being buffeted so much. A trailer, blown over and off the road, lay abandoned.

We stopped at Grímsnes to see the volcanic crater lake, Kerið. We'd to walk up its steep side to the rim of the now dormant volcano to see the lake inside.

"Be careful," the guide warned us. "It's very windy so hold onto your hats – and especially hold onto the children."

The wind was now horrendously strong.

Douglas and I held the hand of David (10) and Andrew (8) respectively while pushing our whole weight backwards to stop ourselves being blown up the hill more quickly than we wanted to walk. It was hard to feel in control. Through the wind I tried to shout words of reassurance to Andrew, but I admit it was a very alarming experience.

We quickly realised it was too much for the young ones. Andrew was scared. David's hat had flown off his head, over the rim of the volcano far above us and into the crater. The fact the snug fitting hat came off was astonishing as it was a cosy winter baseball type hat with closely fitting flaps down his neck and over his ears. It was no match to the wind that day. Unfortunately, it was David's favourite hat, affection-ately called his "Deputy Dawg" hat, which his Uncle David had given him.

We took the boys back to the bus and Douglas and I tried again, this time walking another route hoping the wind would be less severe. At the rim, we managed to take photos of the frozen water in the crater. Here Douglas discovered his gloves (brand new ones) had been ripped out of his pocket by the wind and were nowhere to be seen. Presumably they had joined David's hat in the crater. Yes, this sightseeing stop was quite an experience.

We drove on and stopped at the Haukadalur geothermal area to see the Geysir and Strokkur geysers. It was a little less windy though Andrew was scared when we got out of the minibus. Some of the others in the group didn't get out. As we turned to take Andrew back a lovely lady offered to take him with her to the bus and look after him, giving him a sweet as she did so. Meanwhile the rest of us headed for the geysers.

We expected to see massive spouts of water coming out from the ground and shooting up towards the sky. Instead as soon as the water poked itself out from the ground it was blown horizontally so no vertical fountain display for us.

Our next stop was at Gullfoss waterfall.

"There's a path down to the falls," we were reassured by the guide. But he added, "It's dangerous." Douglas, David and I got out of the minibus, Andrew understandably not wanting to put a foot outside. Thankfully, we quickly realised we were sheltered from the wind and the scenery looked wonderful, so we persuaded him to join us.

By now most of our group were ahead and seemed to be making good progress despite the dangers of the icy path, so we followed. In places the path was very slippery. We would have felt safer had there been a fence between us, and the sheer drop to the icy water below. The walk was one of life's challenges we told ourselves.

At the end of the path we were rewarded with magnificent views of the falls and snow-covered hills that surround them. Along the river bank the snow had been formed into wonderful caverns, ridges and overhangs by the water tumbling in the fast-flowing river and spray from the falls. We think we saw the falls at their best with the sun shining and forming rainbows in the spray. As we stood in awe looking at the sight, we forgot about the dangers experienced earlier.

On a stop on our return journey in the minibus, we saw steam rising from a crack in the pavement. It was escaping from an underground hot water pipe. Something else we'd never seen before. We're only used to frozen water causing burst water pipes.

We were much later arriving back at the hotel because the wind continued, making the driving very difficult and the only way to drive safely, was slowly.

"Today it's Icelandic window weather," the guide told us. "The sun-drenched landscape looks beautiful when inside looking out of windows, but behind windows is where it's best to stay, in the shelter of the house. The tour was nearly cancelled today, and even though it went ahead, it was nearly cut short because of the wind."

This explained the many phone calls the driver received.

Despite the extreme weather we experienced I'm glad we didn't stay indoors looking out, as I wouldn't have missed our trip for the world.

The next day we had a completely different experience. The tour was to end at the airport in time for our flight to New York but included time to swim outdoors in the Blue Lagoon.

"Ninety per cent of the power in Iceland is produced by hydro schemes, the other 10 per cent is thermal energy," the tour guide told us. "The underground hot water is above 100 degrees C and is converted into electricity. This water is full of salt and minerals. Many years previously, when the water had been through the electricity producing process, it flowed out onto the porous lava rock where it drained away. However, the salts and minerals blocked up the pores in the rock and a lake formed. People started coming to bathe in the lake, finding the water good for skin problems. Because of its popularity, a new lagoon, The Blue Lagoon, was formed using fresh underground water – not water discharged from the power station."

It was fantastic being in the hot water. Every now and then we'd to wet our hair and faces with the hot water to heat them up because of the icy cold air. The water was milky-blue, and we couldn't see our hands if they were more than a few inches under the water surface. Wondering what we were standing on, I brought some grains to the surface. It was rough black volcanic sand.

Steam was rising from the surface of the water and the further we walked, the more eerily quiet it got. There was so much steam we almost lost sight of the Blue Lagoon Centre building. Every so often, we walked through an even warmer patch of water. Some patches were so hot we quickly about turned and made our way back to slightly less hot water.

We walked through a cave where one of the walls of rock felt slimy. But it wasn't slime. The build-up of the salts had produced this ultra-smooth finish.

"Let's go to the natural steam room," someone suggested.

To get to it meant leaving the hot water and walking a short distance through the icy cold air from the top of the stairs to the wooden door over the cave entrance.

Once in the cave, we couldn't see a thing, it was so dark and steamy. We could literally only stay there for a few minutes (if that) because of the heat. The others went out of the cave first. At this point, I made a big mistake. "After you," I politely said to a couple of elderly ladies.

I couldn't believe how slowly they walked! The walkway was narrow and there was no way I could pass them as they chatted happily to each other. Remember the air temperature was freezing and I was wearing only my swimming costume. I don't think I've ever come so close to wishing I could push someone out of my way as in those moments. I was desperate to get back into the hot water of the lagoon. Fortunately, I managed to restrain myself from any misdemeanour – just!

In contrast, when we arrived in New York from Iceland the next day, we found ourselves in an Eastertime heat wave. We'd checked the weather forecast before packing our suitcases but discovered American weather-forecasters, like those in the UK, don't always get it right. Never in my wildest dreams did I expect to be wondering on our first day if I should buy shorts for David and Andrew to wear.

How quickly weather can change though. No shorts were required the next day as it was cold and very wet; we got soaked to the skin. David and Andrew's black leather shoes were in such a mess by the end of our time in the city we'd a good reason to give them the experience of sitting on a shoe shiner's high seat before making our way back to the airport. It was wonderful how those shoes shone by the end of the polishing, brushing and buffing making them ready for returning to school when we got home.

"You went to Iceland again, didn't you?" came the question from our friends listening to our tale.

"Yes. For a long time I'd wanted to see the aurora borealis and expert advice was March 2014 was going to offer the highest likelihood of seeing the Northern Lights, better than it had been for many years or likely to be for years to come," I explained, "so we booked a three-night short break."

When we left home heading for Edinburgh Airport, the sun was splitting the sky and it was remarkably warm for March. A great start to our holiday. The drive there was straightforward, and we soon arrived and set about unpacking our belongings before the car was taken to the carpark.

"My warm jacket isn't here," Douglas said despondently. We knew it couldn't possibly be in his suitcase as we were flying with an economy airline and just had small cabin sized suitcases with us.

"Because it was so warm, I didn't put my jacket on when packing the car, and therefore didn't need to take it off before driving as I usually do," he explained.

We knew he would need a jacket in Iceland, and a *warm* one. There was no time to go to any shops in Edinburgh.

"We'll be able buy a jacket in one of the Duty-Free shops at the airport," I assured him.

This promise was one I couldn't keep.

"Look at these ridiculously high prices," he said. "Ridiculous for us anyway. There seems only to be designer shops here. Why aren't there cheaper shops like in Glasgow Airport?"

Finally, he spotted a hoodie for the upcoming Glasgow Commonwealth Games which he optimistically opted for.

"You'll need more than that, but we can buy a waterproof to wear over it in Reykjavik tomorrow morning," I said.

This we did, and the problem was solved.

We repeated the Golden Circle tour, but it was very different to our earlier experience. Firstly, we were in one of several 53 or so seater coaches doing the tour in convoy, rather than the single 19-seater minibus we initially experienced. Plus, we weren't battered by the wind either. Nor did we stop to see Kerið, the volcanic crater lake.

When we and the other coach loads of people got to Gullfoss to see the amazing waterfalls, we found there were official walkways to follow at the top of the cliff with safety railings to look over to the falls below. The icy path we'd walked down to get close to the waterfalls all those years before was no longer an option. This was disappointing and we missed the sense of adventure previously experienced.

I could see the sense of wooden walkways and safety railings, but it was safer to walk beside rather than on them as they were icy and dangerously slippery in places.

On reflection, I'm glad we went to Iceland in 2000, giving us the chance to experience more of the naturalness of the island. It was so much quieter as there were far fewer tourists. The hotel we stayed in this time had been fully booked since a year before – something unheard of until recently. I just hope the island manages to keep a good balance between dealing with increasing numbers of tourists and showing the island off at its wonderful best.

We were looking forward to our night tour to see the Northern Lights. A coach would collect us from the hotel and drive us away from the city where the best sightings of the aurora borealis were expected. We'd been given screeds of instructions, including the need to take plenty of layers of clothes because it would be very cold standing outside the bus. As far as photographs were concerned, we were advised not to use filters on the camera and to take long exposure shots using a tripod to keep the camera steady.

There was one further instruction we'd to follow: ask at the hotel in the late afternoon if the trip would take place. If there was no chance of the aurora borealis being seen, the trip would be cancelled. If the trip was cancelled, we would be booked on a trip on the following night. I liked this contingency plan.

On the first afternoon we were not hopeful because there was total cloud cover above us in Reykjavik. Our fears were confirmed, the tour was cancelled. But there was tomorrow, we told ourselves, remembering the sightings had been amazing so far this season.

We'd another tour the next day, another return trip to the Blue Lagoon. There were differences here too. The facilities had been upgraded.

"Look," I said to Douglas, pointing. "The narrow walkway to the sauna in the cave had been widened! Maybe someone less restrained than me did actually push someone out of the way in their bid to get into the hot water!"

Another new experience was swimming in the hot lagoon water while it was snowing heavily, greatly reducing the visibility while cold snowflakes landed gently on our heads and eyelashes, some tickling as they managed to get into our eyes and up our nostrils.

Back at the hotel reception, a sign told us the Northern Lights tour was cancelled again.

"Is there was any chance conditions will improve and the tour re-scheduled?" I asked hopefully.

"No," was the answer I expected, but hoped not to hear.

The aurora borealis therefore remained hidden behind the clouds and we didn't see the hoped-for spectacle. Receiving a refund for the tour was little consolation, but that's the unpredictability of the weather.

"Las Vegas in 2001 was the complete opposite to the cold we experienced in Iceland. We acclimatised to the warmer weather as we toured from San Francisco and Los Angeles. But driving inland the temperatures reached new heights for us. 111°F (over 43°C) was *way* above our highest temperatures in Scotland," Douglas said, taking my memories back to that holiday.

"*You* in Las Vegas? But David and Andrew would only have been 11 and 9 then, and you took them to a gamblers' mecca!" was the incredulous response.

"Yes," said Douglas happily defending his recommendation. "It's ideal for non-gambling families too. I'd visited Las Vegas many years before and seen the spectacular hotels on The Strip, all vying to outdo each other's design, with amazing light and water features. There's even a simulated erupting volcano. For us it was a great and inexpensive base for touring. Gambling wasn't on the agenda – honestly!"

We stayed at the Circus Circus Hotel, and as we came out of the outdoor swimming pool, we could immediately feel the water evaporating from our skin. The tiles were so hot we felt our feet were burning to a frazzle as we hopped, skipped and jumped and vocally ouch-ed our way across the short distance between the pool and the sun loungers, trying to have as little contact as possible between our feet and the tiles below them.

Before walking along the Las Vegas Strip, we filled bottles with icy cold water from the water dispensers in the hotel to ensure we kept ourselves hydrated. However, we'd only walked from the front door of the hotel to the pavement beyond before the water was no longer icy cold but already warm and soon became hot. We took every opportunity on our walk to refill the bottles with cold water, replacing any remaining unpleasant to drink hot water.

To cool down, we became expert at pouring water down the backs of our necks. Initially the cold water on our hot skin gave us a fright as it trickled down our skin, but it was worth it. The relief was inevitably short lived lasting only a few moments so was often repeated.

After a few days in Las Vegas we continued our tour driving to Bishop. On the way we passed through Death Valley National Park where one of the temperature gauges we saw indicated it was "only" 103°F (just under 40°C).

Driving through some of the high passes, we became aware of a burning smell and began worrying about its origin. Earlier, we'd switched off the air-conditioning, obeying signs along the roadside, to prevent overheating. We wondered if we were going to have to get water from one of huge water tanks containing water specifically for car and truck radiators at the side of the road. Conversation stalled as we each tried to cope with being in an extremely hot car while wanting to keep our thoughts to ourselves about the possible implications of breaking down here – in the middle of nowhere.

"I think the burning smell is from the brakes," Douglas concluded after a while. Stuck behind a very cautiously driven car whose driver kept braking as we drove down the steep passes, Douglas had to do likewise. We stopped for a while to let the car in front get away. Once back in the car, the air-conditioning was put back on and we were pleased the burning smell didn't return.

The temperature continued to drop as we left Death Valley further behind.

"I'll never forget walking back to the hotel after our evening meal in Bishop and wishing I'd put a jumper on as my arms were covered with goose-pimples. I didn't expect to feel chilly," I recalled. "A temperature gauge on a building confirmed a drop in temperature. It was 8 p.m. and the temperature was now *only* 80°F (just 26.67°C). A big drop in temperature, but still equivalent to a hot day-time temperature in Scotland. The goose-pimples proved I was more acclimatized to the heat than I'd realised."

"Right everyone: time to stop the card games and chat and call it a night. Remember we're leaving at 6 a.m. for our next two-day-away adventure."

Just as well one of us was sensible.

The sun setting in Negombo

Start of Tour No 2 and travelling memories

"Douglas – the alarm."

No reaction, so I try again, a bit louder, "Douglas – the alarm."

This time a startled response "What?"

"It's the alarm."

"I can't hear it."

He never hears it, initially anyway. It starts quietly and with each ring gets louder until I can bear it no longer. I've therefore become his "alarm alert-er". Generally, there's some fumbling and muttering before it's switched off. But this time Douglas was right, it wasn't the alarm. I'd imagined it!

"What time is it?" I asked.

He didn't hear me. I didn't think it appropriate to ask again.

I curled up once more wondering, as I often do, why I'm only able to get to sleep lying on my left side. After all, I don't feel any different lying on my right side. Even when telling myself not to be daft, that it's all in my mind, I inevitably find myself turning over onto my left side before falling sleep.

I continued to wonder what time it was. I knew the false alarm occurred after 3.45 a.m., as Douglas had wakened then and wakened me too. But I didn't know how long I'd then slept for before the self-inflicted awakening.

I listened to the familiar sound of a bird's whooping call outside, though had no idea the kind of bird making the sound. Shortly after, I heard the Muslim prayers emanating from the loudspeaker. One thing I knew I didn't miss were the cockerels, ensuring early morning awakenings two years previously in the other guest house.

Unable to sleep, I thought about other journeys and trips I'd been on.

My first big adventure was in June 1979 when I was 18. Jill, my great friend to this day, and I went on holiday touring the Highlands and

Islands of Scotland. We bought a package which included a travel pass for most boats, buses and trains in the region together with vouchers providing accommodation in Youth Hostels. The planning for the tour took hours as we poured over timetables we'd received: Lenzie to Glasgow on our way to Inverness, the islands of Orkney followed by Skye and Mull, with plenty of stopovers in between. Our itinerary was written out to the minute; our train to Inverness would arrive at 13.37 hours precisely.

Trains didn't always run to timetable and our third train of the holiday from Inverness and Culrain left 30 minutes late. The small village of Culrain was where our first Youth Hostel was: the converted Carbisdale Castle (which we were told was haunted).

We weren't worried about the late departure as we didn't have any connections to make. What worried us was Culrain was a "stop on request" station.

"How will we get the train to stop for us?" we asked the guard when he inspected our tickets.

"Don't worry," he said, our anxiousness obvious. "I'll make sure the train stops." And it did.

The next morning, we wanted to board a train at the same station. There were no buildings here, just a platform, and not a railway employee in sight. So again, we wondered how we would stop the train.

Much to our relief there was another couple of tourists already on the platform when we arrived. One literally waved his arms (vigorously) when the train came into view and sure enough the train stopped. It was like hailing a taxi or a bus though it required more exaggerated arm movements. But unlike buses or taxis there was only a handful of trains a day, and if this one hadn't stopped, we would have missed our bus and ferry connection to Orkney, our carefully planned itinerary ruined.

On another ferry route things didn't go so well. It was a very short crossing between Kyle of Lochalsh and Kyleakin. The Skye Bridge replaced the ferry service in 1995 but had the bridge been there we wouldn't have had such excitement on one particular night.

My cousin, Lindsay, was working in the Kyle of Lochalsh hotel. He wasn't at the hotel when we arrived to visit him but one of his friends, Cecil, said we could leave our rucksacks in his room. He would help us find him.

"No need to lock the door," he told us. "No one locks them here."

We eventually found Lindsay but a ferry crossing away – across the water in Kyleakin. Cecil having completed his mission, left us and we'd a great time talking to Lindsay hearing all about his work in the hotel.

At 4.45 p.m. Jill and I decided we'd better make our return ferry crossing to Kyle so we could collect our rucksacks before walking up the road to check in at the hostel.

When we got to Cecil's room the door to the room was now locked! We looked in all the places we thought Cecil might be but couldn't find him. We bought fish suppers to eat as it was teatime, we were hungry, and we thought it would fill in some time before Cecil returned. The fish suppers were horrible. Things weren't going well.

We thought we'd better go to the hostel and explain our situation. The warden wasn't at all helpful telling us, "You have until 10.30 p.m. to collect the rucksacks and get back to the hostel otherwise you will find the doors locked." He obviously couldn't have cared less about our predicament.

What was worrying us was Jill's rucksack contained the cleaning and storing fluid for her contact lenses. It was vital we got her rucksack. No disposable lenses in those days.

We decided to see if Cecil was in Kyleakin. We'd just walked onto the ferry when I found I didn't have my travel pass or the two postcards I'd bought earlier. The postcards were replaceable, unlike the travel pass which we required for the remainder of our holiday.

I rushed off the ferry and headed back to look for my missing property while Jill went to Kyleakin in search of Cecil. I returned to the few shops we'd visited but the missing items weren't in any of them. By this time, I was really worried, and decided as a last resort to go back to the hotel staffrooms. There I found my lost belongings lying on the floor of a bathroom. What a relief!

I met Jill who hadn't found Cecil and we returned to the staffrooms finally finding him.

"I didn't realise you were coming back for the rucksacks and decided I'd better lock the door." Despite this confusion we were relieved, returned to the hostel and checked in.

Had we stayed there we would have had a simple ending to the day. But no, we went out again, took the ferry across to Kyleakin and met up with Lindsay and his friends once more.

"It's 9.50 p.m.," I said. "Time for us to go."

At the jetty, we saw the ferry across the water at our destination a few minutes sail away. We started to get worried when it obviously wasn't leaving the jetty.

"The crew are on a break," someone told us.

The ferry finally left and arrived at 10.15 p.m. just 15 minutes before our 10.30 p.m. curfew. If it had left immediately after arriving and loading, there would have been enough time to get there. It became clear this wasn't going to happen.

"When will the ferry leave?" I asked the captain, and like the relaxed attitude of other locals, there seemed to be no rush. It was highly likely we would arrive at the hostel after the doors had been slammed shut and no doubt double and triple locked to ensure renegades like us were kept out.

I explained our predicament.

"I'll get my friend to drive you to the hostel," he told me, pointing to another passenger. This he did, and we made it – in the nick of time! I don't think I've ever been so pleased to be locked *inside* a building. And Jill was incredibly relieved to have her vital contact lens liquids once more.

I thought about another journey the family made on a bus in 2001; between Stansted and Gatwick Airports before leaving the UK on our way to San Francisco.

There weren't many people on the bus, but there were very few seats we could sit on. Confused? So were we, until we discovered many of the empty seats were soaking wet. There was something wrong with the air conditioning and water was pouring down from above.

The fun started when the bus moved. Rounding corners, the water flooded across the floor from one side of the bus to the other. When the bus accelerated the water headed to the back of the bus. And I'm sure you will have worked out what happened when the driver applied the brakes. Lifting our feet at the right time to avoid the oncoming wave had to be timed to perfection. This wave would have provided ideal indoor-surfing conditions had there been any surfers on board.

The four of us couldn't sit together. Douglas and I sat on seats at the aisles avoiding the wet seats beside the windows. David sat beside a very nice old lady and chatted away to her. I think he told her his 11-year life story.

Andrew sat beside a man but there wasn't much interaction between them. The man was engrossed with text messaging on his phone. Andrew fell asleep. At one point I looked round and saw Andrew's head had fallen over and was resting against the man's arm. Fortunately, the man didn't seem to mind and let him sleep on.

My mind flitted to 1987 when Douglas and I were in Spain on our honeymoon. We were on one of the local buses and, like Andrew, I fell asleep. I was sitting beside Douglas who was at the window. Like Andrew, I keeled over but, in my case, not against Douglas but across the aisle and onto the lap of the person on the seat on the other side of the aisle! Embarrassing or what?

The other passengers on the bus got a real fright – I'm sure thinking there was something seriously wrong with me, either death or some awful illness. As soon as my head made contact with the passenger's lap I wakened.

This was a situation which although embarrassing, wasn't as bad as it could have been. Imagine if it had happened in my hometown, where I know so many people? Imagine being constantly reminded of the incident by all those who heard about it? At least on a Spanish bus I knew I wouldn't meet any of the people again. I could safely walk along the roads for the rest of the holiday with my head held high.

In San Francisco we couldn't not go on the historic cable cars. After breakfast Douglas, David, Andrew and I walked down Powell St to its junction with Market St, where we bought three-day passes at the ticket booth before standing in the queue for the Powell-Hyde route. According to the tourist books, this was the best tram route to go on because of the steep Nob and Russian Hills. Importantly, we would also pass the famous zigzagging Lombard Street. We'd seen it in films, often with cars screeching round the corners. This was our chance to see it in real life.

We didn't have too long to wait before one arrived with space for us. We went to the section open to the elements, the boys and I sitting on the wooden benches looking out while Douglas stood on the running boards at our feet, hanging onto one of the poles. We parents were concerned it was too dangerous for the boys to stand, though needless to say that is what they really wanted to do.

As the tram moved, we soon discovered the wooden benches were very slippery to sit on. We found ourselves sliding into the people on either side of us as we slid up and down on the bench at speed, leaving Douglas stationary as we passed him first one way, then the other, while the tram went up and down the hills. We waved to him as we passed so he knew we were still onboard. (OK – a slight exaggeration about the distance we slid. There were too many people sitting on the same bench for this to actually happen, but I pitied the people who sat at either end of the bench who were bound to be squashed against the end walls.)

We soon discovered riding on the cable car is not a quiet, peaceful experience. There was the regular ringing of bells indicating starting and stopping at various pick-up points along the route. More agitated ringing alerted pedestrians to get out of the way as we careered towards them. (Another exaggeration, we travelled at a sedate pace even down the steep inclines when the creaking handbrake was applied. I've been watching too many high-drama films!)

The cable car travelled on rails on Hyde Street. Lombard Street crosses it. On one side, Lombard Street is straight like other streets in the city. It's on the opposite side of Hyde Street where the zigzagging section of Lombard Street is found. As we looked from our prime viewing position in the cable car, we saw a queue of cars on the straight section of Lombard Street waiting patiently to cross Hyde Street before starting the challenging descent down the famous hairpin bends on the hill opposite.

As we passed the eight tight switchback turns on Lombard Street, we noticed the edges of the road had small walls, set back from the kerb. These walls formed raised beds and were filled with beautiful flowers. The negative aspect of the walls was drivers had to ensure they didn't bump into them. Going by the evidence, many drivers aimed to drive down the zigzagging section as quickly as possible, with no regard for the walls. Alternatively, they weren't very good drivers. My deductions were based on the many indentations in the white walls which could only have been caused by motor vehicles. Each gouge contained a colourful memento of the car involved.

We travelled on down the hill on Hyde Street towards the harbour seeing Alcatraz and the Fisherman's Wharf where ships and boats were safely anchored; a great sight as we approached the end of our first San Francisco cable car experience.

We experienced dangerous driving in Gerona in 2003 between the airport and our hotel. I was pleased I'd contacted the hotel and asked about options for this journey. Otherwise, we would have been ripped off by the taxi driver we approached who quoted twice the amount we'd been told it should cost. We opted instead to get a bus and a short taxi ride to the hotel. However, neither were without concern for our safety.

In the bus, the driver immediately went onto his mobile phone, and talked for five minutes, whilst steering the bus round twisty roads with one hand. David had a full view of the driver and told us he was steering with the back of his hand, as he was quoting from some notes written on the palm of his hand. Some things are better not known about.

The taxi driver drove extremely quickly and through red lights, where if he had stopped, would have provided us with an opportunity to let out our held breath and inhale once again. Thankfully, despite these two unwanted driving experiences, we arrived safely at the hotel.

However, this was nothing compared to the driving Douglas and I experienced in 2013 when on a tour in India. This was a special holiday to celebrate his early retirement from the Scottish Air Traffic Control Centre.

During the first part of the holiday we were in a small coach with the others in the tour group. In the latter part of the holiday four cars replaced the coach which wouldn't have been able to navigate the terrain on the way to Shimla. Initially I thought this was a change for the better, but I soon changed my mind. The experience of being driven in the cars turned out to be a terrifying one.

As we drove early one morning, we quickly realised the thick fog at the hotel had no intention of lifting. Visibility was 50 metres (164 feet) at the most and often much less. Very few of the enormous lorries had headlights on and so would suddenly appear out of nowhere, abruptly entering our visibility zone.

The problem was our driver was determined to keep up with the other cars in our group. His driving technique was to tail-gate whatever vehicle was in front of him. Every time the red brake light illuminated on the vehicle ahead, we passengers found ourselves being flung forward in our seats as he slammed on his brake to prevent us crashing into said vehicle.

He also thought nothing of pulling out to overtake a bus or a lorry in these very busy roads. In the UK, this generally wouldn't be a problem. Drivers look ahead to make sure there's nothing coming towards them and space for them to overtake before crossing the central line in the road. But we were in India in the midst of thick fog. At times we couldn't see beyond the front of the vehicle we were overtaking. The driver had no way of knowing if there was anything coming towards us – and generally a large lorry or bus was doing just that! The incessantly beeping horns became more frantic as either we or they swerved to avoid a collision.

I watched the rapid movement of our driver's foot. One instant he was pushing the accelerator pedal to the floor with all his might to overtake, the next it was slammed onto the brake pedal when he realised there was something emerging through the fog and heading towards us.

"Please, slow down," each of the four of us individually said numerous times. "We don't mind arriving later than the others."

This request was ignored.

"Please can you blast the horn less; it's giving us headaches." We felt this was a reasonable request as it wasn't used as a warning of danger. It was used constantly just to say to each of the thousands of other drivers "Hey – just to let you know I'm here". This request was ignored too. We concluded he was new to the route and it would have been much better if he hadn't been at the end of the convoy.

There were lane markings painted on the road. Our experience in India however, was "lanes" are used differently from those in the UK. The roads we were driven on had two lanes marked in each direction, but drivers created additional lanes within the space provided. Two lanes became three narrower lanes of traffic. If three huge lorries were heading towards us there was no way they could fit into the official two lanes on their side of the road. They simply spilled over onto our side of the road. They had no intention of giving way to the unofficial three lanes of traffic approaching them. More frantic beeping of horns. I shut my eyes until the danger had passed.

This together with the bumpy, pot-holed road meant I was extremely pleased I'd taken a travel pill. But this wasn't enough to keep the nausea away and I was relieved when we were forced to stop for four minutes at a level crossing, waiting for a train to pass. Time for some deep breathing and an opportunity to relax – briefly. I wished I'd taken some tablets for headaches too.

As we waited for the train, I noticed the traffic had its own way of doing things here too. This road had only two lanes, a single lane going in each direction. However, vehicles moved into both lanes on both sides of the railway line, effectively meaning two lanes of traffic were facing each other as if in a stand-off. Which cars would manage to get into the single lane on the other side of the railway track when the barriers lifted, ideally without colliding with one of the vehicles currently facing it?

When the train passed, a man put a flimsy red banner across the track and the barricades were lifted. The battle of the road traffic commenced. I'm not sure what the etiquette was but somehow, with much horn blasting, things seemed to work out and soon traffic was moving in both directions as the road layout intended.

We arrived relieved and without injury at the hotel.

As I lay, sleep still evading me, waiting for the real alarm to go off, I wondered if we would have as interesting a journey as Douglas and I had when in Vietnam in 2015. We were going to Halong Bay for an overnight cruise. I headed for the bus waiting outside the hotel but saw our suitcase being taken to a car behind the bus. We were to be driven by car to Halong Bay. I felt like royalty!

"Four-hour journey. Break in two hours," the driver told us.

Having left at 8 a.m., the first part of the journey was through Hanoi rush hour traffic. I quickly realised it was much safer being in a car than being a pedestrian as we'd been when exploring Hanoi.

We passed several cyclists with their bikes laden with bread. Later we discovered why. At the side of the highway, ladies had stalls selling bread to travellers. There were no lay-bys to offer an element of safety to either party or for other vehicles on the road when someone suddenly decided to stop. Many of those riding on two wheels wore face masks made of thick decorative material. We'd seen market stalls selling literally thousands of them. I was glad the bread was stored in large plastic bags to protect it from the exhaust fumes.

Umbrellas were another accessory used by cyclists. When it started to rain, they held the umbrella in one hand while steering with the other. If there was a passenger on a motorcycle, he or she held the umbrella by the handle while the driver held the material canopy to stop the umbrella blowing inside out and to keep them both protected from the rain. It looked very dangerous.

Not everyone had an umbrella though. When it rained, most bikers wore the cheap plastic see-through capes tourists often wear. As they flapped about, inflated by the passing air they made a colourful sight. A different vibrant display occurred at night. The plastic capes were draped over the handlebar and headlight so instead of white headlights coming towards us, we saw an array of different coloured lights.

We passed a line of newly parked motorbikes, the drivers taking off their capes and draping them over their motorbikes ready to be put on again later.

One thing I really didn't like seeing was small children on the motorbikes – generally without crash-helmets. Usually one or two children sat in front of the parent who was driving, but I saw a very young girl sitting behind her mother, holding onto her round her waist.

It looked very dangerous.

Adults generally wear helmets which is good. But I saw a teenager who must have thought it wasn't trendy to wear the chinstrap of her helmet so had buckled the strap over the top of her pink helmet. It wouldn't do much good if she crashed, I thought. Many of the helmets looked like those worn by jockeys so do not cover the whole head. Some ladies had a curved cut-out at the back of their helmets, to allow their ponytails to hang down their backs.

The motorbikes also performed the function of vans. One had a cage strapped to it containing piglets. On another we saw a contented looking calf lying curled up in a cage. A dead pig was strapped across the back of one motorbike. Another had enormous steel frames strapped to the sides suitable for sheets of plasterboard or plywood.

Once in the countryside the roads were much quieter. But even here we saw some crazy driving. Traffic drives on the right-hand side of the road. A car ahead wanted to turn left. Instead of the driver staying in his lane until he reached the required turn-off then waiting for a break in the oncoming traffic, he moved over to the left-hand lane and drove for several hundred metres with traffic coming towards him. All the oncoming traffic moved out of *his* way until he finally made his left turn.

Later there was a bus in front of us overtaking a lorry. The bus had crossed over into the lane of oncoming traffic. This would have been fine if there was no traffic, but a van was coming straight towards him. The van driver hooted his horn, but it was he who had to drive off the road to make way for the bus.

"Is there a driving test here and what age do people sit the test?" I asked our driver.

"Yes," and a little chuckle, was his reply. As the journey progressed, I realised I was none the wiser as "yes" meant he hadn't a clue what I was talking about but was too polite to say.

We passed paddy fields and banana palms and lotus flowers growing by the roadside. The driver explained with a few words and lots of gestures, that lotus flowers are grown as an edible crop and everything from flower to root can be eaten.

The driver tended to point to things he wanted us to see, and one such thing was duck farms – hundreds of ducks sitting beside or swimming in a pond. Their eggs and meat provide income for the small farms. Another thing pointed out to us were small cemeteries in the corner of the paddy fields. It's the custom to have burial grounds in the family property as they believe ancestors protect the family.

The driver pointed occasionally to buildings including Nike and Canon factories, ceramics and brick manufacturers, sawmill and what he referred to as "government buildings".

"What does 'bo' on shop signs mean?" I asked him, thinking I could learn some Vietnamese words.

"Beef," he told me.

Despite trying hard, I quickly forgot the words for chicken, beer, noodles and motorbike he translated for me. I thought I'd mastered the word for noodles, but I was flung into a state of confusion when I was told two different words for noodles. Vietnamese proved no more straightforward for me to learn than French at school.

We stopped at Hong Ngoc Shopping Centre which looked like a garden centre because of all the stone garden ornaments outside. However, it was a massive craft centre giving employment to less abled and disadvantaged people. The 30-minute stop was for a cuppa. For once we would have liked a great deal longer. There was so much to see: people making statues, clothes and a variety of stitched pictures and other crafts.

We liked watching the speciality eggshell pictures being made. A plaque had glue applied before a large piece of broken eggshell was placed on it and pushed down so it broke. A small hammer was used to totally flatten it. This cracked surface formed the base for a painting added later.

There were also beautiful decorative plates, boxes and vases all finished with very shiny lacquer. When we saw "similar" ones later in the markets even we could see they were fakes.

We enjoyed an iced coffee here. I noted how it was made. Firstly, put lots of ice cubes in a glass and pour over strong black coffee. Add some condensed milk (not a lot required) and stir well. If you want smaller lumps of ice, put it in a liquidiser.

We'd one other short stop where tourists listened to a short talk about cultured pearls followed by time to look around a large sales room. This wasn't of much interest to us, so 10 minutes was plenty of time here. Then it was back into the car to complete the journey to Halong Bay.

At the end of our wonderful overnight cruise in Halong Bay, our driver met us when we disembarked from the tender and our drive back to Hanoi began. The roads were much quieter and because of the language barrier, it took a while to establish it was a holiday, so people were not travelling on the roads. On route, the driver remembered I'd asked on the previous journey if we could stop to take a picture of the lotus plants and he kindly did.

We negotiated a longer stop at Hong Ngoc Shopping Centre and opted to buy take-away iced coffees so we could spend more time doing ethical tourist shopping.

The final vehicle the driver pointed out was a hearse. It was like no funeral car I'd ever seen. If we'd been told it was an ice cream van, we would have believed it. It was so brightly coloured, painted all over with flowers using every colour imaginable. Much more cheerful than the black hearses in the UK.

Finally, our 5.15 a.m. alarm really did go off ... time to get ready for our next Sri Lankan adventure.

The overnight humidity meant the few clothes I'd washed and put on the railings outside our room the night before were still damp. I decided our beach towels and swimwear would have to dry in the minibus as we travelled. There would be plenty of room to hang them.

As we were too early for breakfast we had a DIY one consisting of leftovers: a banana, some curd and a dod[17] of Madeira cake, left over from when I was on the road to recovery after being ill a few days prior.

We expected to find our driver waiting for us at the front of the guest house, but he wasn't. At 6.05 a.m. I phoned the number on the receipt and discovered he *was* waiting but at a different guest house with a similar name.

"We're going travellin'," Sylvia said excitedly in her lovely Newcastle accent. And so, off we set.

We thought a 6 a.m. start was early, but in Sri Lanka it isn't. Our driver told us schools start at 7.30 a.m. and finish at 1.30 p.m., with many children taking packed breakfast and lunch with them. The roads were busy with children walking, cycling, waiting at the side of the road for local buses or being taken to school by parents on bicycles, motor-bikes or scooters. Some children either sat on the cross bar or on the luggage rack behind the seat of the parent's bike. Very uncomfortable for them, I thought, but I supposed they'd got used to it. Those walking were assisted in crossing the road by policemen ensuring traffic stopped at the zebra crossings.

As in Vietnam, we only occasionally saw children wearing crash helmets. Some of the helmets the parents wore had serious cracks and

17 Dod is Scottish for "chunk".

chunks missing from them, so I wasn't convinced of their effectiveness. No other protective clothes were worn. Flip-flops were the usual footwear along with light cotton clothing. This will be much cooler than leathers and boots worn in the UK but I'm sure accidents here are likely to result in serious injury.

As I watched the children, I wondered what they were thinking about. Were they looking forward to or dreading the day ahead? Were they facing tests or was today going to include their favourite subject – perhaps PE or art? Or were they just thinking about what they were going to do after school?

"We've noticed the children all wear white uniforms," I said to the driver. "In the UK different schools have different colours of uniform."

"The government pays for all uniforms and textbooks. Going to school here is free," explained the driver. "Some schools are better and there's great competition to get into them."

Few children were seen after 7.30 a.m. so punctuality was taken seriously. At 7.28 a.m. I saw one young boy being hurriedly made ready by his dad outside the large closed school gates, watched by the gate attendants. Only when the straps on his backpack were put in place over his shoulders were the gates opened.

We passed through an area famous for making roof tiles and bricks, and saw all the finished products piled up at the roadside ready for purchase.

"We've heard some areas in Sri Lanka are facing terrible water shortages."

"There has not been enough rain over the last two years and wells had dried up," the driver told us. As we drove, he pointed out specific areas affected. Driving along we wouldn't have known there was a problem as houses generally have shutters over the windows during the day.

"The people have left their homes and moved away. The government is trying to fix the problem by laying new water pipelines, but this will take a long time to complete."

We passed Tabbowa Wewa, which should have been a massive reservoir (approximately 4.6 square kilometres or 1.8 square miles) but we could only see water in the far distance, most of the reservoir was green with vegetation.

"See the water storage tanks?" the driver said pointing to the side of some isolated houses. "They've been donated by other countries so people can collect rainwater from their roofs."

Our conversation flitted to other holiday travelling experiences. Douglas and I did a lot of travelling in Australia and some of it seemed just like of home. One day we decided to go from Perth (in Australia that is, not Perth in Scotland) to Fremantle by train. Rottnest Island had been our first choice, but this was the finishing point of the annual 20km (approximately 16 miles) Rottnest Channel swim. As thousands of people take part and many more go to Rottnest as spectators, we were told it would be difficult to get on the ferries. So, we jumped on one of the free buses in the central zone of the city which took us to the station for the train to Fremantle.

We found the ticket machines without any problem and didn't think for a moment we would need help to operate them. After all, a ticket machine is a ticket machine

We quickly established we weren't entitled to a concession fare as these were for children only and not oldies like Douglas. Boosted by the realisation we obviously had a natural talent for mastering unfamiliar ticket machines we moved onto the next part of the procedure – selecting where we were going to. We knew this of course – Fremantle. But we hit a problem. "Fremantle" wasn't an option on the machine. It wanted to know which "zone" we were going to.

"I'll go and ask for help," was my immediate decision in response to this dilemma.

Three members of staff were standing at the ticket barrier.

"Can you help us with the ticket machine, please?" I thought there was no point asking which zone we needed as goodness knows what the next Mensa-type question would be.

The response I received wasn't what I expected.

"There are no trains to Fremantle this weekend due to engineering works."

I've heard this excuse many a time in Scotland but somehow thought this was exclusive to the UK. Clearly not.

"Och, you're joking!" was my reply, whilst planning to ask him where else we could go instead.

But I didn't have an opportunity to pose my question.

"It's OK. There's a replacement bus service." Another all too familiar turn of phrase for us in Scotland.

"It's straightforward," he said as he walked with me out of the station to the ticket machines where he directed us to the nearby bus station, the stand to go to and the number of the bus. And sure enough, everything was straightforward and our trip to Fremantle a success.

A week later in Melbourne we met Suzy, my cousin's daughter. She recommended the free tourist tram and in less than an hour we went round the full circuit, helping us get our bearings, converting the 2D street maps we'd been using into 3D in our minds. There was a commentary during the journey, so we were able to plan what we wanted to do next.

"Let's go to Treasury Gardens and the adjacent Fitzroy Gardens."

The gardens were a great place for a stroll, and we enjoyed seeing the miniature Tudor village, conservatory full of beautiful flowers, fountains and historic Cooks' cottage. The cottage belonged to the Cook family in Yorkshire, England, was bought in 1934, dismantled, transported halfway round the world before being rebuilt in Fitzroy Gardens.

We intended having morning coffee in the café, but by the time we got there realised it was too near lunchtime and we were going to Queen Victoria Market for lunch. Outside the café, under the overhanging roof was a man in a red uniform, complete with a red hat, standing behind a table.

I'd been watching for a while but hadn't seen anyone speaking to him. I felt sorry for him. Fancy doing a job in which everyone ignored you – it must be awful. I saw a pile of maps of the city on his table, so I contrived to make myself feel less sorry for him and hopefully make him feel wanted.

"What's the best way was to get to the Queen Victoria Market?" I asked him. He told me it was best to use the tourist tram again and told me which paths through the parks to take to get to the stop outside the parliament building. I thanked him very much and off I went.

"We could just go back to the stop opposite the one we got off when coming to the park," Douglas told me. "We'd know exactly where we were going and wouldn't get lost."

"Yes, I know. But the man I got the instructions from has a clear view of us. It would be very hurtful if we didn't follow his instructions. He was so helpful."

After a slight diversion off the planned route for a visit to the toilets, Douglas again suggested we went onto our known route.

"But the man can still see us, and anyway who knows, he may have a tracking drone watching our every move and would get upset if we ignored his directions. Anyway, the new route will allow you to take different photos."

Douglas grunted.

Once at the road, we started making our way up the hill to the tram stop hoping to reach it before the tram. We wanted to maximise our time at the market before going on a tour to see the penguins returning from the sea to their nests on Phillip Island. We got to the brow of the hill and continued towards the stop. I realised the tram could be catching us without me knowing as I could no longer see over the brow behind me. I started walking more quickly not wanting to run feeling this would give Douglas the impression I was losing faith in my choice of route and tram stop. Surreptitiously, I kept having a sneaky look over my shoulder.

Finally, we arrived at the stop with me trying to give the impression I wasn't at all out of breath. As we stood it became clear the advertised 12-minute service wasn't strictly adhered to.

After what seemed like ages, the tram arrived, and we went to the market. It was brilliant. We started off in the food court buying lunch from various stalls, all at much lower prices than we'd experienced so far in Australia. It was great wandering round the meat, fish and fruit sections before finishing in an enormous hangar with stalls of clothes and all sorts of other interesting items for sale. The time came for us to get another tram back to our apartment to get ready for Phillip Island and the nightly return of the penguins.

At this tram stop several 12-minute time slots passed in which we expected trams to arrive. I found myself thinking about the "Clockwork Orange" in Glasgow, the affectionate name given to the underground subway trains that circle the route every few minutes. Here, even if the trains are delayed by a minute or two, people notice.

"The wait has obviously been too long for that old man," Douglas said nodding in the direction. "He has wet himself."

"Oh no!" I said horrified but unable to stop myself turning to look. Sure enough, there was a puddle at his feet and a stream of liquid running to the kerb. I felt awful for the man.

Douglas on the other hand burst out laughing, hardly able to stop his merriment or speak to me. Not an appropriate reaction I felt.

When finally able to take a breather for long enough to speak he said, "The liquid is from a spilt juice carton behind the man." Said carton was out of my line of vision.

"I can't believe you believed me!" he said and we both chuckled about it throughout the rest of the day.

The tram thankfully came and off we set.

Another memorable journey was between Alice Springs and Yulara, Australia. Douglas and I were looking forward to seeing Uluru (at one time called Ayers Rock).

The journey was straightforward. The coach driver told us, tongue in cheek, she had a very complicated six and a half hour journey ahead of her. She needed to concentrate to ensure she didn't miss the two right and one left turns she required to make. This timescale included a couple of half hour stops, the first at a camel farm, the second at an emu farm, both with welcome café facilities.

At the first stop, there was an option to ride a camel "round the yard" which made me think of donkey rides on the beach in years gone by, but we didn't take up this option. Nor did we buy seed to feed the emus, which was just as well as the nearest emus we saw were specks on the horizon.

The driver was very good at telling us facts and stories including about Coober Pedy, a town famous for opal mining. She told us that though opals are less expensive to buy, they are rarer than diamonds. It's believed only five per cent of the opals there have been found.

Coober Pedy has a desert climate: it's extremely hot in summer and cold in winter. To cope, at least 80 per cent of the people live in underground houses.

The owners can extend their homes by digging extra underground rooms but now must get permission. Previously people were digging their way into other people's homes as there was no record kept of where houses began and finished.

One of the driver's friends extended his home and, as is common, found opals in the soil being dug out. A shop owner who was rebuilding and upgrading part of the shop found enough opals to cover the cost of all the planned construction work.

Later in the journey the driver set us a challenge – to see who could see Uluru first. She would buy the person a drink, but anyone who got it wrong would have to buy her a drink.

"People are often wrong," she warned.

A lady in front of me was the first to point out a flat-topped stone outcrop way in the distance but was told she owed the driver a drink. I was convinced the driver had mistaken what the lady was referring to. I was sure she was right.

Douglas and I fell asleep and later I awoke to find we were right at a flat-topped rock. I took some photos as this was obviously Uluru, I told myself. I was surprised I'd been in such a deep sleep I hadn't heard the driver announce, "This is it." I was sorry Douglas had missed this first sighting. But I had a niggling doubt in my mind. I didn't want to waken Douglas and point out Uluru – just in case I became the laughing stock of the bus.

The journey continued for ages, before a lady behind me shouted out "Uluru." She was right, and I'd been wrong! Thank goodness I hadn't woken Douglas.

As promised, after a couple of hours on the Sri Lankan road, the driver told us, "We'll stop here. This is the last good place for a toilet break, for a long time." The immaculate toilets were part of a new restaurant opened only a month earlier.

"Can we have coffee and toast please?" we asked the owner.

"I will give you egg roti too," he kindly said, obviously keen to make us feel welcome.

The toast with coconut honey was delicious though the honey's taste reminded me of maple syrup. The egg roti wasn't as flavoursome as Douglas and I tasted previously in Hikkaduwa, and unfortunately just as stodgy.

We were too late in the morning to see elephants crossing the road at a location often used by them, but our journey wasn't devoid of wildlife. The driver braked sharply sending us flying from our seats as a mongoose took its life in its paws and scurried across the road. A couple of monkeys lolloped across, attracted by a bag of abandoned food which they happily tucked into.

We stopped at the sacred ancient city of Anuradhapura to take some photos. Anuradhapura dates from the 4th century BC and is now a UNESCO World Heritage Site. The vast area contains Buddhist temples, huge brick hemispherical stupas, ruins of historic palaces and pools to name but a few of the features. It covers a massive area and we could easily have spent a whole day exploring, but instead, we just jumped in and out of the car taking photos. Much of what we saw were archaeological ruins though we saw restoration work too.

One of our photo stops was at the huge Mirisawetiya Stupa which has a diameter of about 51 metres (168 feet) at its base and was an example of amazing restoration work. It was originally built in 2nd century BC by King Dutugemunu. We learned an Englishman, Parker, started the renovation in 1888 after discovering what had become a mound of trees and undergrowth. Funds ran out and the gleaming white domed structure wasn't completed until 1993.

Isurumuniya Temple was another stop. This temple was built between two rocks, connected to a cave and surrounded by lakes and paddy fields. The sign outside told us the temple was built by King Devanapiyatissa (who reigned from 250-210BC) for 500 high-caste children to live in after they were ordained. This Buddhist temple is famous for its stone carvings. Unfortunately, we didn't have time to go in and see them but enjoyed photographing the outside.

Our final stop was at Rankoth Vehera, another stupa. To get close to it, we walked through the remains of a large square terrace with only isolated columns remaining to line the path, the roof long gone. Other old weathered structures and artefacts scattered the site. This stupa is the fourth largest in Sri Lanka with a diameter of about 170 metres (550 feet) and a height of approximately 33 metres (108 feet) to its tip. The only material used to build it was brick, the bricks left exposed and without the gleaming white finish of the Mirisawetiya Stupa. Rankoth Vehera isn't as old having been built by King Nissanka Malla who ruled from 1187AD to 1196AD.

We were keen to get to Trincomalee, a seaport on the north-eastern coast of Sri Lanka, where we would be spending the rest of the day and night, so off we set.

At the Silver Beach Hotel, we were shown to our cabanas with their palm branch roofs. Very exotic and romantic until we looked at them closely. The palm branches had all slid down, revealing corrugated metal sheeting underneath. Not the intricate thatching I expected.

Cabana rooms in Trincomalee; roofs in need of repair!

Inside our room, the original wall shower had broken but remained in situ. The water on-off lever was anchored to the shower head above with a piece of thick wire to stop people trying to switch it on. An electric shower had been installed beside the broken one, but its electric plug and socket were also in the shower cubicle. Water and electricity to my understanding shouldn't meet and it was hard to see how this could be avoided in a shower cubicle. Fortunately, we lived to tell the tale and didn't end up electrocuted. Just as well or I wouldn't be writing this!

On the plus side, there were two cakes of soap, so we could have one in the shower and the other at the wash hand basin, plus bottles of water were provided, both more than in our Negombo guest house.

We'd lunch in one of the hotel's three restaurants pointed out to us on arrival. We wondered if there might be international options such as an Italian or Chinese restaurant in addition to one serving Sri Lankan food. It transpired the "three restaurants" meant there were three different pagodas each serving the same fare but we could choose which one to sit in.

A wander along the beach followed by a swim, or more accurately a play in the waves, were our post arrival pursuits. Originally, we'd thought of going to Pigeon Island where we would be able to do some snorkelling. However, the sea looked rough and based on the inability of the others to see any fish when they went on the fishing trip in similar conditions, we felt it wasn't worth risking a two-hour boat trip for.

There were other things to see in Trincomalee – the fort and the harbour (where many ships were attacked and sunk during World War Two). The driver was called upon again. Before the fort, we spotted and got out to see the brightly coloured and ornate Pathirakali Amman Hindu Temple (see photo on front cover).

There was a ceremony taking place and we watched as six men wearing sarongs walked round the outside of the temple. The musical accompaniment was produced by one man blowing into a nadaswaram, a long tube-like wind instrument with seven finger holes, while another hit a thavil, a barrel shaped drum. The third instrumentalist rang a hand bell. A fourth man was carrying a red and gold umbrella which he was holding above a man who was carrying what looked a large bunch of flowers.

We were aware of an elderly lady hovering around outside the temple door. Her long white hair was neatly pleated, the plait falling down the back of her brown and cream sari. When the procession of men went in through the door of the temple, the lady suddenly raised her arms above her head and with effort, forcefully threw something to the ground. It made an almighty bang as it smashed. It was a coconut. The lady nonchalantly sauntered away. We learned a coconut is smashed as a symbolic act to represent complete submission to the Hindu gods. The coconut represents the person's head and ego. When smashed the person lets go of their ego along with pride felt in a future achievement.

Brightly coloured and ornate Pathirakali Amman Hindu Temple, Trincomalee

There was a cow wandering around and as we were leaving it took a dislike to Sylvia, walking up and head butting her! Time for us to go.

The Fort wasn't what we expected. There was a Buddhist temple and army barracks there, but no opportunity to explore as we'd done in Galle. Next on the list was the harbour and it wasn't as we expected. It turned out to be a secure area, so we couldn't go to it either.

But we'd another option up our sleeves: the Trincomalee British War Cemetery. Sylvia and George had heard about it the night before. Apparently after it was established, a local man, without any payment, took it upon himself to keep it maintained. The cemetery is now maintained by Sri Lankan Ministry of Defence on behalf of the Commonwealth War Graves Commission, but it's the son of the original man who now keeps it beautifully maintained.

The driver didn't know where the cemetery was but asked a tuk-tuk driver and received directions, 10km from where we were, beyond our accommodation. Off we set. After a while, the driver asked for more directions, and we were pointed on in the same direction. At the next request for directions, we were told we'd come too far and needed to go back the way we'd come. Next two requests for directions confirmed we were now going in the right direction but had further to go. I'd noticed a graveyard close to our accommodation earlier and began to wonder if this was where we were meant to go. If so, it wasn't 10km away as the driver had originally been told. And yes, we soon discovered it was the graveyard I'd seen. We could have walked to it!

The peaceful cemetery was on a grassy hillside and beautifully maintained with many different shrubs beside the rows of gravestones. Over 140 white gravestones represented military and some civilian personnel who were killed during the war or died afterwards because of the war. As we were leaving, the sun was setting and, in my mind, I could hear *The Last Post* being played on a bugle. It was very poignant.

The tranquility of Trincomalee British War Cemetery

On returning to the hotel, we quickly headed out in search of somewhere to eat. Before entering the restaurant, we asked the crucial question: "Do you have Lion beer?"

"Yes," was the enthusiastic response. We were warmly welcomed and invited to sit upstairs in the wooden Beach Restaurant (which despite the name wasn't at the beach). A tablecloth was put on our table, "We bring a candle to make it very, very nice," we were promised.

Drinks were ordered, and the waiter disappeared downstairs. Returning a while later he said, "The beer not cold. We put it in freezer. Ready in five minutes."

"OK, that's fine," we reassured him.

Five minutes became twenty minutes. We were now suspicious. Had they gone to buy the beer first? Never mind, we'd ordered our food, so things were moving in a positive direction.

Three meals were eventually delivered to the table.

"The chef make yours now," I was told. "Ready in a few minutes."

The "few minutes" extended and extended. The three others in our band of intrepid explorers had nearly finished their meal and my prawn spaghetti still hadn't arrived. I no longer felt hungry.

We felt we hadn't been treated well. Delayed beers for the men, no promised candles and no meal for me. l got up from the table and went downstairs to cancel my meal. I was met with all sorts of protestations and assurances it was just coming.

"Gas for cookers ran out. But it all fixed now. Spaghetti just coming."

I stuck to my guns. "I don't want spaghetti now. It's too late. The others have finished their meals. Just give me some ice cream." (Now there's a surprise!)

More beer was ordered, and one bottle was brought to the table.

"What about the second bottle?" he was asked.

"Beer run out. End of season. We usually only sell five bottles a day. They all been sold."

This was the final straw. We paid and left, going instead to a real beach restaurant, one *on* the beach, for a final drink of the evening and a chat about our hopes for the following day.

Up, down and over

We'd asked to have breakfast at 7.30 a.m. wanting to leave at 8 a.m. for the busy day ahead. However, well before breakfast Sylvia knocked on our door.

"The fishermen are on the beach pulling in the long fishing net like in Negombo," she told us. Another photo opportunity beckoned.

The fishermen used a different technique. We couldn't help feeling disappointed as they didn't sing while they worked as the fishermen in Negombo did. The in unison foot-stamping technique to anchor their feet while they moved backwards was the same though. Here the rope wasn't neatly coiled but instead, like the long net was laid out in a single long line along the shore meaning more frequent changes in direction were required as they walked (see photo on front cover).

Sylvia and I stood at a distance but not for long.

"Lady, come," we were ushered by one of the men. Sylvia was soon allocated a position in the line of men and joined the stamping and net pulling. Next it was my turn. Our wee shots made us realise how heavy the men's task was despite the large number pulling. I know we didn't lessen their workload, but it was fun for all involved, even if the accompanying amusement was at our expense. How they laughed at our efforts! Hopefully we broke what appeared to be a monotonous, time-consuming job.

We returned for breakfast but encountered Sri Lankan timescales. Our order was quickly taken for fruit juice, two eggs and a hot drink. After 15 minutes, our hot drinks arrived. More waiting followed before firstly the fried eggs and toast were brought. Later the boiled eggs arrived and eventually the fruit juice. Had the three restaurants been mobbed we could have understood the delays, but we and another couple were the only people to be served. Our curiosity about what caused the hold-ups remained unanswered.

While my three amigos were finishing breakfast, I nipped along to take more photos, this time of the landed catch. Some fishermen were down on their hunkers around a circular pile of small silver fish emptied from the net onto the sand. Fish were sorted into piles of different varieties. Other men checked the net removing the minute fish stuck in it before throwing them into the sorting pile. A third group of men carefully loaded the long net back into a boat ready to be taken out to sea again. The catch was much bigger than the one in Negombo but I'm sure once divided, the men wouldn't receive much here either.

Seeing these fishermen far exceeded our original desire to see the stick fishermen. These men showed us *real* fishing.

"Just buy a postcard of stick fishermen," George suggested. A great idea I thought.

After breakfast, George came from his room next door to ours and kindly offered to take our case to the car. This offer, however, led to devastating news about differences in our accommodation.

"Our room is bigger than yours," he told us. "*And* ours is a semi-detached cabana whereas yours is only a terraced one."

"Semi-detached does sound posher than 'end of terrace'," I laughed. "Maybe this is to make up for our bigger fridge in Negombo!"

"And the superior wash-hand basin with a rack under it for toilet bags which ours doesn't have," Sylvia added jokingly.

"Even-stevens then?" I suggested, and all agreed.

As we drove, we passed through a famous curd making area, with stalls along the roadside selling curd in fireclay pots covered with what looked like cotton material. I was amazed it wasn't refrigerated but the driver told us buffalo milk curd will last for two weeks without refrigeration, and longer when refrigerated.

We drove over the dam wall of a massive reservoir which stretched out on our right-hand side. It was hard to believe it was first built 500 years ago. During the intervening period the dam has been breached several times and the reservoir emptied. Fortunately, successful repair work was possible.

Wildlife on this journey included peacocks and mongoose (or is it mongeese for plural?). The driver told us about the electric fences which restrict elephant movement.

"Elephants are clever animals. They won't let an electric fence stop them," he told us.

We were intrigued to learn they fell a tree or find a large branch, take it to the fence, place it so the wood is angled from the ground, up and over the top of the fence. The elephant obviously can't walk up this and jump down to the ground on the other side of the fence, but it can stamp on the tree trunk or branch. The force breaks the fence giving the elephant an opening through which to travel. Clever creative creatures.

"Elephant," the driver shouted shortly afterwards. We looked up excitedly only to hear him correcting himself, "Oh no, it's a poster." It was a roadside billboard advertising the nearby safari park. We were all disappointed, including the driver.

The final part of the journey to see the ruins of the ancient city of Sigiriya was along an 8km (5 miles) single-track road, on which we regularly had to pull over to allow those exiting to pass.

"People will ask to be your guide. You need to pay for this, but you don't need a guide," our driver warned. "It will be easy for you." This was good advice, though he didn't mention we foreigners would have to pay 75 times the amount locals pay for entry. But we didn't mind paying for this once-in-a-lifetime experience.

Sigiriya is a UNESCO World Heritage Site. In the middle of a forest, protruding above the tree canopy, stands 200 metres (656 feet) high rock. The rock is a lava plug left behind when a volcano exploded. The volcano is extinct – thankfully. If it hadn't been, the chosen location of the palace would have been very dangerous – it was on the rock's summit!

The rock we climbed to see the remains of the palace, Sigiriya

King Kasyapa (Kashyapa) (477 – 495AD) built this new capital city after killing his father and seizing the throne from Moggallana, his half-brother and rightful heir. The rock with the palace on top was surrounded by gardens, reservoirs and other buildings. In 495AD Moggallana attacked and despite the elaborate defences, killed Kasyapa. Moggallana didn't remain in Sigiriya, instead making Anuradhapura the capital city once again. Sigiriya became a Buddhist Monastery until the 13th or 14th century. We were going to be exploring what remained, which required us to climb the rock after walking through the gardens with immaculate grass and flower beds being tended by numerous people.

The rock resembled the shape of an upturned mug – without the handle. The sides were shear. We'd prepared ourselves for a long hard climb up many, many steps. Our ascent began.

As usual on the first flight I counted the steps and continued to do so all the way to the summit. However, I can't tell you the total number. Every time I stopped to take a photo, catch my breath or have a drink of water I thought carefully about the number I'd reached so when I restarted, I could continue. But every time I restarted; I'd forgotten the number I'd so carefully tried to remember. Clearly lack of oxygen was taking its toll. (That's my excuse and I'm sticking to it.)

One of the famous features we stopped at was the "Mirror Wall". I'd expected something I could see my reflection in. It wasn't, not anymore at least. Originally the white plaster covering the wall was so highly polished the king could see himself when he walked past. Perhaps it wasn't ever like looking in a modern-day mirror, but it was impressive none the less.

At one point we went up a cast iron spiral staircase fixed to the cliff face. This took us to a platform from which we could see ancient paintings on the wall. Egg yolks were one of the paint ingredients.

Then, in terms of my puffing and panting, and aching legs, the cruellest thing happened, the route took us *down* 53 steps in an adjacent spiral staircase (yes, I counted them). The ascent began again, using a different route but we had to go up *exactly* 53 steps again before we could make any real progress.

"You will know you're halfway there when you reach the elephant's feet carved in the rock," I remembered the driver telling us.

"We're halfway up," Sylvia said when we reached a plaza, pointing to carved animal's feet.

Half-way point of our climb, at the plaza with lion's feet

"No, we can't be," I said. "These are lion's feet, not elephant's feet." But I was wrong. I'd incorrectly "remembered" the creature whose feet we were to look for. It was therefore a pleasant surprise to realise we were further up than I thought.

Many people were having a rest at the plaza. Monkeys attracted the attention of those with cameras. Doing people watching, I was very aware it was possible to differentiate between those heading for the summit and those who had reached the top and were making their way back down. Those going up were subdued by the heat, exertion and thoughts of the climb to come, while those coming down were chatting, laughing and smiling. We were in the former group.

There was nothing for it but to start on the second half of our "rock-climbing" expedition. This time most of the climb was up cast-iron stairs. I could understand people getting scared doing this. The staircases are held in place with only rods fixed into the rock. The rods don't look very big or strong, and their rusty appearance showed they had been there a long time. I quickly put the thought of the structural stability of this staircase out of my mind, focusing instead on my counting.

Finally, we reached the top, very out of breath, hot and tired. Douglas' t-shirt was soaked through with sweat. But importantly, we'd made it.

On top of the rock were the impressive ruins of the palace and ancillary buildings. I was astonished wondering how all the labour and materials were brought to the summit, knowing how exhausted I felt just walking up once. There was even an outdoor swimming pool containing now stagnant water. We'd been told it was the first ever outdoor swimming pool in Sri Lanka.

We were amazed at our abilities when we were told later the climb involved about 1,200 steps. This is like climbing the stairs to the top of a 60-storey building.

We stayed at the top for a while to recover and take in the amazing views before making our descent. Even going down needed care. In places there were new stainless-steel handrails which looked good but were very slippery and extremely hot to touch. The old rusty cast iron handrails were cooler, rougher and felt safer. Some of the stone steps were so well worn they were like polished stone, so also slippery.

After we passed the half-way point – of lion's feet fame, we discovered there were two routes. We'd to follow signs to the "foreigner's car park", another example of differentiation between us and the locals. We therefore didn't return to the entrance area and so missed visiting the large café and museum. Instead we walked the gauntlet of men selling guidebooks, souvenirs and postcards. The pictures on the postcards looked as though they had been taken 50 years before. We saw a snake charmer too before we finally arrived at an area with a few stalls selling drinks and ice cream at, we assumed, foreigners' prices. George was so scunnered[18] at the price requested for a bottle of juice, he told the man to take it back.

In the car again, a half hour drive took us to Dambulla, to see the Buddhist rock temple. The driver stopped at the ticket office to buy our entrance tickets. A conversation ensued.

"They've run out of tickets," he translated.

Our hearts sank as we'd wanted to see this temple. He explained the solution, "At the entrance just say they've run out of tickets and you will be let in." Strange, we thought.

We were driven to the entrance where more stalls awaited. These ones were selling drinks at normal prices, so our water supplies were thankfully replenished.

[18] Scunnered = Scottish for "disgusted".

I was apprehensive; would we be let in without the $10 tickets? But sure enough, when told they had run out of tickets, we were ushered into the grounds. Unlike Sigiriya we had unexpected free access but still steps to climb; just 153 stone ones this time. Yet I could feel the muscles at the tops of my legs complaining, and the heat was making the climb exhausting.

"Shoes off," we were told at the top. We popped them into our bags rather than leaving them in the shoe racks. Walking the 75 metres or so (82 yards) to the temple entrance was torture. The stone underfoot was burning hot. We half ran, preferring to risk standing on stray stones, to reach the shaded entrance ahead. Once there, we realised others had waited until this point to take their shoes off, leaving them in a pile beside the door; something we could laugh about once our feet recovered! But at least we now knew we could put our shoes back on for the return journey.

Inside there was a courtyard to cross, again of burning stone. We paused, got into a huddle, reviewed our options and finally planned in minute detail a route taking us to the shaded area in as short a distance as possible.

The temple itself consisted of several huge caves each lined with dozens and dozens of differently sized statues of Buddha. The ceilings were totally covered in paintings of Buddha. It was fascinating to wander through the caves and wonderful to be in the cool atmosphere where, on the cool stone floor, our feet weren't burnt to cinders.

Returning to the entrance, we sat on a stone step to put our footwear back on. In normal circumstances this would be straightforward. What we'd forgotten was the temperature of the stone step we sat on. While trying not to dwell on the severe bottom burning going on and focusing instead on putting our shoes on as quickly as possible, a young lad came and asked for chocolate. In these temperatures, I visualised the runny mess the chocolate would have been in had we been carrying any! Douglas remembered about a bar of chewy sesame seed we'd bought yesterday when at the fort in Trincomalee. We'd broken a little bit off to try but found it too sweet for us. The lad was delighted to accept this.

After stopping for lunch, the journey back to Negombo resumed. We passed the entrance to the International Cricket Ground in Sri Lanka, where England come to play, sometimes winning, sometimes losing. I was surprised to learn the national sport in Sri Lanka is volleyball having thought it would be cricket. This explained why I'd seen so many volleyball courts during the holiday.

The drive back was on busier roads than the one we'd taken to Trincomalee. We passed through far more towns and villages where we encountered more vehicles and the associated increase in horn tooting. As George commented, there was also an increase in the number of near misses between vehicles. At times it was much less stressful to focus our eyes on anything other than the traffic around us.

We got back to the guest house in Negombo about 6.15 p.m. and enjoyed another excellent meal at Coconut Lodge Restaurant. This has become the favourite place to eat for all of us. Because we didn't have many days left of our holiday, we were reluctant to experiment elsewhere for fear of being disappointed. Here we knew anything we ordered would be delicious.

I'd a notion for something plain to eat. Twice Sylvia had ordered shepherd's pie and said it was brilliant. It seemed strange ordering this, it being such a staple meal back home. However, going against all my normal instincts to try local dishes when abroad, I ordered shepherd's pie.

"We've had quite a day of climbing," I said as we waited for our meals.

"If there's a building or tower with steps, the Moore family likes to climb them," Douglas said. "And bridges have to be walked across. Remember when we visited Newcastle in February 2002, we walked along the riverside paths criss-crossing the river on three of the bridges – the Tyne Bridge, the Hydraulic Swing Bridge, and the Gateshead Millennium Bridge. Maybe a daft activity, but we saw things we would otherwise have missed, like the rickety looking Medieval timber framed buildings between the Swing and Millennium bridges. And now whenever scenes from Newcastle appear on the television, we can shout,

"We've crossed those bridges! Shouting at the TV is another of our daft activities."

"Our short stay in New York in 2000, was ideal for our love of walking across bridges and going to the tops of buildings," I added. "Though in most buildings lifts transported us upwards; or should I say, 'elevators' as I'm talking about America?"

The first challenge was to buy the Metro cards for the subway journey to the Brooklyn Bridge. We felt very knowledgeable having read Metro cards were sold in shops and not at the subway station. The trouble was we couldn't see signs outside any shops indicating they sold said cards.

"Where can I buy Metro cards?" I asked a police officer.

"I'm not sure," was the reply I didn't expect to hear.

Undaunted, I asked at newspaper kiosk.

"Here," was the welcome reply.

And so, we made our first journey on the New York subway.

On the Brooklyn Bridge we found ourselves on a wooden planked pedestrian walkway above the lanes of traffic crossing the East River between Brooklyn and Manhattan. This we shared with cyclists with whistles in their mouths. Strange, we thought. When we heard the whistles being blown loudly, we realised they were instead of the gentler handlebar bicycle bells we're familiar with, a warning to pedestrians who happen to be in their way.

We caught up with some refuse collectors emptying the bins on the walkway. They lifted the bags of rubbish out of the bin, tied and threw them over the railings into a refuse lorry slowly driving on the road below.

When we got to the opposite side of the Bridge, we'd hoped to get a boat back across the water, but we couldn't find any boats. It wasn't a problem, though, to do a 180-degree turn and walk back across the just-over-one-mile long bridge.

We could now add the Brooklyn Bridge to the list of bridges we'd walked across.

The next day our challenge was the Statue of Liberty. Knowing it was very popular, we prepared a plan.

I got up early and went to the bus station to buy two-day bus tour passes. We'd been told the office opened at 7 a.m. Still benefitting from jetlag, I walked the ten-minute route to the bus station for opening time. Arriving there, I discovered the office opened at 7 a.m., but bus tickets weren't sold until 8 a.m. Back to the hotel I went for breakfast.

With stomachs full, we all went to the bus station ready for our day's sightseeing, hopping on and off buses. We expected to join a long queue for tickets and were amazed there wasn't one. Queues though had already formed outside for the first departing buses at 9 a.m. with people using day two of their two-day pass.

We took the express bus directly to the Statue of Liberty. We were disappointed there was no commentary as we travelled and wondered if the little red books with maps of the routes and details of all the sights replaced this.

From the bus stop at Battery Park we walked to the water's edge where a ferry was being loaded with folk like us. As we queued and waited, we were amused by the various sellers walking around with briefcases full of sunglasses, "gold" chains, watches etc. trying to tempt us to buy. They were clearly keeping one eye on us while the other watched for approaching policemen.

After waiting for the next boat, we enjoyed the trip to Liberty Island, anticipation of the climb mounting with each passing minute. On the journey, amongst the announcements made, was the warning the queues may be one to two hours long. But this warning didn't dampen our spirits. We prepared ourselves for delays.

It was great seeing the Statue of Liberty at close quarters, though it wasn't as big as we expected.

We got off the ferry as quickly as we could and headed for the entrance – a zigzagging queue in a huge tent. Half the chicane was empty. By the time the next ferry arrived, and those passengers joined the queue, the tent was full. We moved slowly.

Once out of the tent we noticed grooves in the stonework along the side of the statue's base, formed by coins being scored across the stone, a sign many people before us had made similar slow progress, we thought. We put a couple of cents into the grooves to add to those already there.

Trying to fill the slowly passing time Douglas asked David some mental arithmetic sums. (David enjoyed doing sums – honestly!) Overhearing this, a lady next to us started chatting. She was a teacher from North Carolina and was with her daughter. She told us about recent flooding caused by Hurricane Floyd when schools were closed for several weeks. School holidays were shortened to ensure the children didn't miss their schooling. I wonder how happy the children were with this arrangement.

It took an hour just to get to the door into the Statue of Liberty. Inside there was a security check before we joined the next queue which led to an initial short flight of steps.

Very slow progress was made, and we kept wondering what was round the corner at the top of these steps. The answer was revealed as we strained to peer round – the queue continued!

"How far does the queue continue?" an Englishman in front of us asked

"Right to the top," a security guard replied.

There was a lift we could have used with only a tiny queue, but it only went as far as the top of the stone plinth. It wasn't possible to transfer from here to the steps leading to the top of the statue. We knew we would regret it later if we didn't climb the 354 steps. We walked past the lift.

The ascent was extremely slow.

"I've just broken a record," I cried jubilantly to the others. "I've just climbed eight steps without stopping."

We felt a great sense of achievement when we reached the level where the lift stopped.

Very few people were coming down from the top until suddenly a large group of young children descended with their leader. This gave us a boost. We felt sure we would now quickly move up a section. Unfortunately, we didn't experience any burst of speed or quickening of our pace.

Every now and then, there was an announcement over the public address system naming children who "had to return immediately to join their school party who were ready to board the boat." If any of the children were inside the statue, I have no idea how they would get down. In the single file one-way system there was absolutely no room for passing.

Inside the statue it was intriguing to see the means of construction. There was a grid framework made of flat bars at approximately one metre (3 feet) intervals. Beyond this we could see the copper sheeting, shaped for example, into the folds of the dress.

We reached a stainless-steel spiral staircase. Directly above and close to our heads was a similar staircase on which people descending from the top walked. The stair was very steep, and I felt the handrail could have done with being higher up to ensure children didn't fall over it. I'm used to climbing up and down scaffolding and not usually bothered by such things but felt this frightening.

Finally, we made it – after 3.5 hours we reached the top! But it wasn't what we expected. We'd been looking forward to standing on an observation area round the length of the crown. Instead, we were on a tiny platform, on which only about eight people could stand. We hadn't realised we would only be able to see out a few of the windows of the crown. It was therefore a case of taking a few photographs through the unclear windows before starting the descent and letting the next few people up.

It only took half an hour to walk back down including stops at two observation levels in the plinth, going to the shop and for comfort breaks! We think the length of time it took to go up must have been caused by people staying too long on the platform at the top. By the time we were there, everyone moved on quickly spending little time admiring the views.

We walked round the base of the statue and well-manicured grass but decided not to wait in another queue in the restaurant for lunch instead joining the queue for the ferry back across the water!

After the queues at the Statue of Liberty, we were determined to try to avoid queues the next day. As the hop-on hop-off tour bus didn't leave until 9.00 a.m. and the Empire State Building was its 11th stop we decided to walk there.

Although only a 30-minute walk it felt far longer, maybe because the famous building was amongst other buildings and out of sight, so we didn't have the landmark to aim for. We thought we would never arrive.

When we finally did, I was surprised to find an arcade of shops on the ground floor. We didn't stop to look though. We had a mission – to avoid queues – so kept moving quickly. Pre-purchased tickets in hand, we somewhat smugly walked past the already long ticket queue and through the corridors that followed.

As we followed the signs, we felt we were in a three-dimensional maze, going up and down escalators with a nagging suspicion there must be a more direct route. In the end, we arrived at the lifts and were relieved to see only a short queue for several lifts. Our turn soon came, and we entered an enormous lift. The doors shut, but we struggled to know if we were moving. The floor indicator above the doors confirmed we were, showing not individual floor numbers but only every tenth floor as we were travelling so quickly. Our ears popped. It only took about a minute to reach the 86th floor where a shop and a walkway round the outside of the building greeted us. It thrilled us to see the Statue of Liberty and identify other buildings we knew.

My sister Jean and husband David had given our David and Andrew birthday money in advance and suggested they buy something at the Empire State Building and think of them while there, so we did. David bought an Empire State Building number plate, and Andrew an Empire State Building ornament. While in the shop, we saw the teacher and her daughter we met at the Statue of Liberty. They too had planned to come early to avoid the queues!

To go up to the 102nd floor there was a queue. It didn't seem very long. We discovered looks can be deceptive as the queue didn't move for ages, no idea why. Fortunately, once going, the queue moved quickly. This time it was a small lift which only took 6-8 people at a time.

We reached the top and awarded ourselves a gold star for pre-planning. We walked round the indoor Observation Area, taking in all the views before making our way back down in the lifts.

As we were walking through the corridors on the ground floor heading outside, we passed a now enormous queues for tickets.

"You'd have been better off in my tour," we heard a tour guide say to those in the queue as he led his group past them. "I would have pre-booked your tickets and you wouldn't have had to wait in the queue." This was the last thing the people in the queue needed to hear.

Outside we found the bus-stop and waited for the open-topped double-decker. We went upstairs to enjoy the sunshine and see everything at its best. Sun after the previous day's rain was very welcome.

The bus was brought to a halt in a beautiful square with elegant trees and colourful flowerbeds beside the City Hall and Woolworth Building. Cops stood all-round the square.

"What's going on?" a man near us shouted down to a policeman below.

"A politician is coming to make a speech. We're expecting a protest."

While we waited, we were happy to admire the views from our prime viewing seats. But as we've experienced on different holidays, we were left with an unfinished snapshot of something potentially interesting because the bus moved on before we found out who the politician was or if a protest took place.

We got off the tour bus at the stop for the World Trade Center.

Our visit began with the guide on the bus giving us very confusing instructions about how to cross the road, so we were pleased when we arrived inside the enormous building. But we discovered we'd gone wrong somewhere. We were in the wrong "twin tower". It was a magnif-icent building; marble everywhere, carpets we sank into, sunken dining area with a ceiling high enough to allow trees to grow inside.

With more directions we headed for where the guide intended us to be. Like the Empire State Building, we'd pre-paid tickets to go to the top of the building, but the system was different. These had to be exchanged for other tickets and guess what? We'd a large queue to join.

"Only one person for each group needs to queue," an attendant came and told us. "Everyone else should move on and wait." The queue immediately shortened as family members left the queue.

I took David and Andrew to the holding area. We sat on the luxurious carpet and read a book together – very aware of another enormous queue snaking ahead of us. The time came for us to join this and whilst there, we were told to stand against a painted backdrop of the Twin Towers to have our photograph taken. A numbered ticket would allow us to view our photo later. The queue gave the photographers a captive audience, though one family objected strongly. To get their message across after trying repeatedly to tell the photographer they didn't want their photo taken, they turned to face the backdrop. A photo was taken of their backs. It would have been funny if the objectors viewed their photo, liked the picture of their backs and bought it!

Through security, we slowly moved towards the lifts, glad I'd brought the book to read to David and Andrew. Eventually, we reached the lift and went up the 107 floors. Like the Empire State Building, it was a great experience being transported upwards at such speed, taking little over a minute to reach the top.

We made our way to the observation windows round the perimeter, sat on benches looking out at the skyline and identified all the places we'd already visited. A model of Manhattan attracted our attention. Buildings lit up when the integral commentary mentioned them.

An auditorium on this floor was our next port of call. We sat down and fastened our seat belts – literally. It was a simulated helicopter ride, but we hadn't told David and Andrew, waiting instead to see their surprise when the seats started moving. We all enjoyed this.

We felt the cool breeze as the ascending escalator took us higher and outside. Thankfully it wasn't too windy, or the outside area would have been closed. The views were slightly hazy but still worth seeing.

After returning on the escalator, we had some lunch; slices of pizza, heated when we ordered them. Just what we were needing to revive our energy levels.

We all agreed we'd had a good time and cheerfully headed off ready to make our way down. What we hadn't anticipated was a queue for this too! David and Andrew found some computers and played on these while Douglas and I stood in line. They were able to type messages to be displayed outside in lights when it got dark. Unfortunately, our hotel wasn't close enough to see the messages, but we visualised them illuminating the city.

I remember exactly what I was doing less than 17 months later on 11 September 2001 when the 9/11 attacks on the Twin Towers happened. I was in the back room of our house giving a flute lesson. Andrew was in the front room, and yelled, "Come and see what's on the TV!"

We couldn't believe our eyes as the footage of the first plane crashing into the side of the building was repeated. Then we saw the second plane crash into the second tower. The dreadful tragedy was incomprehensible and as we watched our thoughts jumped back and forth to our visit to the Twin Towers such a short time before.

And now all these years later, every time we hear or see anything about the Twin Towers, we not only think of what we were doing when disaster struck, but also the great time we had there before the tragic event. First in our memory for some reason tends to be where we sat and ate pizza!

"I've always wanted to know: why is the Golden Gate Bridge in San Francisco so called when it looks red? Surely it should be gold?" I asked the others as we continued eating our delicious meal in Sri Lanka.

Fortunately, someone more knowledgeable enlightened me. "The name doesn't refer to the colour. It refers to the water it's suspended over – the Golden Gate Strait – the narrow strip of water linking the Pacific Ocean and San Francisco Bay.

"I should have learned that when we were there in 2001, I suppose."

Of course, being us, the Moore clan had to walk across the bridge. Before setting foot on it, we made sure we stopped to take a photo beside the sign telling us the main span between the two supporting towers is 4,200 feet (approximately 1,280 metres).

The walk across and back was brilliant, taking about an hour altogether. There was a breeze blowing but the sky was blue, and the views couldn't have been better. There were many boats sailing and windsurfers zooming along in the water below us. I'm sure all were pleased it was a windy day.

The only problem we had was the lack of eyes in the backs of our heads. The pavement was for both cyclists and pedestrians with no delineation on the pavement to separate the two. As a result, we constantly had to look for cyclists in front and behind us and move out of their way as they clearly weren't going to move round us. We conquered the bridge unharmed and now it brings back great memories whenever we see it on TV.

Towards the end of the same self-drive holiday we stopped at a tourist information office and a very helpful lady told us about a wonderful waterfall we *had* to visit. According to the leaflet it was an "incredible 80-foot waterfall" in the Julia Pfeiffer Burns State Park. Armed with the leaflet, we set off and found without difficulty the carpark off Highway 1.

At the car park, directions evaporated but we saw one sign for a waterfall and uncertainly followed it, heading into the forest. Along the way we saw several people who all confirmed we were going in the right direction. The forest was very pleasant to walk through with a wonderful smell from the pine trees. However, we found ourselves walking up and down steep paths at the end of our day, feeling tired. The cool, calm and collected adults got less so as we debated whether this was the correct way despite all the assurances we'd been given. The leaflet said it was to be 0.64 miles round trip (just over 1km).

After walking about 1.5 miles we met a couple with a map. They showed us where we were and how much further it was to the falls. We realised we were heading for different falls, not the ones we'd come to see.

It was now 5 p.m. We decided not to continue to the alternative falls but instead walked back the way we'd come.

At the bottom, right in front of our noses was the path we should have followed. It went in the opposite direction and not into the forest, but instead through an underpass below the main road we'd driven along.

In the end, we found what we were looking for. The falls were not the spectacular sight we'd built ourselves up for. To be honest, we wouldn't have called them falls at all. What we saw was little more than a trickle of water coming down the rock face. They were certainly not "incredible" as we'd been led to believe. The forest walk turned out to be better.

"What about our walk and climb in Oslo in May 2002 when we went to the ski jump with David and Andrew," Douglas prompted.

"Just to make it clear, we didn't try ski jumping ourselves, but we had fun, even though the day started with a big disappointment for Andrew – there were no fried eggs at the breakfast buffet. For some reason, the chefs in the hotel didn't make them at the weekend, at Andrew's age and stage, not having fried eggs *mattered*!

Undeterred, we made our way to the Metro station, clutching our Oslo cards allowing us free use of the trains. The station was close to the hotel, and we were soon on our way to Holmenkollen – the ski jump. It was a stop-start journey, as there were many stations along the way; one way to build up our levels of anticipation.

When we arrived at Holmenkollen station, there was an exodus as hordes of people got off. We quickly assumed they were also heading for the ski jump as there was a lack of good signposting to tell us the way to go. We were therefore happy to find ourselves walking in the middle of the crowd. A while later without having realised what was happening, we found ourselves no longer in this middle. Somehow, while we were blethering, we'd overtaken many of those who were taking things at a gentler pace. We were second from the front which suited us. Suddenly the couple in front changed direction and headed off along a different road. What should we do? Follow them or take up the lead ourselves? After a quick confab, we decided not to follow as our instinct told us the other couple were going in the wrong direction.

This decision would have been fine if we were on our own. However, to our horror, we noticed everyone was following us! Bearing in mind the signposting was non-existent, and we were following our "instincts" we hoped we were right, and the other couple were wrong. Feeling like the Pied Piper, the pressure was on. This eased slightly when the original leading couple re-joined the crowd. We tried to convince ourselves they had realised the error of their ways and concluded we were right. But we still weren't 100 per cent sure.

This uncertainty continued as other people split from the group and went in different directions. We thought we were getting closer to the ski jump but still no signs. We were determined not to give the impression we didn't have a clue where we were going. On we went, resolutely, thankfully arriving shortly thereafter at the ski jump with our "followers". Only a rolled-up umbrella held aloft was missing from our self-awarded elevated position of tour guides.

It was strange seeing the ski jump and surrounding area in May. There wasn't a flake of snow in sight. The basin area at the bottom of the slope where skiers landed was a lake of water. We walked round the seating area surrounding the "lake", still with the band of loyal followers behind us. In front of us steep concrete steps loomed. Our ascent was about to begin as was another challenge.

The challenge was to maintain our position as the leaders. We couldn't possibly let anyone overtake us now. The climb was tough, but we were not going to be beaten. Douglas and I soon found ourselves unable to speak, our focus being on breathing – deeply. As ever, David and Andrew chatted away, quite the thing just as they did every day in life. Oh, for the fitness of youth. Our determination paid off. We kept our leading position. Douglas and I tried to give the impression to those we met at the top we were just as fit as David and Andrew. I have a feeling they might have seen through the pretence.

At the top of the stairs was the visitor centre and museum but we by-passed these. After all, we'd to get to the top of the ski jump. We got into the lift for the next part of the ascent. Beside the lift were stairs and David and Andrew were disappointed we couldn't walk up them. It turned out, there were plenty of stairs still to climb after the lift. We wondered how the ski jumpers managed every time they wanted to jump.

Finally, we got our first sight of the view from the top. It was breathtaking to look down the route the ski jumpers take. From the top, the slope they land on after leaving the take-off point was so steep, we couldn't see the landing area. Ski jumping is not for the faint hearted and as far as we were concerned it looked terrifying.

Having reached the top and admired the view we made our way back down all the steps. Our legs felt like jelly when we reached the bottom.

We took time to look round the very interesting museum, particularly liking the models showing how the ski jump had been altered over the years to make it longer and steeper.

"How old were you when you were here on a school cruise excursion?" I asked Douglas.

"Fifteen."

"There've been two alterations to the design of the ski jump since then," I established looking at the dated models of the jump. "Each one looks more terrifying than the last."

We returned to the train station and continued to the end of the Metro line so we could go to Tryvannstarnet, a tower where, we'd read, we would see a "panoramic view over Oslo".

We'd no sooner started to walk to the tower than the heavens opened, the rain started – and boy did it pour. The road became a river, but as we were by now wet, we decided to continue to our second ascending adventure of the day.

We passed enormous car parks on our walk from the metro to the tower. I was surprised this tower was popular enough to warrant so many parking spaces.

We arrived at the tower drookit.[19] There was a tearoom and though we would like to have been served, the three young members of staff were deep in conversation and ignored us. Due to this inattention we decided to go up the tower first. Perhaps, we reasoned, when we returned, they would notice and be prepared to serve us. However, like the ski jump, there was a lack of signposting and we ended up interrupting them to

19 Drookit is Scottish for "extremely wet; drenched".

ask where we were to go.

We weren't allowed to climb the stairs but instead had to use the lift. But never mind, we were going to be seeing a "panoramic view over Oslo" we reminded ourselves. The little negativities of the experience so far, would soon be forgotten.

And what can I say about the view? Well, we found ourselves amongst the clouds, only catching glimpses of our surroundings for milliseconds when the clouds parted. These glimpses revealed we were at the same altitude as the tops of surrounding ski slopes. Seeing the tops of chair lifts made me quickly put two and two together: the enormous car parks were for the chair lifts and not for Tryvannstarnet Tower as I'd thought!

We returned to ground level and were met with a similar reception as when we arrived. This was enough to make us decide not to bother with a cuppa and instead head back to the Metro. We hadn't gone far when the rain stopped and the sky cleared a bit, but we opted not to return to the tower for the hoped-for panoramic view. We were 99 per cent sure we wouldn't be welcomed like long lost friends by the tearoom staff, so continued, going instead to the excellent Maritime Museums.

"We'd experiences of queuing, lifts and stairs in Barcelona too, when we went to the Temple de la Sagrada Familia – Gaudi's, at the moment, Unfinished Cathedral," Douglas continued the topic.

There was a queue at the tourist information office, another waiting to get on the hop-on hop-off tourist bus, one waiting to buy entry tickets for the Cathedral then a final one waiting for a lift to take us up one of its towers.

We waited in the final queue for about half an hour, in full sun and heat, and were so grateful when we got into the lift as unexpectedly, it was air-conditioned. As one lady passenger commented, it was worth the two Euros each to go up the lift, just for the air-conditioning – short time though it was.

Out of the lift were stairs to climb. It's impossible to describe the wonderful sights we saw, both the surrounding landscape, and the construction of the cathedral. To see up close the different features and multitude of colours in the building was mind-blowing. We hadn't seen such intricate stone carving or variety of designs and detailing in one building before. Finally, we forced ourselves to move on and walked down the 426 steps, turning down the option of the air-conditioned lift.

Some of the descent was frightening. There was a narrow spiral staircase which didn't have a central support or protection. Fortunately, there was a stainless-steel handrail on the left-hand side which we could hold on to, tightly(!), as we looked down the central hole to see all the spirals of stone stairs, all the way down to ground level.

Next, we went inside the cathedral, and I was taken aback by what I saw. I knew the cathedral wasn't finished, but I hadn't realised we would be walking into a building site, with porta-cabins, hoardings, scaffolding etc. We could see where the next batch of concrete would be poured into moulds for some of the ceiling panels. There was very little of the ceiling completed, so we looked up to the sky.

In an enormous museum underneath the cathedral, was a multitude of drawings, models and photos showing the various stages of construction. The 1:10 scaled Plaster of Paris models showed sections of the cathedral, some now competed, others yet to be built. We saw the workshop where the models were made, ensuring the designs could be replicated in the finished building.

It will be interesting to go back one day to see how the construction of this amazing building is progressing or maybe we'll go when it's no longer "unfinished".

Douglas and I experienced a different climb in Halong Bay, Vietnam.

Despite the thunder and lightning, we'd slept during our one-night mini cruise aboard *Jasmine*, built in the style of a traditional Vietnamese junk with dark wood cladding and three brown sails.

On wakening, we knew we'd a strict timetable to adhere to:

6.30 a.m.: croissants, muffins, tea and coffee would be served.

7 a.m.: tai chi in the dining room (the pouring rain making the upper deck unsuitable for this pursuit).

7.30 a.m.: board the tender to go to Ti Top Island, climb the 430 steps for a great view from the top. Go down again to water's edge for a swim before returning to Jasmine.

9.30 a.m.: check out of room, ready for breakfast in the dining room

It was still raining as we boarded the tender, but we were given long capes to wear. Almost immediately after stepping onto the island, I discovered mine wasn't waterproof. By the end of the outing my skirt and t-shirt underneath were soaking.

Seven of us from the cruise made the trip, the weather I'm sure putting others off. As we were the first group to arrive at the island, it was quiet, which suited us.

It was a steep climb, and one lady was struggling as we neared the top. Douglas and I slowed down.

"Are you OK?" Douglas asked.

"Yes," she assured us. "No need for you to wait," she insisted.

Instead we increased our speed, anxious to reach the top to tell our guide we were concerned about her. I'd assumed he was leading us, but I was wrong; he wasn't there. What I thought was terrible, was the lady's husband *was* at the top, having walked on leaving her on her own. When she reached the top, her face was an awful colour. She sat down on the ground. Her husband disappeared off down the hill, hopefully going for help, I thought. We didn't want to leave her.

"I'm fine," she again reassured. "I'm just feeling a bit seasick."

I could relate to how awful seasickness can be, but I know Douglas wouldn't have abandoned me as she had been. For me though, getting off the boat and doing this climb would have cleared any feelings of seasickness. Everyone's different I suppose.

Her husband returned but alone. He must have gone for some extra exercise rather than for help, we reckoned. He didn't seem in the least bit concerned about his wife.

Returning to the shore, we went for a paddle while others swam. We hadn't known about the swimming so hadn't brought costumes on this holiday.

Back at the boat we saw the lady we'd worried about. She assured us she was fine, which was a relief.

"There are some seemingly uncaring people in the world," I concluded. "Just as well we're perfect! And talking about perfection, so was my shepherd's pie."

Unlike my version of mince with carrot and onion, this had tomato and mild herbs too. The meat was exceptionally lean, just as I like it, and the mashed potato and cheese topping was perfect.

More napkin folding tuition followed, with me struggling to achieve the waiter's aspirations in creating a perfect "Bird of Paradise".

"Hey, I've just realised it's well past my bedtime. Perfecting my 'Bird of Paradise' can wait for another night."

Tablecloths and fine dining

Our second last breakfast beside the canal. How quickly the days have passed. A huge monitor lizard greeted us – in the water thankfully.

The waitress amused us. No matter what she brought to the table for Douglas, she always walked slowly behind him, right round the square table before arriving back to where she started and carefully placed the item on the table. She's never in a hurry.

The uneven steps up to the kitchen are simply cut into the soil bank. I'm always relieved when I see her safely at the top of the steps; I worry her flip-flop sandals are not ideal footwear for this terrain.

Douglas decided to have the strange tasting eggs again, unlike the lovely ones in Trincomalee. We wonder what these egg-laying hens are being fed.

I asked for curd to accompany the fruit. Having heard my request, Sylvia from their separate table, also asked for curd. As time went by, I reckoned someone must have been sent to buy the curd. Finally, the tub (as it comes from the shop) and a bowl were taken to Sylvia. Was this favouritism or were the staff trying to make up for the fact we'd a better fridge in our room?

After Sylvia scooped out the curd she wanted, the tub was brought to me, but without a bowl.

"Can I have a bowl please?" I asked.

The waitress looked a bit confused, but I assumed she understood when the shaking of her head started and she said, "Yes."

No bowl materialised and eventually I gave up waiting. I used my tea plate instead. I'd just about finished eating when she carefully and slowly came down the earth steps again, this time carrying a tray. I was surprised when she came to our table because on the tray wasn't the bowl asked for but two cups and saucers. The "yes" in this case hadn't meant she'd understood.

"It's OK," I said, pointing to the curd to show I'd managed without a bowl and off she went returning up the earth steps with the laden tray and, as ever, a broad smile.

"I'm thinking about the breakfast I loved in India," I said to Douglas. "The one in the heritage hotel where the restaurant waiting staff wore wonderful traditional costumes including stunning turbans and white gloves. The boiled egg I ordered was served in a silver egg cup, complete with a cover which the waiter removed revealing the egg. It was cooked to perfection – cooked white and runny yolk. When I finished, I said to you the egg had been so delicious I wished I could have had another, even though one is my normal limit."

"Yes, and I told you it was easily solved, and you should just order another one," Douglas remembered.

"And for once in my life I did what I was told! I attracted the attention of the waiter and asked if I could please have another egg. When he reached in front of me, I thought he was about to remove my empty egg cup, but no, he lifted off the top half of the silver egg cup revealing a hidden compartment in which sat another egg. I'd never seen anything like it before. And the second was just as good as the first."

It was a different experience and an education for David and Andrew when ordering eggs in New York in 2000. They hadn't heard the expressions "over-easy" or "sunny side up" which made them laugh.

We always went to the same café for breakfast having been so well treated on the first occasion by William the waiter. On the final morning William said to Andrew, "Don't tell me: chocolate milk and eggs over-easy," and on finishing them Andrew told William, "They get better every day. They're even better than Granny's."

They must have been amazing for this to be the case.

But all was not perfect in this café. The pancakes were disappointing, much stodgier than we like and most certainly not as good as Granny's! After the first morning pancakes didn't even get a second chance.

Our favourite breakfast bread experience was in Iceland in 2014. Douglas and I were on a tour, and we stopped at Fontana Laugarvatn, a spa and wellness centre. But before enjoying the warmth of the outdoors geothermal mineral baths with views over the still water of the lake, breakfast was served.

"The rye bread is ready. Follow me," the now spade-carrying guide instructed.

Strange, we thought as we were led outside, then watched as he dug a stainless-steel pot out of the black sand. Beneath the surface, the ground was so hot the loaf of bread had baked there overnight. The wonderful smell of freshly baked, hot bread reached our noses as it was sliced, and while being smothered with butter our mouths couldn't help but water. We were told Icelanders have a simple formula for knowing how much butter to spread on the bread; the butter should be the same thickness as the bread. We were happy to have a bit less butter than this.

"I've just thought about a toast experience," I said to Douglas "Remember breakfast at the Kulata Academy Café in Yulara town square (Australia)?"

This had become a special place for us. It was staffed by trainees of Ayers Rock Resort's National Indigenous Training Academy. They were all so friendly and eager to please and the food was good too.

We placed our breakfast order then sat outside where I was fascinated watching a man sitting on a grass cutting machine. The lawn had been cut but here was one small patch of long blades of grass he'd missed, and I found myself focusing on it wondering if he'd notice too. He didn't and instead went rapidly round and round in circles over a particular strip of the lawn. It looked fun but made no difference to the grass length. Finally, he sped away to his next task.

A waitress approached and asked, "Do you want your toast toasted?"

I was confused wondering if this was something different in Australia.

"Don't you normally toast the toast?" I asked.

"Yes, it's usually toasted, but we just wanted to check," was her reply.

"Yes please, I would like my toast toasted," I confirmed.

Douglas' order, I think, had caused the confusion. At least I'll blame him. He ordered a ham and egg pane, though not sure what a pane was.

"Do you want it toasted?" he was asked

"Yes please."

But just before he paid, he changed his mind and asked for it not to be toasted. This change didn't seem to cause any problem at the till but might have been mixed up with my order further down the production line, resulting in my toast order being changed to one for non-toasted toast.

"Fortunately, the misunderstanding was resolved, I got my toasted toast, and you got the amazing untoasted pane, a large piece of crusty topped soda bread, cut in half and stuffed full of ham and egg. Delicious I recall."

With the end of the holiday now rapidly approaching, I happily placed the last bundle of clothes outside on the veranda to our Sri Lanka room knowing the next time I saw them they'd be clean and carefully folded ready to be packed. This self-indulgence fills me with joy when I arrive home with fresh, clean clothes ready to be put away. A similar "laundry glow" arises when taking washing in from the line in our garden, dried by the sun and the ozone breeze from the nearby sandy beach providing a wonderful fresh smell as I iron.

Douglas and I headed for the bus stop for our final trip to the CIB department store, me still smiling from ear to ear thinking about the laundry.

The bus was busy, and we stood until a couple of stops later, we were offered a seat. It was whilst on the bus a sudden realisation struck me.

"I've forgotten to bring the discount card for the CIB store," I said, trying my best to hide the teasing mirth inside.

Local bus, showing signs of wear and tear

"Tragedy," was his response in a rather non-plus, flat tone of voice. Clearly, he didn't consider the level of "tragedy" warranted getting off the bus and returning to the guest house to collect it.

"But we'll lose out on points on our purchases today." I persevered but even this didn't appear to sway him. Finally, he cottoned on and we laughed at my nonsensical chat.

I decided to have one last look at fabric, not for my mother-of-the-groom wedding outfit but genuinely for a tablecloth this time. Those sewn for me in Sri Lanka two years previously unexpectedly shrank when washed. Loving the matching placemats, I wanted to buy material of a suitable colour to co-ordinate with them.

After much deliberation, we decided on orange material and it was readied for us as before. After paying, we returned to the baker/coffee shop we discovered on our previous shopping trip. We ordered white coffee, and our favourite coconut filled crepe, plus something new: an apple cake made to look like an apple. It was round, about 7.5cm (3") in diameter, smothered in crimson red icing with a little piece of green icing for the stalk. Cutlery wasn't provided and knowing we wanted to try both, the waiter kindly cut both in two. Beneath the red icing, was a cross between a brown sponge cake and a truffle. The flavour was a mystery to us, but it beautifully balanced the intense sweetness of the icing.

"I'm feeling really tired," Douglas said.

"Don't worry, with the sugar intake from the cake and the caffeine in the coffee you will soon be wide awake and probably for a long, long time," the unqualified medic in me advised.

"I'm just thinking about the morning coffees we had with David and Andrew when we were on holiday at our caravan," I continued. "Our first outing of the day after breakfast had to include a morning coffee somewhere."

"Not many days went past without a morning coffee," Douglas acknowledged. "Scones and a coffee for us, toast and a drink for them."

As Andrew grew older, he discovered the delights of hot chocolate. In one café in Kirkcudbright not only was there ordinary hot-chocolate on the menu, but also a large special hot-chocolate which included marsh-mallows, cream and chocolate sprinkles.

I liked to show the boys they were treated equally and even at an early age, encouraged them to understand the value of money. I offered him a choice: special hot chocolate but forego the toast or ordinary hot chocolate and toast as normal. After all the hot chocolate included "food" (albeit marshmallows, cream and sprinkles). With all those calories I knew he wouldn't starve as it would soon be lunchtime. He opted for the special hot chocolate without toast.

Being a parent isn't easy I've decided. It would have been so much easier just to let Andrew have both the special hot chocolate and the toast and not think about the fairness dilemma. Andrew seemed happy with the choices, and I haven't faced accusations of cruelty from him in his now adult years. I suppose therefore I wasn't being unreasonable, though even writing this now, I wonder if I did the right thing.

We also loved walking through the forest at the back of the caravan park to Rockcliffe with its sandy beach. David and Andrew were great walkers right from when they were very young, constantly talking as we walked along.

It was my sister Jean and her family who first experienced the delights of Baron's Craig Hotel in Rockcliffe. We'd seen it many times but hadn't thought it the kind of place to welcome young children, especially ones who were generally wearing wellies to keep feet dry as we walked. However, Jean assured me neither was a problem.

To let you understand the reason for our concerns, the hotel was a magnificent stone building complete with square embattled tower and was positioned on a hill overlooking specular views of the Solway Firth. Its gardens were carefully manicured and on three sides it was surrounded by forests. It looked far too posh for the likes of us.

We made our first visit, little wellies left at the outside door, and were shown into a magnificent lounge with enormous windows looking out across the water. Yes, it was posh. Jean said it would be a real treat for us. We told David and Andrew they had to pretend they were princes (the hotel did look like a castle after all) and they had to be on their best behaviour.

We were the only people in the lounge. The lady who came to take our order was delightful and had an air about her suggesting she had worked there for many years. We ordered coke and crisps for David and Andrew and coffee for Douglas and me.

Nothing was rushed. We relaxed, absorbing the atmosphere as we waited. The crisps and coke were brought from the bar. The lady returned with the tray and carefully placed in front of us a silver coffee pot, teapot and pot of hot water. A silver bowl containing white and brown sugar cubes and jugs of hot and cold milk followed. Next, a two-tier cake stand with four warmed miniature scones and four small rounds of melt in the mouth shortbread, was put on the table. The jam was none of your mass-produced kind, but home-made and delicious.

It was a treat, having wonderful service in amazing surroundings and feeling we were special to the staff. The boys behaved just like good princes and were allowed one final treat before we left: a cube of brown and white sugar from the sugar bowl.

We returned during subsequent holidays but unfortunately, the hotel changed hands several times over the years, and though we kept going it was never the same. One occasion particularly sticks in our memory.

David and Andrew were much older by this time which in some ways was a disadvantage.

As usual, we went in and stopped at the reception desk where we asked for morning coffee. The man, who we learned was the new owner, got in a flap on hearing our request, moving uneasily from side to side and looking as though he didn't know what to do.

"That's a bit of a problem," he started by saying, going on to explain, "You've sort of caught us between breakfast and lunch."

We inwardly agree; morning coffee *is* between breakfast and lunch but wondered why this was a problem. He went on to explain further, "You see we've stopped serving breakfast and we haven't started serving lunch yet."

Still this didn't make sense. After all, isn't the whole point of morning coffee to have something different to eat and drink between the two?

"Does this mean you don't serve morning coffee?" I asked, sensing David and Andrew's amusement behind me and trying not to laugh myself.

"Well I can give you cups of coffee," he told me.

"So, you don't have any scones?" I further asked, by now hearing David and Andrew sniggering.

"Eh ... no. The delivery hasn't arrived yet." he replied, wringing his hand, just like the character Basil Fawlty (played by John Cleese), in the TV series *Fawlty Towers*.

"Any shortbread then?" Shortbread is after all, a traditional Scottish nibble.

"We don't have shortbread either."

"What about biscuits?" I asked as a last resort, by now trying desperately to choke back the laughter bubbling up inside me.

"Well I'm not sure. I'll see what I can come up with." And off he disappeared.

We went and sat down, unable to believe the scenarios we had seen in a comedy programme on TV now happening in real life. Ever since, we've referred to the hotel as *Fawlty Towers*.

Coffee and biscuits were brought to the table by a lovely waitress, but we realised David and Andrew needed more sustenance.

"Can we have some crisps too, please?" I asked.

"You want crips?" was the reply in broken English.

"Yes please, two packets of salt and vinegar crisps."

While eating these, David and Andrew noticed the date on the packet:

they were well past the use by date.

The owner came later to ask if everything was OK, "Yes, thank you, though I think you should check the crisps behind the bar, as they're out of date."

"Oh," he replied with exasperation. "That's the waitress. She's Polish you know."

Clearly, he was Basil Fawlty in disguise we concluded.

Another in-between-meals snack I remember was in one of the landside restaurants in Glasgow airport the night before we flew to Madeira in 2012. David and Andrew had a plate of chips and, as ever, Andrew added copious amounts of tomato sauce to his. He accidently dropped a chip on the floor and picked it up carefully wrapping it in a serviette. This package ended up looking like a chopped off finger, the tomato sauce without doubt looking very much like fresh blood. They were highly amused.

"You can't leave it on the table," I said.

"Why not?" Andrew said.

"Because it might give the waitress a fright."

Unsurprisingly David and Andrew thought it was very funny, imagining and verbalizing possible outcomes; screams from a terrified waitress as she fainted and collapsed in a heap on the floor followed by panic 999 phone calls to the police and ambulance services and so on.

"Can we hide and see what happens?"

"No," I said much to their disappointment.

"I'm glad we tried Sri Lankan apple cake, even if it was a bit sweet for us," Douglas said, and I agreed. "Time to go now for the bus back to the guest house with this tablecloth material."

Purchases dropped off, we made our way to the Beach Lodge Hotel where we joined Sylvia, George, Jacqui and Paul for lunch.

"Did you get your material?" I was asked

"Yes, but I think I've bought too much. Because the last material shrank, I didn't want to get too little, so I asked for five metres. There was only a little left on the bale after this was measured, so I said I'd take six metres, to be on the safe side. Seeing there was still a bit left, I increased this to seven metres and was given the last remaining bit of material. Even allowing for shrinkage, the table and its extension will be well and truly covered. Mind you, I think I could cover the whole kitchen/dining room extension too! Here's me a Quantity Surveyor and I don't know how much material to buy. I'll stick to counting bricks."

I ordered a plate of crab and sweet corn soup.

"The taste of this soup has transported me to a sea food lunch I will never forget. In July 2001 we'd just returned from a fantastic tour of Alcatraz Island, a place I think anyone visiting San Francisco should go to."

We went to the *Sour Dough Bread Company* at Fisherman's Wharf. Douglas and I ordered clam chowder, something I hadn't eaten before. What made it special and memorable was the truly delicious chowder was served in a hollowed out circular loaf. The bread removed to create the "bowl" was served at the side so could be eaten with the soup. Nothing was wasted. No washing up required either as we ate the bread bowl too!

Several days later, having driven in our rented car through Death Valley and Yosemite, we got a pleasant surprise in Oakhurst. We were nearing the end of our meal, and a couple in the table next to us rose to leave. They came over and told us how well-behaved David and Andrew were. They said what a pleasure it had been because often their mealtime is spoiled by dreadfully behaved children at nearby tables. Inside ourselves, we beamed with pride. David and Andrew's heads fortunately didn't swell too much – they were still able to get out of the restaurant door as we left!

Later in the holiday, we were in Monterey. We saw a tempting restaurant and went in.

"Can I have a mint julep," Douglas asked when the drinks order was being taken.

"I'll ask," the waitress replied but returned saying, "I'm sorry but unfortunately the barman doesn't have any fresh mint, but he would make it with mint cordial."

"No. Thanks anyway. I'll order something else," he said.

Douglas went out of the restaurant to put more money into the meter where the car was parked. While he was away, the waitress came over with the drink he had ordered plus a mint julip.[20]

"The barman said he would like him to try the mint julip made with the mint cordial and let him know how it compared with the 'real thing' made with mint leaves. He's never made a mint julip before and wants views on this variation. He won't charge for this cocktail."

When Douglas returned, I explained all this to him. He was embarrassed and confessed to me and the waitress, "Just as the barman

[20] Mint julip = a cocktail with a Bourbon Whiskey base and fresh mint leaves.

hasn't made one before, I haven't drunk a mint julip before, so I won't be able to offer any comparison." He thoroughly enjoyed it and try as he might to pay for it, they wouldn't accept any money.

The food, location and staff were fantastic, but we were about to learn something new when we returned to the car. We noticed something on the windscreen, a parking ticket. We couldn't understand this, as there was still 17 minutes on the meter.

After examining the ticket in detail, we discovered we were wrongly parked, facing oncoming traffic and we were also more than the maximum distance away from the kerb. We didn't know these rules. We were more than the permitted 18" (nearly 46cm) away from the kerb. Yes, I know, 18" is a significant distance, but there was a reason. There was a fence at the edge of the pavement, so if we'd parked any closer, we wouldn't have been able to open the car doors.

This was an upsetting end to the day plus hassle the next day. Douglas phoned to pay the fine, only to be told the ticket wasn't yet in the computer system, so he couldn't pay over the phone, so we had to go to the appropriate office to pay. Later, we saw a traffic warden using a measuring rod: lesson learned.

My crab and sweet corn soup and the other's lunches finished, we went for a swim in the sea before Sylvia and I arranged transport to collect us from the Beach Lodge Hotel and take us to Jasmine Beauty and Massage Centre.

When we arrived at the Centre, we discovered the person at the hotel had booked massages rather than a facial and flower bath for Sylvia, and a pedicure plus a flower bath for me. I was determined to find someone who could give my feet the tender loving care they deserved. We would have to wait two hours for the treatments we wanted. Plus, we were advised, only herbal baths were available as there was a lack of flowers at this time of year. We were puzzled by the shortage of flowers and didn't want to hang around for two hours so booked the facial and pedicures for the next morning. There was no point having herbal baths. Having a bath before a relaxing dinner was what we'd wanted; having one the next day before a final holiday swim seemed to defeat the purpose. The minibus took us back to meet our respective husbands.

The task of checking-in online for our homeward journey made our departure seem all the closer.

My face lit up when I saw my last batch of pristine, neatly folded laundry.

"It's great I have a wife who is so easily pleased," Douglas said smiling, as I lifted the pile into our room.

This was Paul and Jacqui's last night and at the Coconut Lodge Restaurant, the waiter excitedly met us before showing us to a specially decorated table. Diagonally across the usual orange, green and pink checked tablecloth, he had placed a small square black tablecloth and on top of this, along the length of the table, was a green table cloth scrunched up to form a table runner resembling ocean waves. On this were posies of artificial flowers and a candle stood tall in a glass lantern. All our napkins were folded and looked just like lit candles.

"Look, we got a real candle!" Sylvia spotted. "More that we got in the Trincomalee restaurant, even though we were promised one."

Yes, the waiter had gone out of his way to make our time here memorable.

We all ordered and were delighted with our varied meals. Douglas had jumbo prawns served with mayonnaise and wedges of lime along with an upturned bowlful of rice decorated with a flowerhead. I had garlic prawns served with mashed potatoes and salad. I know it sounds ridiculous having mashed potatoes, but this was at my request as I needed a change from rice and noodles. The potatoes where fantastic; I could easily have had a plate of them only.

Sylvia and George both had steaks, each perfectly cooked to their own requirements. Paul opted for the enormous mixed grill which included steak, chicken, pork, sausage and liver (I think I've remembered every-thing – well except the chips) and Jacqui had lemon chicken. I give details of all of these to give an idea of the range and versatility of dishes available. And this is just a fraction of the menu which extended to include a wide range of the Sri Lankan and Italian dishes. We think the chef is amazing. While other restaurants offer varied menus, none consistently provided us with delicious food, no matter what we chose. We could relax and enjoy our evening.

Our napkin folding skills continued to develop under the watchful eye and instruction of our waiter who showed us even more designs.

We parted company with Jacqui and Paul who returned to the guest house as they were due to leave in the middle of the night for their flight. The rest of us headed for Rodeo Bar for a drink, but it was too busy, so we went to one next door. This was very fortunate as on one of the walls was a large canvas painting of stick fishermen. I hadn't managed to buy a postcard of them so was happy to be able to take a photo of the canvas as a reminder of the sentimental image I had in my mind.

"I can't believe how much I enjoyed the potatoes tonight," I said to Douglas as we walked back to the guest house.

"Sometimes the simple meals are the best. We've had some wonderful meals abroad; like the one in the Dubai fish market restaurant on our way back from your teaching session in Hong Kong in 2013," Douglas recalled.

"Oh yes. It wasn't at all what I expected. I thought we were going to a fish market with a restaurant attached to it, not a restaurant in the hotel next to ours."

So, where did the "fish market" aspect of the restaurant come from? Well in the restaurant were a few imitation market stalls, complete with thatched canopies.

"It was funny being given a dish of French fries when we sat at the table, rather than a basket of bread we tend to get in the UK," I remarked.

We were taken to the "market stalls" and shown the many varieties of fresh fish.

"Which would you like?" we were asked.

We chose a massive tiger prawn, some squid, and a locally caught fish. All were weighed and carefully placed in a wicker shopping basket after which we were asked to choose accompanying vegetables from a separate stall. This was the last we saw of the ingredients until they were brought cooked and beautifully presented from the kitchen.

We'd waited in anticipation of the chef's creativity as we sat overlooking the Creek watching all the well-lit tourist boats passing by. We were not disappointed. The tiger prawn was cooked in lemon and garlic sauce and the squid, deep-fried. The fish was cooked in oyster sauce and served with stir fried vegetables and rice. I was surprised the fish was filleted, having expected it to come to the table head and all.

"And then a sample tray of deserts was brought to the table," I recalled. "You chose crème caramel with fruit and were surprised to receive two varieties of crème caramel: vanilla and chocolate. I was full so didn't order anything. But because the waitress brought me a spoon too, I *had* to sample yours. And finally, you enjoyed a Turkish coffee."

"It was a wonderful experience," Douglas said. "And the *Sounds of Silence* experience at Yulara in Australia was another night to remember."

When the coach arrived at the hotel, I was surprised to learn the journey would only take 15 minutes. I was expecting to be taken closer to Uluru. Seeing road signs indicating "water treatment" and "refuse disposal" then passing the industrial looking coach station continued my uneasy feelings. Much of the journey thereafter was on an unmade road, and for us passengers it was like going over corrugated steel sheeting, setting our teeth a-chattering. The bus driver did his best to drive on the very edges of the track where there was a bit more soil with fewer undulations.

The coach stopped. We'd arrived in the desert in the middle of nowhere, so I felt things were looking up. We climbed some steps and found ourselves on a platform on top of a dune overlooking the Uluru-Kata Tjuta National Park, where we were greeted by waiting staff with trays of bubbly. Uluru was in the distance in front of us and behind the sun was lowering itself for the night beside Kata Tjuta. Sounds of a man playing a didgeridoo filled the air.

We soon found ourselves talking to a lovely couple, Diane and Philip, while canapés were brought round and the sound of happy chitchat joined the didgeridoo. Watching the sun slowly setting was very relaxing and seeing the varying light and colour effects on Uluru somewhat hypnotic. Once the sun set, the red, green and golden colours around us further intensified.

We were led down another path to a lower area where ten large round tables lay before us on the red desert sand, each bedecked with white tablecloths and central light. (Cutlery, napkins and glasses were also included – just in case you were wondering.) We found everyone at our table friendly and easy to talk to as the cloudless blue sky changed to intense black which lit with countless twinkling stars.

Dining began with a soup starter followed by a "Bush Tucker Inspired" buffet. While at the buffet, the waitresses went round refolding all the napkins, always an indication of top-level service I feel. Must remember to do this when I next have guests.

After the main course, the central battery-operated light on each table and similar buffet lights were switched off and we found ourselves in complete darkness. At this point we were asked to be silent for a minute or two and look up at the sky. Above us was a mass of stars with the Milky Way stretching from one side of the sky to the other. It reminded me of caravan holidays in Kippford where I saw the Milky Way for the first time. Initially I thought I was looking up at clouds before realising it was a mass of stars. Being in Kippford meant we got away from light pollution allowing us to see the wonders of the night sky,

A man came and gave us a talk about the stars in this southern hemisphere sky. More surprises as I hadn't expected such a humorous explanation of what we could see as we looked skyward. It was also very easy to identify the stars he was talking about because he had a couple of special torches with long beams which he used as pointers. Otherwise I don't think I would have been able to pick out the Southern Cross amongst the innumerable stars, planets and galaxies this exceptionally clear atmosphere allowed us to see.

At the end of the talk we were given the opportunity to look through a powerful telescope set up away from the tables. Douglas and I went while waiting for our table's turn to go to the dessert buffet. There were a few people in front of us and I listened to their "Oo-s" and "Aa-s" as they looked at the stars the telescope was trained on: Orion's belt.

My turn came. All I could see through the telescope was a black circle so couldn't join in the "Oo-s" and "Aa-s". Was this a modern version of *The Emperor's New Clothes* story, I wondered, in which everyone in the crowd said how wonderful he looked when actually he was naked, but no one except finally a little boy said so?

I kept jiggling my position and every so often had a fleeting glimpse of stars before my view returned to blackness. Finally, I mastered the technique and saw what I was supposed to see and furthermore managed to keep it in sight. Yes, it was amazing to think the light we were seeing was 175,000 light years away, but I wasn't as amazed at what I saw as the others had been. From the exclamations I heard I was expecting to see much more detail, like looking at the moon and seeing the craters. This turned out to be an unrealistic expectation.

The dessert buffet offered a good selection and I wasn't disappointed. We'd plenty of liquid refreshments too as coffee and port joined the continually topped-up wine and juice glasses we'd had throughout the meal.

Despite my initial misgivings as we travelled, this was a very special evening and a fantastic way to spend our last evening in Yulara.

"That was a unique experience, but I think it's also special when we eat as locals do when we travel," Douglas said.

"Yes, me too, like our first family experience of eating in Hong Kong in 2007. Choosing a restaurant was far from easy as there were so many! The narrow roads were filled with small restaurants cheek by jowl on both sides. We ended up choosing one with lots of locals eating in it, sure this was a sign of good food, and, very importantly one with pictures of the food on the menus. Otherwise, we wouldn't have had a clue what to order."

David's meal arrived first, and he sat patiently waiting for our other meals to be served. Mine arrived. We waited some more. Andrew's came and after another wait, Douglas told us to start before it got cold. This we did and had eaten most of our food, before catching the waiter's attention to say we were still waiting on one meal. He nodded and disappeared, finally arriving with Douglas' meal.

Then, looking around we saw all the tables were served one plate at a time. This was put in the middle of the table and everyone shared each dish as it came, rather than all food being brought at the same time or each person having a meal to themselves as we were accustomed to. We'd learned something new.

In 2013, Douglas and I along with another lecturer Richard went out with Gabriel the college's Hong Kong local representative for a meal in a small restaurant, very popular with Hongkongers. Douglas, Richard and I were the only foreigners and even though we'd booked a table, we'd a while to wait. We did so standing beside a large tank of shellfish and swimming fish. Like us they were waiting, but for them it was waiting to be consumed!

We sat back as Gabriel kindly ordered, selecting dishes this restaurant was famous for. We had no idea what had been ordered but were not disappointed with the array of dishes.

First, a different variety of abalone from the one I had in soup previously in the Jumbo King Floating Restaurant in Aberdeen (Hong Kong). Soup and several main dishes followed. Douglas and I weren't sure what the "meat" was and didn't like to ask as it tasted good and we might have been put off if we discovered what it was.

We'd just finished eating and I turned to Douglas to say it was amazing all the dishes had arrived more or less together, and in an order we would expect in the UK. However, a dish of kai lan (Chinese broccoli) unexpectedly arrived. It was very good but strange to eat it on its own rather than with the main dishes.

Watermelon was a refreshing end to the meal – except it wasn't the end. Bowls of sweet lentil soup (which is a dessert) appeared. I was stuffed full so just had a taste but found the lentil soup was the only thing I wasn't keen on.

"We were surrounded by Chinese restaurants when we rented an apartment in Melbourne's China Town, in Australia, too," Douglas said.

And I cringed as I remembered my poor observation skills during our first meal there.

We walked down the narrow roads looking at pictures of food on menus of the innumerable restaurants as there were no English translations. Finally, we decided which one to eat in.

It was like a fast food restaurant; we ordered our food at a counter, it was made, we paid and took our trays of food to a basic bench table at the window. We sat with our trays in front of us, watching the world go by as we ate.

"It's nice eating a Chinese meal in amongst all the locals. It reminds me of Hong Kong," I said to Douglas, to which he replied, "But this is a Japanese restaurant!"

"What?" I said, surprised at his reply. "How do you know?"

"Well there are Japanese flags, and Rising Sun Ensigns decorating the place to begin with."

I hadn't noticed these, but I suppose I wasn't looking for them assuming all restaurants in China Town would be Chinese. It wasn't the Chinese food I expected, but it was a brilliant meal.

We were in Melbourne for five nights and by our last night we were yet to have a Chinese meal so clearly this had to be rectified. We crossed the courtyard outside our apartment and chose to turn right to begin the task of selecting a restaurant. At most doors someone stood holding a menu inviting passers-by in. Finally, we chose one based on the delightful smile we got from the girl outside. We were eating early as is our norm, so the restaurant wasn't busy, but reassuringly there was a large Chinese family sitting at a huge round table.

The smiles we received outside continued inside with the waiting staff. We were shown to a table for two and sat down. I immediately realised there was something wrong with my chair as it wobbled perilously when I moved. Not wanting to spend the rest of the meal trying to balance on the chair, I decided to swap it for one at the unoccupied table next to us. Sitting down, I discovered it also wobbled.

I stood up again and was making my way to another empty table when one of the smiling waitresses came over wondering, I'm sure, what I was up to. I explained about the wobbly chairs, with hand signals and demonstrations as she had difficulty understanding my English and my Chinese is non-existent. On realising what was wrong, she quickly brought me another chair. Gratefully I sat down – and wobbled.

By this point I was getting a bit embarrassed and said it didn't matter. I would perfect my balancing technique I thought. But she would have none of it and insisted we moved to another table. Apologetically we did as we were told. Unfortunately, I knew I was going to be sitting on the wobbly chair I'd initially swapped, but decided I wasn't going to say anything. But low and behold it didn't wobble! We realised it was an uneven floor causing the wobble and not any of the chairs. We'd originally been sitting where a wall had been demolished and unevenly floored over.

The waitresses continued to keep an unobtrusive, watchful eye on us. I didn't notice until I accidentally dropped my napkin and bent down to pick it up. Before I could reach it, a waitress was at my side saying she would get me a new one.

We had such a happy time; the food was great, and we successfully ate a Chinese meal in China Town.

"We've had fun when eating out with David and Andrew too," I said, feeling a happy glow as I remembered. "Do you remember the puzzle booklet I took one evening when we were in Madeira in 2012? It was a 12-year-old freebie from a newspaper with its dated quiz questions. The highlight was the question requiring us to calculate how many Robin Reliant cars were equivalent to two Mercedes and two Porches, basing our answer on other considerations of these car types."

David set to, writing out mathematical formulae on the white paper tablecloth while Douglas and Andrew became engrossed discussing the problem finally agreeing it was seven Robin Reliants. David eventually arrived at an answer too: six and two-thirds. I agreed with Douglas and Andrew having used simultaneous equations.

Fortunately, the quiz booklet came with answers, so we turned to the back to see who was right. The answer was four! So much for my memory of school maths!

David was determined to work out where he had gone wrong. Soon, not one but two table covers were covered with his calculations.

The rest of us felt there was another possibility: the back of the book was wrong. (Unlikely I know, but we were happy with this solution to our dilemma). Fortunately, David agreed to give up when the food arrived and before we'd to ask for a third tablecloth.

Andrew said he would ask his flat mates who were studying mathematical subjects at university. Come to think about it, he didn't ever tell us the answer. As a result, none of us are any the wiser about how to establish the number of Reliant Robin cars equivalent to two Mercedes and two Porches. (2+2 = 4)

Another night we made a return visit to a restaurant up the hill from the hotel. The owner didn't speak English but his gentle nature meant we really liked him. That night he had a lot of fun with us showing language isn't a barrier to humour. For example, I (teetotal person that I am) had a glass of beer put down in front of me instead of Douglas. He knew exactly how to tease us.

This teasing continued with David and Andrew. The best was when we asked for the bill. He came with a printed bill from the cash register. It was about a metre (3 feet) long. He gave it to Andrew along with the credit card payment machine and waited.

Andrew swiftly passed it all to his Dad who was relieved to find most of the strip of paper was blank.

As we left, he shook our hands warmly, appearing to have enjoyed his time with us as much as we'd had with him.

"Happy times," we agreed and said night-night, sad our Sri Lankan holiday was so nearly at an end.

Tranquil surroundings for beauty treatments

Beauty treatments and
time to say goodbye

Take Two: our second trip to the Jasmine Beauty and Massage Centre. Sylvia and I were once again taken by minibus to the Centre and this time escorted to one of the many treatment rooms. I was surprised we were both taken to the same room, me having a pedicure and Sylvia a face massage. Part of the experience of a face massage, I think, is to relax – without background noises such as someone like me screaming in pain while having a pedicure. The pain refers to our last experiences of having a pedicure in Sri Lanka two years previously. I think I need to explain.

Sylvia and I decided to go for a pedicure. Our friend Iain recommended a man on the Main Street.

"He is very thorough," he told us, adding, "It might be a little bit sore." But we women are made of sterner stuff and what was a little pain to the likes of us?

In the door we went, and Sylvia was ushered to sit in the dentist-like chair. A foot spa was brought for her to soak her feet in. A little chatting began, but his English wasn't very good, and our Sri Lankan language was non-existent. I sat on a big leather couch, flicking through magazines from the coffee table in front of me.

The pedicure started and I became aware Sylvia wasn't looking very relaxed. She looked intently at what the pedicurist was doing and every so often her face contorted. I now had to fulfil my role as distractionist. I started chatting to her, trying to draw her attention away from her feet – for a few nanoseconds anyway. The prodding and cutting, scraping and snipping quickly drew her attention back. She even got to the stage of saying, "Ouch – that's sore," at which point he looked up, smiled, rubbed her leg and said, "It's OK."

Clearly it wasn't OK, but she soldiered on as my thoughts turned to it being me next.

The man took much longer than we expected. It had been our intention to go back to the guest house, have a shower and come back into town with George, Douglas and Iain for a meal. I realised, there wouldn't be time to do this if Sylvia waited for me. I told her to go back on her own and come back with the men on their way to the meal, by which time I should be finished. I would forego the shower.

And so, my torture began. I received the same treatment – and pain – as Sylvia. He even managed to draw blood from one of my toes. I too got the same smile and rubbing of leg treatment when I told him he had hurt me.

I was still sitting in the chair when the others returned, and Iain came in to see how I was getting on.

"I don't think your description of 'a little bit sore' comes close to an appropriate description of the pain we've endured!" I teased.

Afterwards I found walking sore. My toenails had been cut far too short and were digging into the flesh at the top of my toes. My cut toe started to swell and looked as though it was infected. I'm not convinced sterilisation of equipment was part of the normal routine in the establishment.

It's because of my experience Douglas and I said, "No, don't go there" when we saw other tourists looking at the pricelist.

The treatment room in the Jasmine Beauty and Massage Centre was extremely hot. A disadvantage of being the first morning customers was the air conditioning was only switched on when we went into the room. I wondered if I would be able to cope with the heat. Fortunately, it eventually began to make an impact and the temperature decreased to a more acceptable level.

Because Sylvia and I were in the same room and I didn't want to disturb her I didn't speak much to the girl who was doing my pedicure. If I did, I spoke quietly. Sylvia was lying next to me, eyes shut, looking very relaxed and peaceful. She had an ear infection in both ears so had drops and big dods of cotton wool in them. As a result, she couldn't hear when the girl doing her face massage asked her a question. She was effectively dead to the world and oblivious to being spoken to.

It was therefore just as well we were in the same room, and even better we were close to one another. I took on new roles; interpreter and message relay-er. My first task was to understand what she was trying to say or ask as her English was limited. My next task, in the absence of a microphone or megaphone, was to yell at the top of my voice, to stir

Sylvia from her slumbers. She removed the handfuls of cotton wool from her ears, looked over, bleary eyed, and sleepily said, "What?"

I explained the "Would you like …" question she needed to answer.

"Yes, OK," she invariably replied. The cotton wool was carefully replaced, and the previous relaxed state resumed.

On one occasion the question was, "Do you want your eyebrows threaded?"

"OK," came the reply.

The problem was there was a follow-on instruction, but the cotton wool was already repositioned in her ear. A further yell was required from me. This time Sylvia tried to understand me without removing the cotton wool, so it took several attempts with miming from me to convey the girl wanted Sylvia to stretch the skin round her eyebrows with her fingers. During all this, work on my feet continued.

What was this pedicure like? I must admit I had a flashback to the experience two years previously when I saw the tray of what can genuinely be called instruments of torture. However, there wasn't much pain this time. At one point the girl clearly recognised I was pulling my foot away from her. This was before I worked out Sylvia couldn't hear, and I was still trying not to speak so actions rather than words were required.

"Am I tickling?" My beautician enquired.

"No, you're hurting me," I replied quietly, still thinking of Sylvia. Either I spoke too quietly, or she didn't understand as she did the same thing again. The outcome was Sylvia was no longer uppermost in my mind and I made sure the beautician heard and understood me. Afterwards the treatment continued pain free.

"Everything fine?" I was asked at the end of the treatment. Disappointed, I had to say, "No." Remedial work followed to rectify the problems I've become accustomed to.

My treatment finished before Sylvia, so I went to the lounge area where I was given a cup of herbal tea. I can honestly say it was totally and utterly disgusting. Being herbal it must be good for me, I thought, so persevered. But good for me or not, I was beaten, only taking about half of it. Sylvia wasn't offered this delight, but I made sure she didn't miss out. She took one sip of what was left of mine and agreed 100 per cent with my verdict.

We were driven back to the guest house where Douglas and George swooned (or so we liked to think) when they saw us two beauties. I'm sure they didn't notice any difference whatsoever.

Douglas was concerned about my wellbeing though. "Did you get on OK? Suffer any injuries this time?"

Smiling I reassured him, "I've come through the ordeal unscathed."

"I don't understand why you put yourself through these treatments."

"I keep hoping things will work out well and one day my nails will look like Andrew's lovely ones."

"Well they didn't a couple of years ago when we were on the cruise in Halong Bay, Vietnam, did they?"

"That's true. I ended up being the instructor, though the only knowledge I have is based on filing my own fingernails!"

"Yes, and there was blood gushing out your thumb by the end of it."

"Slight exaggeration, but everything was sorted, and I ended up not having to pay for the manicure which was maybe a good thing as I'm not convinced there was any improvement. My nails certainly weren't any closer to looking like Andrew's as I'd hoped. He can't have inherited his nails from me."

"We've had some good experiences though," I said to Douglas, "like in Ranthambore in India, in 2013."

Some of the tour group were going on an optional tiger spotting game drive to Ranthambore National Park. As we were going to be doing two such drives the next day, we decided to have a time of relaxation at the hotel.

We went for a swim before checking out the availability for massages. Amazingly we could be taken straight away. We opted to assume this wasn't an indication of the masseurs' lack of skill giving rise to everyone else in the hotel avoiding her.

I chose a Classical Abhyanga which promised "great benefits to body, mind, skin and immune system". What more could I ask for? I hadn't had such a massage before, but I'm always prepared to try something new. Copious amounts of warm oil were used in this full body massage, and I had an hour of total relaxation.

At the end, the lady asked, "How old you are?"

"Nearly 52," I replied after deducting my year of birth from the current year. I never remember how old I am.

"How many children you have?"

"Two."

"No way: you lie. You 30-year-old!" Patter or not, I decided to believe every word she said.

I couldn't say if all the promised benefits were achieved but the sense of relaxation and such a laughable comment were good enough for me.

Douglas had a head and shoulder massage which he enjoyed too but didn't come away having received compliments like me. (I told myself I was the only person she had ever said such a thing to.)

We went out of the hotel and looked in a few shops before Douglas decided to have his hair cut. We'd been told a hair cut in India was an experience not to be missed, though the details were kept secret from us. Suffice to say, Douglas was curious, and we had time to spare.

Leaving the main road, walking past a wandering cow and up an unmade dusty lane we found a barber, who looked about 18, in an open-fronted hut. The hut had three ancient looking barber's chairs in it and a band of mirrors round the three walls, the fourth being open to the lane outside.

To begin with everything was familiar. Douglas had his hair raised with a comb and cut with scissors, but things changed as a cutthroat razor blade tidied up the edges.

I'd been videoing the procedure and at this point the barber brushed away the cut hairs, removed the gown from Douglas and stepped away from the chair. Douglas looked up with a contented, relaxed smile on his face. He was enjoying this pampering.

A towel was put across his chest and I watched as the young barber rubbed oil in his hands before massaging it onto Douglas' scalp using his fingertips. He sprayed something on Douglas' hair before continuing the vigorous rubbing. Douglas was having trouble keeping his head in an upright position, such was the force of the rubbing. Every now and then the barber looked round at the video camera and smiled broadly. He was putting on a show for me.

The next part of the "treatment" involved the barber putting his hands together, fingers straight, like in a praying position. Keeping both hands together, he slapped Douglas' head all over with the back of one of the hands. As if this wasn't enough, pinching his scalp all over followed. My comment on the video, in between laughing, was Douglas didn't get treatment like this from his barber back home. A rub with his palms, a few more slaps and it was time for a neck massage. A rub down with the towel followed before combing through his hair to allow him to check everything looked the way it should.

Things didn't end there. The beard had to be trimmed with a few more smiles directed to the camera. The young man clearly liked being a film star as he grinned from ear to ear. When Douglas' whole body stopped reverberating from the "massage" and the blade swishing had stopped, he too had a broad smile on his face.

"And what about the great time we had with Chris and Dave in Dubai in 2014? A week of relaxation in a beach-side hotel. Just what we were needing!" I said to Douglas, trying to balance dubious experiences with positive ones.

There, going outside to sun-bathe was a pampering session in itself. Sun loungers were positioned by an attendant, meeting our individual level of shade requirements, and we were presented with towels. Much appreciated cold, wet face clothes were brought at regular intervals to wipe our fever-like brows along with ice-cold bottles of water.

The sandy beach was immaculate having been carefully raked before we arrived in the morning. Wearing shoes was essential to prevent feet burning on the sand as we walked down to the sea for a swim. It was like walking into a hot bath – very different from the temperature of the water around the UK coast, which could often be politely described as "chilly". Chris told us the previous time they had been there the sea was too hot to go into.

The waves were just right for us to enjoy activities we associated with our childhood – jumping as the waves came towards us and launching ourselves forward on our fronts to be swept towards the water's edge. Great fun!

One day, Douglas and I decided to try a more adult activity indoors. There was a spa in the hotel with Hammam pools in it. Not having heard of Hammam pools before we didn't know what to expect.

After putting on our swimming costumes, we went through the door from our respective changing rooms into a large captivating space within which were five different pools. Four smaller ones were spaced round the perimeter of the room with a larger pool in the middle.

The whole room was very tastefully decorated in a Roman theme. Mosaic tiles decorated the floor and panels around the four small pools. Marble pillars surrounded the main central pool, and these supported a feature ceiling which looked like the sky. Between the pillars were graceful statues of Roman figures. Lighting was subdued with up and down-lighters in the floor, walls and pools creating a tranquil atmosphere.

An attendant appeared and explained we should start in the hottest pool before going into each of the pools in order of their temperature until we finished in the coolest one. On the side of each pool was a sign detailing the water temperature. We felt our bodies relax as we rested on the underwater seat ledges around the hottest pool which was about 100°F (37.8°C).

Thereafter we noticed the length of time spent in each pool was directly proportional to the temperature of the water. By the time we got to the fifth and final pool, which had a temperature of 59°F (15°C), I didn't want to get in at all. Douglas bravely stepped in and reassured me it wasn't as bad as I thought. I listened to his advice and stepped in but immediately realised it was a mistake to trust my husband so implicitly. The water felt freezing after the other pools. I forced myself to sit down so I could say I'd not chickened out.

Apparently, the coldest pool did "wonders for our blood circulation" though I suspect the miniscule number of seconds I managed are not likely to have had much impact!

Yes, "beauty" treatments can be good, bad or ugly, but all provide some "me time" plus invariably a story to tell. And in the case of the Hammam pools, a fun experience to be recommended.

"We need to finish packing," I said. Realisation of the time had struck. Our Sri Lanka room had to be vacated by 12.30 p.m. so we were glad to be able to leave our cases in George and Sylvia's room as they were flying the next day.

It was time for lunch. Off we went to our favourite restaurant where our equally favourite waiter had decorated the table for our departure and presented us each with a little box of Ceylon teabags. I've never received a gift from a waiter and was so touched by this. We'd a lovely meal before returning to the guest house for a final swim and game of cards, after which we said our goodbyes.

A good-bye that never brings me sadness is to the mosquitoes I leave behind! Despite all the precautions I took this holiday I still got bitten, ending up with big red marks which remained on my skin for several weeks. So, did the vitamin B supplements and spray I used work? I suppose it would be easy to say no they didn't, but I'm inclined to say I could have been worse had I not swallowed and sprayed. I'm less convinced the ankle and wrist bands worked. At least one determined and subsequently happy and sated mosquito made its way under an ankle band for some of my delicious blood.

On the other hand, the UV light precautions i.e. SF40 throughout the holiday rather than reducing the SF level as I normally do, plus staying in the shade whenever possible, were 100 per cent successful. No rash or itchy skin. No need to take antihistamine or steroid tablets prescribed for me in case these precautions didn't work. Success.

Janaka took us by car from the guest house to Colombo airport, leaving at 6.30 p.m. for our flight at 10.05 p.m.

The journey was straightforward. "This is more relaxing than our transfer from Yulara to Sydney, Australia," I said, enjoying sitting back and watching the world go by.

"That's an understatement," was Douglas' reply.

"There aren't taxis in Yulara," we'd been well warned on the coach from Alice Springs to Yulara. "The nearest taxi is in Alice Springs; five hours' drive away – without stops. So, don't miss the coach to the airport at the end of your stay in Yulara."

We were in plenty of time for the coach but didn't want to get on first. I'd hatched a plan and wanted our cases to be loaded on last, so we would get them first at the airport, meaning we would get to the front of the check-in queue. Unfortunately, the coach went on to another hotel, so our cases were pushed back. As soon as mine was unloaded, I went ahead and waited for Douglas in the queue. It's amazing how long it can take a second case to be unloaded even though it was initially beside mine.

Douglas eventually joined me. Online check-in wasn't available for this flight and I suddenly remembered our booking reference was in a folder in my case. Because the case had been damaged on a previous flight, I'd spent ages taping it up to keep it secure and didn't want to take the tape off. Douglas had the mini travel booklet with all our itinerary in it, but on checking this it only included our flight times and not our booking reference. I wasn't sure they would accept this.

"Our passports will confirm our identity, so I don't think they'll need the booking reference," I said inspirationally.

Douglas started taking things out of his backpack to get his travel-document bag. I thought it strange he was taking so many things out and as he got decidedly nearer the bottom of the rucksack, I saw a worrying note of realisation on his face. At the same time, I thought about the room safe back at the hotel: the room safe where he so carefully stores our passports. The passports were still in the safe, there were no taxis to get us back to the hotel and we'd a flight to catch. This was a small airport, not one we'd arrived at three hours before flight departure time. It was more like going to a bus station in time to catch a local bus. We didn't have much time.

We left the queue and I quickly headed for an AAT Kings travel agent; the company which had organised many of our tours and our transfer to the airport. He suggested I speak to one of the bus drivers still outside as he would be able to contact the hotel and get another bus coming later, to bring the passport to the airport.

This seemed a good idea, but when I asked, the bus driver didn't have a direct telephone number for the hotel. Instead it connected Douglas to the hotel group's call centre. Worse, he was put in a queue of people similarly wanting to speak to someone. He kept dialling the number and each time tried selecting a different option from the menu recited to him but always ended up hearing, "All our agents are busy right now. Your call is important to us, please hold and we will be with you as soon as possible." Not the response you want to hear when you *really* need to speak to someone.

I spoke to the bus driver again. He found a different number on his phone, but it reached the same travel centre.

Another AAT Kings agent asked us if we were getting on the bus outside. I explained we needed to get back to the hotel for our passports.

"Get on the bus," he said to Douglas.

"But how will I get back? There aren't any taxis."

"The hotel will organise something."

So, Douglas got on the coach, clutching the phone, waiting for an agent "not to be taking other calls" so he could hopefully speak to someone at the hotel.

Meanwhile, I moved our cases near to but not in the ever-diminishing queue of people checking in. I thought, when there was no one left in the queue, I could go and explain what had happened. Perhaps because it was such a small airport (six flights out a day) and me looking such an honest person they would check us in with Douglas *in absentia* thus allowing the plane to be loaded with our two cases. A long shot I supposed. I resigned myself to just waiting for Douglas. There were now very few people left in the queue.

I don't think I have ever been pleased to see a queue lengthen. Another bus load of passengers arrived and went ahead of me. The check-in procedure wasn't imminently going to close. I was convinced Douglas would get back in time.

Douglas meanwhile was on the coach, phone in hand and finally got to speak to someone at the hotel and explained our predicament. On arrival at the hotel, one of the managers had the black travel pouch in his hand.

"How will I get back to the airport?" Douglas asked.

"Don't worry," was the welcome reply as a white minibus drew up outside and he was whisked back to the airport. We both now joined the few remaining folk waiting to check-in.

"I'm so sorry," he kept saying. To which my response was, "It doesn't matter, and anyway, it gives me something to write about."

"That's why I'm sorry!" he replied.

A very long queue at security wasn't moving when we joined it. After a while, Douglas went exploring, walking to the other end of the airport. When he returned, he asked, "Have you moved?"

"One step."

Later, we heard a garbled announcement. It was about our flight and we were on the wrong side of security. I went and asked if there was enough time for us to get through security.

"Which flight are you on to Sydney?"

"The first one."

"No there's not time. Come with me."

She took us and others on our flight to the front of the queue where we formed a small crowd around the single security station. No one was sitting in front of the screen of the hand baggage x-ray machine, and nothing on the conveyor belt was moving. A frequent flier told us the man behind the conveyor belt who was making sure we put all electronic goods in trays was one of the airport managers. He was clearly relaxed about the situation even though our flight was due to depart in 30 minutes.

"Will we get on the plane?" someone asked him.

"Sure," he said. "It would be too much hassle to remove your cases from the plane's hold."

We waited, and we waited, and we waited. Finally, a man appeared from a small room, sat down in front of his screen and the conveyor belt started moving once more. No explanation of the delay was provided. Perhaps there had be a computer error. Perhaps he had gone for a coffee. We'll never know.

We only had a few minutes to wait in the departure lounge before we walked across the tarmac to the plane, on the way, spotting our first snake of the trip.

In comparison, at Sri Lanka's Colombo airport we enjoyed a wander round the shops after a very lengthy process of security checks, though what level of security they achieved I'm not sure.

The first check was immediately after we entered the airport building. A short distance away was baggage screening. This was where I got the first feeling screening was not as rigorous as in other airports. We both had bottles of water with us. According to the posters, as we expected, they were not be allowed. Stopping, we started to drink the water but were waved through by a lady officer saying it was OK to take them with us.

Over to the check-in area we went. There were masses of people. The queue for those who like us, had checked-in online wasn't moving. As printouts of boarding passes weren't issued, I'm not sure what the purpose of online check-in was.

Eventually, after the queues for business class and upwards depleted to zero, our queue started moving as staff invited those in our queue forward. We were ushered over by the lady at the platinum top-of-the-range (and price) passengers. So, in the end we had an upgrade, at check-in anyway.

Close by, people for flights to Saudi Arabia were waiting to be checked in. Virtually all the passengers were wearing white gowns, ladies with their heads covered too. I noticed many of the ladies had large signs on the back of their long head scarves. I was inquisitive and wanted to know what the signs were for. Having deposited our hold luggage and with boarding cards in hand I walked close to a group with large orange signs on their backs to see if I could solve the mystery. It turned out they were all part of a travel tour group. The orange signs had been sewn on, but other groups had their different signs pinned with safety pins. Presumably this was to make each group easily identifiable.

Our next check was at emigration. I remembered from the last time the quickest queues were at the far end of the room we were now in. We passed through quickly finding this was still the case.

Onward to our final checkpoint, putting all appropriate clothing and loose bits and pieces into the trays. Unusually, bearing in mind the major operation involved for Douglas emptying his multiple pockets, removing his belts, watches, shoes etc. we both got through this security check without being stopped. To be fair, this was probably assisted by the fact most of the staff were standing chatting to each other and basically ignoring all passengers. As I said, "security" didn't seem to be a very big issue here.

"A different experience to the one we had leaving Hong Kong in 2013," Douglas said.

"Oh yes," I replied, sheepishly.

Having arrived in Kowloon safely, we'd of course to return to the UK. Douglas and I found the train journey from Kowloon to the airport uneventful. We went smoothly through the first part of security with nothing untoward found in our hand luggage or on our persons. Next was passport control.

Have you seen immigration programmes on TV, and how people are stopped and escorted to grotty little rooms and interrogated? Well so were we – or at least I was – but Douglas wouldn't leave me so came too. On arriving in Hong Kong on this trip, you may recall I was nervous thinking about the possibility of there being something wrong with my work visa. It didn't dawn on me there would be a problem when trying to leave the country.

My work visa lasted seven days and we'd been in the country for longer than this.

"But I was only working for five days," I assured the men showing them my timetable. "I'd a rest day on arrival and we've had a few days holiday after my lectures finished."

I learned it didn't matter I was only working for five days. I should have left the country after seven days and re-entered for the remainder of our time there. A visit to Macau would have solved the problem – something Douglas had asked if I wanted to do, but as I hadn't fancied doing so said "no". If only I'd said "yes," and we'd gone there instead of somewhere else, we wouldn't have been in this predicament.

There was nothing we could do except wait until they sorted out the paperwork. The clock ticked on.

"You go without me," I suggested to Douglas. "I can get a later flight." Needless to say, he refused to abandon me.

One thing concerning Douglas was he wouldn't have time to change into his travelling clothes as planned. I checked the "cell" for CCTV cameras and couldn't see any.

"Get changed here. I will use diversionary tactics if anyone comes back into the room," I said trying to make light of our situation. Boy, did he change quickly!

When a man eventually came back, there was another problem to overcome. We didn't have enough cash to pay the HK$ 160 required to adjust my visa (less than £15). We only had HK$120 as we'd deliberately used up the currency to avoid changing it when we got home. They wouldn't accept credit cards.

"Do you have any sterling?" we were asked. Fortunately, Douglas did. One of the many men involved in sorting things for us took some to a bureau de change as we weren't allowed to leave to do it ourselves. What was really kind was he gave us enough HK money to pay for the visa and the remaining change was in UK notes.

We were "released" 45 minutes before the flight was due to depart, so very little time to look round duty free as planned. We fitted in as much as we could before arriving at our gate at the "final call". We were going home after all.

"Yes, an experience hopefully not to be repeated. The security here in Sri Lanka is definitely more relaxed."

On the flight from Colombo to Dubai, the time passed gently as I watched a couple of films: *The Whole Truth* a courtroom drama, and *Queen of Katie* which was based on a true story about a man who set up a chess club for children in a slum area in Uganda. I enjoyed the second film, though wondered if others watching the film felt, like me, that the film settings and clothes worn by many of the children looked too perfect and perhaps didn't represent the true living conditions in this impoverished area in Uganda. My hope is the film will help alleviate the poverty.

The flight was good and uneventful. We hadn't wanted to build our hopes up so were extremely relieved when the plane taxied to a gate on landing, avoiding the lengthy process of being bussed the long distance from a remote gate as we've experienced in the past. A few steps later, we were in Dubai airport terminal.

Still travelling but arriving home, suitcases full of clean clothes

We'd seven hours to wait in Dubai airport before our flight to Glasgow. Once through security, we looked round the shops in Terminal A before heading for the train to take us to Terminal B. Two adjacent lifts arrived at the same time. Standing in front of the opening lift doors, I thought it would be fun if Douglas and I went in different lifts and raced down to the train platform. My competitive streak meant I sincerely hoped I would win.

Douglas went in the right-hand set of doors, so I headed for the left-hand ones. On entering, I immediately turned to the left looking for the button to press to shut the doors as quickly as possible. After all, this was a race – though I hadn't actually told Douglas this detail. No buttons on the left side. Realising they must be on the other side, I speedily turned and what a shock I got! Who should be standing facing me, but Douglas. Both sets of doors opened into the same enormous lift. The race was a draw.

I needn't have looked for buttons to push anyway as the lift was automatic, as was the train which took us to terminal B. As we travelled, another train ran on a parallel track. We edged ahead of it and it was a bit disconcerting to pass a driver's cabin without a driver in it.

We wandered round Terminal B. One of our time-filling exercises was to find an aftershave I smelled as I passed a man sitting on the beach at Trincomalee. Turning back to him, I'd boldly said, "I really like your aftershave. What's it called?"

"*Azzaro*," he replied.

Easy, thought I, we'll find it in the airport and Douglas can try it on to make sure I like it on him.

However, it wasn't straightforward. *Azzaro*, I discovered, was the manufacturer's brand and there were 12 varieties in the duty-free shop. The sampling began, but Douglas ran out of areas of skin on his hands and wrists and had to move to spraying patches on his shirt sleeves, down his front, his back, on his legs before taking off his shoes so his feet got a skoosh. (OK not totally accurate but gives an idea of the process we went through.) And of course, it was very difficult to know if any of the ones we were smelling was the one I'd liked on the man at the beach.

"Is it five or six different scents our noses can differentiate before the sense begins to fail?" I asked. As we'd exceeded the limit and in our sleepy state, we decided it was too risky to make a purchase.

"How often we've come a cropper when it comes to sampling perfumes or aftershaves," I said laughing. "We're very good at skooshing but hopeless at remembering which is which. Even if we identify one we like, we invariably can't remember its name when we want to buy it another time. We need personal shoppers to keep us right."

By now our aim was to find some couchettes to lie on and have a sleep. The seven-hour wait was because of Colombo airport being shut during the day and the resultant changes to flight times we'd booked. It wasn't enough time to make it worth booking into a hotel room as we've done when travelling between the UK and Hong Kong. We were very grateful for such a room after one flight when we had travelled in an enormous double decker A380 plane. On that occasion we hadn't managed to get one of the pairs of seats at the back of the plane and I was in the middle seat between Douglas and a man at the aisle. He suffered from major BO, so I was happy he wasn't also an animated speaker, flapping his arms as he spoke.

The cabin crew were awful. We hardly saw them. Possibly they'd gone into hiding as some passengers had been very demanding at the beginning of the flight.

The horrible, cramping, twitching feeling in my legs when I'm tired started. I couldn't sleep. I desperately wanted to get off the plane and lie down knowing this was the solution to relieve the symptoms. Circling round and round Dubai in the holding pattern waiting for a landing slot was horrendous. I watched the inflight maps. Seeing us travelling *away* from the airport rather than towards it as we circled was awful. When would it circle for the last time, I kept wondering?

Finally, we got off the plane. What a relief to see a man with our name on a card. He led us directly to the airport hotel reception on a much shorter route than we would have followed if left to our own devices. There wasn't a queue at reception so in no time we were in bed and asleep for five hours. Fantastic! After checking out and getting in the lift at reception it amazed us when the doors opened, and we found ourselves in the departure lounge of the airport. No security checks required. Bliss!

On the follow-on flight from Hong Kong I was again in the middle of three seats. As the plane filled no one came to the aisle seat beside me. The doors closed but I didn't want to raise my hopes.

It was only when the plane started to taxi, I felt sure the seat was going to remain empty. Once airborne but before I moved to the aisle seat a man asked if he could sit in the empty seat. I felt bad saying, "Sorry, no. I'm about to move into it." Just like me he wanted to move from a middle into an aisle seat. He found another seat somewhere else in the plane, so I didn't feel bad for long.

Although I'd two seats, I didn't want to embarrass myself trying to lie down in case I didn't fit. I was sure everyone near me would be watching my every move and would laugh at my efforts before I admitted defeat. However, later I noticed a lady curled up in two similar seats. If she could do it, so could I. Curl up I did, and managed to get some sleep, and my legs behaved themselves.

But after finding couchettes in Dubai airport, sleep was elusive. Unfortunately, I'd packed my eye mask in my suitcase instead of hand luggage, so I didn't have a blackout environment to make sleep come more easily. I also discovered I hadn't brought my lightweight jacket; I could have used this to cover my eyes. The only cloth item I found was a spare pair of underpants, which I didn't think was suitable to use.

As I lay on the couchette, I became aware of all the sounds around me, starting with the moving walkway. It whirred and had a quiet, regular squeak, the squeak slowing as the walkway itself slowed down when no one was on it; an energy saving measure. A tired young child some distance away cried every once in a while. I couldn't resist opening my eyes when I heard what sounded like a large laundry trolley from a hospital with a wobbly wheel. My ears hadn't deceived me. It looked just like a hospital laundry trolley. After a while, another sound was added to the collage. The man next to me started snoring – loudly.

Another sense came to the fore. I was feeling cold and had to remedy this situation. I noticed one well-prepared traveller inside a lightweight sleeping bag. If only I'd thought about it, I could have borrowed a blanket from the plane we arrived on and returned it by taking it onto the plane to Glasgow. In my half-asleep state, I found myself thinking of ridiculous implications of such an act. I imagined the Glasgow plane being unable to take off due to the extra unexpected load of the blanket. Or the extra weight and accompanying higher fuel usage might make the plane drop out of the sky during the flight when the fuel ran out. I smiled at these nonsensical thoughts.

The seven hours between flights went by surprisingly quickly and it seemed no time till we were heading to board our plane for Glasgow.

"No ice cream like we did on our way to Australia," Douglas warned.

"We only got the ice cream because the shop selling the frozen yoghurt we love was in a different terminal," I tried to justify. We had ended up buying strawberry ice cream sundaes from McDonald's, a poor second best but a lot better than nothing. The gate for our flight to Perth was open and the plane boarding.

"There's no rush," Douglas said. "We can take our time and eat the ice cream before going to the gate."

"I think it would be lovely to sit on the plane eating the ice cream as we wait for take-off. Let's put the sundaes in our rucksacks."

Douglas shook his head in dismay, but off we set, sundaes in our rucksacks.

Having been through security when we landed, we'd yet another security check before reaching gate 20. Rucksacks had to be presented at a row of tables and opened. I showed my bag of liquids before the lady rummaged around inside my rucksack where she found the ice cream.

"Not allowed on the plane," I was told. "Eat it now."

It hadn't dawned on me ice cream would be classified as a liquid. We back tracked and ate our already melting ice cream standing a few paces away from the security desks.

Ready for yet another security check we approached the row of tables once again. We stood waiting our turn but were approached by the man who had been directing the queue. He had watched us eating our ice cream and told us we could go through saying we'd already had our bags checked.

And I admit now we didn't tell the whole truth and nothing but the truth. We thanked him and walked past the security desks. What we didn't divulge was only my bag had been checked. Douglas had been waiting behind me and his security check wasn't carried out. But we knew there wasn't anything of interest to the security folk.

Once seated in the plane for our final flight home from Sri Lanka, I said to Douglas, "Thankfully getting our seats on a plane today was more straightforward than on the return flight from Florida before David was born."

"It certainly was!"

Douglas worked as an Air Traffic Control Assistant at the time and was entitled to buy staff stand-by tickets for flights and had done so before he met me. Staff stand-by tickets meant a cheap holiday in Florida we otherwise wouldn't have been able to contemplate.

We experienced no problems on our flight from Glasgow and I thought it would be the same on our return journey. The check-in procedure initially was no different from normal.

"Go through security and to the flight departure gate when called," we were told but this was followed with, "There's no guarantee you will get seats on the plane."

Strange, I thought. I assumed we wouldn't be checked-in unless there were seats available. I hadn't anticipated this period of uncertainty.

The wait began, with little conversation between us. I was quietly confident we would get seats, but was conscious Douglas was less so. He had experienced such things whereas I hadn't.

"Seats for staff stand-by tickets are allocated after normal stand-by tickets," he warned.

The announcement instructing all passengers to go to the gate was heard. We found seats in the departure area and sat facing the desks at the gate, surrounded by a plane-full of people. Eventually, sour faced ladies at the desks started shouting surnames one at a time and the person or family group went to the desk. It was a slow process but those approaching the desk returned with boarding passes. I started listening closely to the names thinking they must be in alphabetical order. I was therefore startled when "Moore" was bypassed.

We waited another interminably long time. Other people approached and left the desk before eventually we heard, "Moore" (though pronounced "More" rather than the Scottish "Moor"). Were we taking the 15 paces to the desk to be told we wouldn't get on the flight? Douglas had work to go to as soon as we got home so this was a situation we didn't want to contemplate.

The sour faced woman spoke. We listened.

"You will get on the flight," she told sternly. What a relief!

"But you will not get seats together," she continued. Not a problem, we thought. After all it was an overnight flight and we'll be sleeping.

"You won't get any food on the plane. There's only enough for those who had confirmed tickets," she added as a parting shot. This was OK too. A little less food wouldn't do us any harm, I reasoned.

Boy, we were relieved as we walked away from the desk, our spirits immediately lifted. We were going home!

On the flight we took our seats and once at cruising altitude the air stewardess came offering me drinks and a meal. There were various codes of conduct to be followed when using staff stand-by tickets; be smartly dressed, including a shirt and tie for Douglas, and we weren't to tell other passengers we'd cheap stand-by tickets. I faced a dilemma. The food being offered wasn't for me, but how I could I pass on this information to the stewardess without others knowing?

"I'm a staff stand-by passenger," I whispered to her. "I've been told there's no food for me."

"Sorry could you repeat, I can't hear you."

I repeated my message a bit louder.

"Of course there's food for you. There was enough food on the plane for the total number of seats. Ground staff shouldn't have been told that."

"Oh, thank you," I said. "My husband is sitting over there. He'll also be concerned when offered food." She assured me she would explain the situation.

This conversation drew the attention of the man next to me. It turned out he was an airline captain who had been given the same information as us. His wife was also sitting elsewhere. Where was she sitting? Next to Douglas! A stewardess immediately rearranged our seats.

"We got home, and I got to work, thank goodness, but no more stand-by flights for us!" Douglas correctly concluded.

On this final flight from Sri Lanka I watched my favourite film of the flights, Dolly Parton's *Coat of many colours* about some of her childhood. A tearjerker for me and I was pleased I'd hankies in my pocket. I got a few concerned glances from members of the flight-crew as they saw my puffed-up eyes and tears streaming down my face.

I'd a different wetting experience on our return journey flight from San Francisco to Gatwick in 2001 at the end of a fantastic family holiday.

Not long after take-off I was aware of liquid dripping on me and staining my white cardigan. I got up. Trying to find the source, I opened the overhead locker. This caused a torrent of liquid to flood onto my seat. I quickly shut the locker and called a stewardess.

It was from a flask of iced tea. The stewardess was far from happy. There had been an announcement as we boarded, "No liquids are to be placed in the overhead lockers."

She identified the culprit, a lady sitting on the opposite side of the aisle from us. Theoretically she was using *my* locker, I felt. The poor stewardess was ignored as she tried to tell the lady she was removing the flask and putting it into a floor level cabinet elsewhere in the plane. The woman wasn't in the least bit concerned about the flask or stains all over my white cardigan or my very wet seat. She wasn't pleased her film watching was interrupted. I got a pillow to sit on, no upgrade to First Class unfortunately!

A while later, there was an ear-piercing sound and members of the cabin crew rushed around trying to establish what was making the horrendous noise. Finally, they descended upon and surrounded the same lady still happily watching the film. Once they finally managed to interrupt her film watching, they found she had a personal alarm. Somehow the pin had come out setting the alarm off.

A steward frantically tried to muffle the screeching sound, holding the alarm tightly between his hands. Meanwhile several stewardesses were down on their hands and knees while another one body-searched the lady, all looking for the missing pin. Fortunately, they eventually found it and put it back into the alarm. Peace resumed.

I wonder what they would have done if the pin hadn't been found? It's not as though they could have opened the door of the plane and thrown the alarm away at 33,000ft!

It's fun and can be educating watching other passengers on long flights. Douglas and I experienced this once when surrounded by a group of Chinese folk. They talked loudly and ate *so* much food. Between the served meals they each ate three pots of noodles. Their last request for nine pots couldn't be fulfilled as there were only four pots left on the whole plane. They also had a supply of very pungent food they added to the meals which wasn't very pleasant for those close by.

On that flight, Douglas was sitting at the window and I was sitting in the middle seat of the group of three. The lady next to me in the aisle seat was up and down like a yoyo. Her preparations for leaving her seat were funny. She dramatically threw her blanket onto me before giving me a farewell dig in my arm with her elbow. Her headphones went flying, also landing on me, because she had forgotten to take them off before standing. Oh, the delights of flying!

In contrast, we'd a straightforward final leg flight to Glasgow with no difficult or awkward passengers. The last part of the flight offered great views of the UK's snow-covered landscape below, with the sun shining on it. The two degrees temperature announced by the captain as we landed was a big change from the 30 degrees plus temperatures left behind in Sri Lanka, hot even in the air-conditioned car and airport. At 11.20 a.m. we touched down.

Arriving at the stand, a pleasant surprise unfolded. The rear door was opened and as our seats were two rows from the back, we were some of the first off the plane. We walked across the tarmac and were at immigration before any of the passengers from the posh seats at the front of the plane. However, this advantage didn't help with getting our luggage as machinery on the plane had broken down. An unfortunate happening but one we could have done without.

A lovely taxi driver took us from the airport to Paisley Gilmour Street train station. I couldn't believe it when he deliberately rounded *down* the fare when we arrived. How kind, we thought. It meant he got a bigger tip as we gave him what we planned to give him anyway.

Our final experience of the holiday related to our house keys. Douglas didn't know where he had put them for safe keeping after he locked the front door as we left home at the start of our holiday. While we were waiting for our train in Gilmour Street station, the search began.

As ever, there were many pockets to look through – his rucksack, two jackets and holiday over-the-shoulder bag. I double checked what he had already checked. I remembered I hadn't looked inside his credit card wallet, but no joy.

"We'll be able to get a spare key from one of the various people who have one," he rightly said. But who? David would be working, our next-door neighbour had one, but I remembered she only had one for the conservatory door and I'd also locked the double doors into the house from the conservatory, and I couldn't remember if our other next-door neighbour had a key.

"We'll go home with the cases, check with neighbours and if necessary, we'll walk to your Mum and Dad's for the spare key they have," Douglas said.

"Hopefully Mum and Dad will be in, but the one-mile walk will give me time to remember the secret place where they keep their spare house key to let us get in for our spare key!"

For some reason while we were still on the train, Douglas decided to look in his wallet, in the pocket which he normally keeps the key for the front door and guess what? There was the key: where it's always kept. He hadn't put it in a different "safe" place after all. No need to put our plan into action.

The journey from the guest house in Sri Lanka to our front door at home took approximately 24.5 hours.

We'd had a great holiday but were glad to be home, complete with two suitcases of clean clothes, ready to be put away in readiness for our next travelling adventure.

Final thought from Douglas: it would be great if all airports looked after ministers like in Colombo, Sri Lanka.
Sign reads: "Reserved for Clergy"

Postscript

The joy of this postscript is I have the opportunity to update you on what happened to all those metres and metres of fabric bought with my Mother-of-the-Groom wedding outfit in mind for Andrew and Julia's wedding.

The problem with the fabric was when I got home, I didn't have a clue where to find a pattern or someone to make the dress for me. An exciting prospect became a stressful situation. I'd no idea what a Mother-of-the-Groom should wear.

Some friends came to my rescue. While out for a meal, they took me in hand, telling me what I already knew: I *had* to get my outfit organised.

"What kind of outfit are you thinking of?" they wanted to know.

"All I've decided is that I want to wear a dress, maybe navy blue."

They were so kind offering all sorts of advice, one offering to lend me a dress, others telling me where I could go to buy an outfit.

Unfortunately, Mum was very ill about this time and I knew I needed to get something bought as simply as possible. So, I asked friends Chris and Roberta and David's then girlfriend and now fiancée, Leah, to come with me to one of the suggested shops, a large factory outlet not far from where we live.

It was the best thing I could have done. They set to work, taking things off rails, telling me I'd to try things on and not just assume I wouldn't like it and to be prepared to go out of my usual comfort zone. The changing room became a mecca of activity. They were good at telling me when something wasn't right but equally reassured me when something I wasn't sure about, suited me. I tried on pink and red dresses, but decided they clashed with the colour of my rosy cheeks and not being a make-up wearer, I felt this was a problem.

I love the dress we decided upon; knee length, darker than navy – somewhere between navy and black, two layers of fabric with the top layer a lacy material with white ribbon flowers up one side of the front and back.

Dress chosen, my team selected jacket options while one of the shop assistants disappeared and returned with bags and hats – yes hats. This was well and truly out of my comfort zone, but I got one. The only thing I couldn't get in the shop was shoes. One pair were perfect in style but not colour.

It was wonderful to achieve so much in one shop and in a short period of time. We even fitted in a cuppa in the tearoom before heading home.

If only getting the shoes had been as straightforward. I hate shoe shopping at the best of times as my feet are broad and often shoes are uncomfortable. In addition, I'm not prepared to have painful feet just to look the part (even though in one shop this is what I was told had to be done for a wedding). By the end of the designated afternoon I'd spent trailing round shoe shops in a nearby town, I was nearly in tears as I entered the last possible shop. An assistant in a shoe shop I'd been in earlier had suggested it. If I didn't get anything here, I would have to travel to Glasgow and start all over again.

The shop wasn't one I would have considered as it sold fashion clothes; not somewhere I would expect to find comfortable footwear. I didn't hold out much hope but went in.

And lo and behold I found a pair of white sandals with a wide fitting and importantly, they didn't have high heels. It took far longer to buy shoes than the rest of my outfit.

The only question in my mind was did they go with the outfit and were they fancy enough? Leah was called upon for expert advice. She knew I was prepared for a negative, honest answer. But she said they were shoes she would wear, so I was sorted. What a relief!

As for the fabric I bought all those thousands of miles away in Sri Lanka; so far, I've only made the white lining material into a tablecloth. The other material still awaits conversion.

The white tablecloth came about when friend Jan suggested we have a tea and cake afternoon before the wedding. Great idea! Afternoon tea though, required not only home baking, but a white tablecloth, so my sewing machine was put to work hemming the two frayed edges.

Andrew and Julia's wedding was wonderful. Douglas carried out the wedding ceremony, the hotel arranged everything expertly, the photographer was sensitive, the meal excellent, dancing afterwards fun, and there was such a friendly and happy atmosphere. And lastly, I felt very comfortable in my outfit. All in all, we'd a very happy day.

And now with an extended family, who knows what holiday adventures I will have with my dearly loved Douglas, David, Leah, Andrew and Julia and the tales I will tell of the travelling Moores.

My amazing family: David, me, Andrew, Julia, Douglas and Leah.
A wonderful, happy wedding day.
(Thanks for the photo Julia and Andrew)

L - #0267 - 280920 - C0 - 210/148/14 - PB - DID2915012